Where Angels Fear to Tread

SALLY BECKER

Where Angels Fear to Tread

THE MEMOIR OF A HUMANITARIAN AID WORKER

HARPER
element

HarperElement
An imprint of HarperCollins*Publishers*
1 London Bridge Street
London SE1 9GF

www.harpercollins.co.uk

HarperCollins*Publishers*
Macken House, 39/40 Mayor Street Upper
Dublin 1, D01 C9W8, Ireland

First published by HarperElement 2025

1 3 5 7 9 10 8 6 4 2

Sections of this book have been previously published under the
title *Sunflowers and Snipers: Saving Children in the Balkan War*
(The History Press, 2021)

A catalogue record of this book is
available from the British Library

ISBN 978-0-00-874157-0

Printed and bound in the UK using 100%
renewable electricity at CPI Group (UK) Ltd

For Billie

Whom shall I send and who will go for us?
Then said I, Here am I; send me.
Isaiah 6:8

PART I
Operation Angel

1

'You can't get insurance for dismemberment!' called my father from the hall. I ignored him and continued to place the last few items in my holdall, wondering if I'd overlooked anything of vital importance; it isn't easy packing for a war zone. Dog tags, engraved with my name and blood group and given to me for luck by a friend, were the last items to enter the bag. We'd be travelling by road across Europe without any overnight stops, so I also packed a sleeping bag.

When my parents learned that I planned to go to Bosnia they reacted in different ways. I left home when I was sixteen, so my mother was used to me travelling, and although concerned about the danger, she accepted my decision. My father thought I'd 'lost my mind', though, and tried to dissuade me from going by describing in detail the horrific injuries caused by anti-personnel mines, which ultimately resulted in the loss of one or more limbs.

When it was time to say goodbye I found him in the sitting-room watching a rerun of *Laurel and Hardy*. He held up a dark object, opening it to reveal a wicked-looking blade. 'It's a killing knife,' he stated sombrely, and proceeded to demonstrate its locking device. 'Carry it with you always; you never know when you might need it.'

'I couldn't kill anyone,' I said.

'You might need to use it in self-defence,' he persisted. 'There are a lot of fascists out there!'

3

I agreed to take it with me, although I was sure it would never be used.

A Croatian organisation called Suncokret (Sunflowers) had accepted me as a volunteer delivering humanitarian aid to refugee camps, and they'd arranged for me to join a convoy funded by the Medjugorje Appeal, a Catholic organisation run by local businessman Bernard Ellis. Bernard was a convert to Catholicism whose charity was named after a small village in Bosnia-Herzegovina that had become a famous place of pilgrimage since 1981, when a group of children claimed to have seen visions of the Virgin Mary.

Arriving at the base in Godstone, Surrey, my heart began to beat a little faster when I saw ten white trucks and a bus with red crosses painted on the sides. I entered a very large, dimly lit warehouse packed from floor to ceiling with humanitarian aid: boxes of tinned food, flour, medical supplies, mattresses, blankets and clothes of all kinds. I was introduced to Sean Vatcher, my co-driver on the bus.

Sean was in his mid-twenties, tall, slim and with brooding good looks, olive skin and short black hair. He aspired to be a war photographer and planned to use this mission to add to his portfolio. Apart from a young woman called Lynne Gillette the volunteers were all men. Lynne, who was twenty-six, had travelled down from Manchester, where she worked as a temp while also running a collection point for the Medjugorje Appeal together with her boyfriend. She was dressed in a flared skirt and flat pumps, and had curly brown hair and brown eyes. Bright, bubbly and with a great sense of humour, I liked her immediately.

Before heading off, Sean suggested I drive the bus around the car park. It was hard to judge the vehicle's length, but he assured me I'd soon get the hang of it. The bus would normally have required an HGV or PSV licence, but as the fleet of vehicles were all painted white with red crosses, they were classified as ambulances. I familiarised myself with the bus's controls, including the air brakes, and practised turning, parking and reversing. I was driving by the seat of my pants for a while but by the time we reached France I'd got the hang of it.

On the bus's dashboard was a large portrait photo of Collette, a volunteer Sean had met on a previous trip. The photo was displayed so that he could see it throughout our journey to Bosnia, where he hoped she would be waiting. I teased him mercilessly whenever I caught him gazing adoringly at her photograph instead of the road.

The journey through France, Italy and into the Balkans was long and arduous, so there was plenty of time to think about the events that culminated in this convoy heading out east. I'd been working as an artist on the Costa del Sol when I first became aware of the conflict in the former Yugoslavia. Terms such as 'genocide' and 'ethnic cleansing' that I'd only previously heard in relation to the Holocaust were becoming commonplace. Night after night the television news would be full of harrowing pictures, and I watched with mounting concern.

One afternoon in April 1993 I was applying the finishing touches to a painting when I caught a news report from Sarajevo. The Bosnian capital was encircled by forces from the Bosnian Serb Army, which was preventing supplies from reaching the city and bombarding the area with artillery and mortars from the surrounding hills and picking off people far down below with sniper fire. A young woman was waiting to cross the road while a man with PRESS printed on his helmet was reporting on the bodies of an elderly couple who'd been shot by a sniper. Noticing the film crew, the woman suddenly turned to the camera. Looking straight into the lens, she cried out: 'Why is no one helping us?' I felt like she was talking directly to me.

Before setting off I was determined to learn as much as possible about the Balkans conflict, not an easy task considering the enormous complexity of the region. Following the end of the Second World War, a Communist regime was established in

Yugoslavia headed by Josip Broz Tito. The communist doctrine of 'brotherhood and unity' helped to bind the diverse and multi-ethnic society of Bosnia-Herzegovina, which was made up of three main groups: Serbs, Muslims and Croats. Tito's death in 1980, however, created an opportunity for nationalist elements in the society to spread their malign influence, hastened by the rise of Serb nationalist Slobodan Milošević, intent on creating a Greater Serbia.

After the collapse of the Soviet Union, democratic movements swept across much of Eastern Europe, including Yugoslavia. Each of the Yugoslav republics held multi-party elections, and on 25 June 1991 Slovenia and Croatia became the first to declare their independence. Because of its military strength and its small population of Serbs, Milošević allowed Slovenia to secede with relatively little resistance, but Croatia's declaration of independence was met less congenially. As fighting broke out to the north, Alija Izetbegović, the Muslim leader of the Bosnian multi-ethnic government party, was concerned that Bosnia would soon become embroiled in the conflict. He initially proposed a loose confederation to preserve a unitary Bosnian state, but with its parliament fragmented along ethnic lines, tensions continued to rise. Radovan Karadžić, leader of the SDP, the largest Serb faction in the Bosnian parliament, gave a warning to Izetbegović on the fate of the Muslims should Bosnia try to separate from the federation:

> Don't think that you won't take Bosnia and Herzegovina to Hell and the Bosnian Muslim people perhaps to annihilation; because the Muslim people would not be able to defend themselves if there were a war here.

On 9 January 1992 the Bosnian Serb assembly proclaimed a separate republic for the Serbian people of Bosnia and Herzegovina, and proceeded to form autonomous regions throughout the state. Milošević vowed to defend his people from what he described as 'Croatian genocide' and 'Islamic fundamentalism'. Fearing the drive for a Greater Serbia, the Muslims and Croats called for a referendum for Bosnian independence and the Serbs responded by launching a military offensive. Towns and villages were surrounded, with many who didn't manage to escape being burned to death inside their homes. Men were detained in camps and women systematically raped, all part of the infamous 'ethnic cleansing' whose horrors were shown on television. Muslim enclaves in central Bosnia were crowded with refugees but access was blocked by Serb forces, leading to acute shortages of food, fuel and medicines.

An arms embargo imposed by the UN Security Council affected Bosnia's Muslims the most. The Serbs had inherited the lion's share of the Cold War-era Yugoslav People's Army (JNA) arsenal and the Croats were able to smuggle Western arms, but just as Karadžić predicted, the Bosnian Muslims were unable to defend themselves and thousands were killed. The international community viewed the conflict with a certain lack of interest, and US Secretary of State Warren Christopher stated: 'Since the conflict in Bosnia does not affect our vital national interests, America will not intervene.'

During that first year of the conflict the predominantly Catholic Croats fought alongside the Bosnian Muslims, but by the time I set off in May 1993 the situation had started to change. Disillusioned with the Bosnian government in Sarajevo and supported militarily and financially by Croatia, the Bosnian Croats were planning to establish their own ethnically based state. The armed forces of the Croatian Defence Council known as the HVO began their own 'ethnic cleansing' campaign in an attempt to create a homogenous Croatian population in parts of Herzegovina. This included the strategic city of Mostar, which they intended to be their capital. As with all civil wars, people fought those who'd once been their friends, neighbours became bitter adversaries, and families divided according to ethnic origins.

Thousands of Muslims were now being rounded up and driven into camps or forced across the river to the east side of the city. Mostar's ethnic and religious divisions soon became a haunting symbol of the war. At the same time 200,000 Croats had been 'cleansed' from central Bosnia by Serbs and Muslims. Neither side seemed to know who started the conflict, though each inevitably blamed the other.

When we boarded the ferry to Split we were finally able to rest, and by the time we sailed into the beautiful Adriatic port I was feeling refreshed and excited to be doing something worthwhile.

The dock was crowded with refugees, mostly elderly women dressed in black, their heads covered with scarves, leaving only their eyes to reveal the horrors they'd witnessed. Many had lost their husbands and children either through separation or death. These were the displaced and dispossessed whose homes had been burned to the ground, their cherished belongings gone forever.

We drove along the glorious Croatian coastline, passing through a succession of idyllic resorts. The sea was calm, reflecting the deep blue of the sky, and it seemed inconceivable that battles were raging just a few miles away; once we crossed the border into Bosnia-Herzegovina, however, we passed trucks filled with soldiers and the road sign to Medjugorje was peppered with bullet holes.

We parked the vehicles in a compound not far from the main street, which was overlooked by the Hill of Crosses, a place pilgrims would climb barefoot or even on their knees, stopping to pray at each way station until they reached the top. It was dominated by a large church and the way was lined with souvenir shops selling crosses, rosaries and postcards.

We were preparing to take one of the ambulances to a hospital under the control of Croat forces on the west side of Mostar when I received a message from Bernard Ellis. He had arranged for me to meet with a doctor who worked at the hospital. Built on a hillside overlooking the city, the hospital at Bijeli Brijeg had been roughed up during the Serb offensive and there was a large hole in the roof.

Dr Vladlena Atijus was an anaesthetist from Zagreb who'd been assigned to work in the hospital as part of the war effort. A robust-looking woman in her late forties with a mass of black hair flattened beneath a green surgical cap, she was already taking charge of the place although she'd not been there for long. The staff seemed to like her demonstrative, no-nonsense approach.

Between operations to remove bullets and shrapnel from a never-ending stream of wounded soldiers, she found time to talk, and I soon learned that, like me, she was Jewish. She told me that since the war first broke out in 1992, many of Bosnia's Jews had gone to live abroad. Only about seventy people still remained in Mostar and, having managed to survive the horrors of the Second World War, they were determined to stay. One or two families still remained on the east side of Mostar but no one had heard from them for several weeks. She told me that the Jews were regarded as neutral by both the Muslims and the Croats, and were respected by both sides.

Vladlena returned to the staff room after a particularly long operation and told me that a man had just died. Her face was flushed and tears rolled down her cheeks. 'You see what they do to us?' she cried. 'These Muslims whom you so pity? They kill us! Our parents, our husbands, even our children. Come with me.'

She led me through wards filled with scarred and bandaged victims of the war raging less than a mile away in the city centre. She showed me the well-equipped casualty and first aid room and the two operating theatres. She told me that they were short of medicines and equipment; the aid organisations donated several tonnes of medicines, but most were out of date.

'We only use them if we really have no choice,' she said, 'because there are times when something, even if it's a year out of

9

date, is better than nothing at all.' Before I left, she gave me a long list of what was needed.

Sean and Collette were inseparable and seemed to be more in love with each passing day. They were lodging in a hotel in Čitluk, a small town on the road between Medjugorje and Mostar, and they suggested that Lynne and I should stay there too. The hotel was being used as a base for soldiers from various units as well as doctors who'd been given military status at the outbreak of war. It was quite disconcerting at mealtimes to find ourselves surrounded by men in uniform, but the hotel had the only functioning kitchen in town – all the others were without electricity.

The room was a little shabby, with just enough space for two single beds, a small couch and a table. There was an en suite shower and toilet, but the water only came on for two hours a day and always at different times. Fortunately, at 200 Deutschmarks per month our room was quite cheap, a major consideration as neither Lynne nor I had much money.

Among the guests were a group of mercenaries from a unit of foreign nationals known as the Grdani – the Crazy Ones. They were a curious bunch who'd originally joined not for financial gain, which was negligible, but to defend the Muslims and Croats against the Serbs. Thierry was a veteran of the French Foreign Legion who'd originally fought with the ARBiH (Army of the Republic of Bosnia-Herzegovina), but when the situation began to change he was assigned to a unit within the HVO. Slightly built, with close-cropped hair parted by a long scar, he had bright twinkling eyes and dimples in his cheeks and spoke English with a sexy French accent. His best friend Dommie – dark hair, brooding good looks – was also French but much more reserved.

Dave, their leader, had served with the British Army. He was short and squat, with arms and shoulders like Martello towers that made him look very tough, an effect enhanced by an old bullet wound in his jaw. There was also a young man called Paul, a real 'Jack the lad', and an Irishman called Paddy, with the requisite birthright sense of humour who wanted to become a game warden in Tanzania.

Having never encountered a mercenary before, I found the boys intriguing. In some ways they seemed so ordinary – laughing, joking, flirting and talking of home – yet I knew that Thierry, who detested cruelty to women, children or old people, was nonetheless a sniper who could target his victims with deadly accuracy, and each of his fellow soldiers was equally ready to kill.

At first we found it difficult to sleep for the sound of missiles being fired from a rocket-propelled grenade (RPG) launcher a couple of miles away and the crowing of a cockerel at dawn. The boys took occasional pot shots at it from their windows, but that only seemed to make the creature crow even louder.

Sean, a member of the Territorial Army in Britain, was training with the Grdani, convinced that any experience alongside the boys would be good for his portfolio. He wore combats and carried a Kalashnikov rifle along with his camera.

Collette was able to strip a gun down faster than most men and was a crack shot. With sun-streaked hair and startling green eyes, she was popular with most of the residents, especially Thierry and the 'boys', who lived just down the hall, and she played a mean game of cards.

Despite her aptitude with guns, Collette was a peacenik by conviction who wanted to see an end to the violence. Originally a grocer from Michigan, she'd come over as a Suncokret volunteer to help the refugees. When the Muslim camps began to close, she started working for the Croat Health Authority, transporting patients to Split where the facilities were much better. Collette was a Catholic and very spiritual. One of the patients didn't make it and died in her arms on the way to hospital. She told me that a few moments later she saw a shooting star and wondered whether it was the dead man's soul on its way to heaven.

2

We'd only been in Čitluk for a few days when a young lad turned up in the hotel reception area where Lynne and I were sitting with 'the boys'. Damir Rozić had a thin, angular face, a mop of thick, curly black hair and big brown eyes. He was only fifteen but had hitchhiked through a highly dangerous area to come and find me as his grandfather had been wounded and he'd been told I might be able to help. He asked us to come with him to Mostar about twenty kilometres to the north-east, but I wasn't sure how we'd get there. The boys had a one-tonne army truck from the Medjugorje appeal, and they offered to let us use it; the vehicle was still painted white with a red cross, so I figured we'd be safe.

Mostar is one of the largest cities in Herzegovina and lies sixty kilometres from the Adriatic coast to the west. Built on the banks of the River Neretva between Hum Hill and the Velez mountains, it was a popular destination with tourists prior to the war, mainly for the famous and extremely picturesque 16th century bridge over the river in the middle of town. As we drove along the winding road leading down into the valley past damaged buildings and a church with a gaping hole in its roof, Damir suggested we keep our heads down as the area was exposed to snipers in the surrounding hills. The west side of the city was a geometric mass of modern high-rise blocks and abandoned shopping malls.

The old city hospital was situated downtown, only 200 metres from the front line. Its walls were pockmarked with shrapnel and ribbons of UN tape were flapping around in the breeze. The patients were housed in the basement – above ground was too dangerous – and as we went down the stairs we had to adjust our eyes to the dim light. We passed the pale, haunted faces of young soldiers, many of whom were prisoners of war. Damir explained that they'd been wounded while being forced to dig trenches on the front line. I must have looked shocked for he immediately assured me that this was common practice on all sides.

'But surely it's against the Geneva Convention?' I said.

Damir laughed wryly. 'The Geneva convention means nothing out here.'

His grandfather Roman was lying on a bed at the far end of the ward. Sitting beside him was Damir's mother Erna, a striking-looking woman in her early forties with dark curly hair and big brown eyes. In broken English she told me that her father, who was eighty-three and quite deaf, had been taking a walk outside his apartment when he was shot in the leg. Somehow, he'd managed to roll beneath a car and take cover, but it was several hours before he was found and taken to hospital.

The bullet had shattered the bone, causing an infection. He had lain there in the basement of the hospital for several weeks and each day Erna braved the snipers and RPGs to visit him. Her mother was crippled with arthritis and unable to walk so she hadn't seen her husband since the shooting. She remained at home, the windows boarded up to protect her from the elements and the constant artillery fire.

I approached the bed, and in the gloom I could see Roman's rheumy eyes staring out from a wrinkled, weathered face. He was so gaunt that his skin looked almost translucent, and he was covered in bed sores as there was no rubbing alcohol available. His leg was propped up on a pillow and metal pins protruded from the external fixator on his shin, holding together the festering wound.

'He needs a special antibiotic which they can't get here, and without it he'll die,' said Erna, her eyes filling with tears.

I was shocked to find a hospital so desperately short of medicine when there were so many aid agencies based in the region, and I wondered where the supplies were going. Rumours of aid being sold on the black market were rife and although evidence emerged of the UN's involvement in the illegal trade, the charges were routinely dismissed.

UN soldiers were also accused of using local brothels. Sylvana Foa, spokesperson for the UN, was quoted as saying that it was no surprise that 'out of 1,400 pimply 18-year-olds, a bunch of them should get up to hanky-panky'. One of these so-called 'brothels' was a Serb-run concentration camp where Bosnian women were routinely raped. When the UN finally investigated, a special commission confirmed that some terrible but 'limited' misdeeds had occurred.

After promising that we'd try to get the antibiotics and other things that were needed, I bent down to kiss the old man goodbye. He seemed to be trying to say something but every time he tried to speak he immediately started coughing. When he eventually fell back, exhausted, he took my hand and asked for a cigarette.

On the way to Erna's apartment, I held my breath as we crossed a small intersection that left us exposed to snipers. The building overlooked the front line, which ran along the main boulevard parallel to the river. It had been hit several times and their balcony door was shattered; nevertheless, their home was clean and tidy, with simple furniture and a small television. Damir's bedroom faced the front line, so he slept on a mattress in his parent's room.

We sat around a large wooden coffee table and drank squash; coffee was only available on the black market and was therefore too expensive. Erna apologised for not serving tea, but they only had electricity for a couple of hours each day. Damir's jeans were old and worn because they hadn't been able to buy him any clothes for almost a year.

Bella, their little dog, jumped onto my lap, but the cat spent most of the time in the bathroom, terrified by the noises outside. Erna explained that the dog had been born after the war began so was used to the noise of battle, but the poor cat was older and remained in a constant state of anxiety. The homeliness of the place felt disorientating, as we were chatting against a background of machine-gun fire and explosions. Lynne and I would flinch when the noises were particularly loud, but Erna and Damir hardly seemed to notice.

There was a knock at the door and a man of about fifty entered the apartment. He had a round face, ruddy cheeks and a broad smile, and was sweating so profusely that his shirt was soaked. 'Zoran Mandlbaum,' he said, shaking my hand until it hurt.

Zoran was an engineer who'd helped construct many of the bridges that were now being systematically destroyed. Speaking in German, a language that Lynne and I could both understand, he explained that he was president of the local Jewish community and Vladlena had suggested he ask for my help. He spoke animatedly, his words accentuated with an occasional prod or thump as he told us that over a hundred aid packages had been sent out from Britain last year. Only half of them had arrived in Mostar and there hadn't been anything since then. Each family received fifty Deutschmarks a month from the authorities, but this wasn't enough to buy even the basics, let alone fruit and vegetables. Only 20 per cent of Bosnia's Jewish population had survived the Second World War, and those still living in Mostar were mostly the elderly. Some suffered badly with their nerves, but there were no sedatives available; others were diabetic or asthmatic, but it was hard to find medication.

Zoran took us to see the warehouse – in reality the front room of an old lady's house – where the aid was stored. It was empty, with just a few sprouting potatoes lying on the floor. As we prepared to leave, I assured him that we'd try to get some aid. Damir guided us back to the road that would take us out of the city, then he headed back alone through the dangerous streets.

While Lynne began phoning around for the antibiotics I went to see Albert Benabou, a UN civil affairs officer based in Medjugorje. Being Israeli, I assumed he'd do his very best to help. I handed him a list with the names and addresses of all the Jewish people still residing in Mostar, and he seemed surprised there were so many. He asked me to make a list of those who might wish to leave the area, and he allowed me to use his phone to call the Central British Fund for World Jewish Relief.

Despite my insistence to the contrary, the person I spoke to remained adamant that the warehouse in Mostar was being filled on a regular basis, a claim repeated to me again in a phone call to my hotel later that evening. This exchange soon became heated as the woman in charge accused me of packing a suitcase and arriving in the region with no foreknowledge and no previous experience.

Although this was true, it was irrelevant – I'd seen the situation with my own eyes. But she wasn't interested. 'This organisation is responsible for the Jewish community in the former Yugoslavia, and we certainly don't need your help,' she said firmly. 'I'm sure you mean well but your information is completely wrong. We transport aid to Croatia every month and Mr Mandlbaum knows that he can collect whatever the community requires from the warehouse in Split.'

'He tried that recently,' I told her, 'but he was turned away and returned to Mostar empty-handed; in any case he doesn't have suitable transport, just a very small car, and the petrol is rationed.'

There was silence at the other end and I drummed my fingers impatiently on the table as I waited for her to reply. 'I suggest you pack up your bags and go home,' the woman said, and hung up.

Throughout the war, members of the Jewish community maintained relatively good relations with all sides and were therefore able to move around more freely than most, and during the siege of Sarajevo the Jewish humanitarian organisation known as La Benevolencija saved many lives. They operated a free pharmacy, opened the city's only clinic where multi-ethnic staff tended thousands of patients, gave away many tonnes of food, served hot meals from the soup kitchen and were the main carrier of mail in and out the city. They also organised several convoys to bring people to safety, less than half of them Jews; people were helped according to need, not creed. None of this would have been possible without the help of the American Jewish Joint Distribution Committee and the Central British Fund for World Jewish Relief. Somehow, though, Mostar was being sidelined and I couldn't seem to get this across.

The *Brighton Argus* newspaper back home ran an appeal on my behalf, sending a truck filled with medical aid and equipment, but it would be another three months before any official aid reached the Jewish warehouse; that it did was solely down to Mike Mendoza, a presenter on Spectrum, a small radio station in London. Apart from raising funds, Mike continued to support and defend my actions as I advanced ever deeper into the chaos of the Bosnian conflict.

3

Lynne contacted all the aid agencies but only one replied, a German organisation based in Zagreb. The man she spoke to assured her that he'd drive down to Čitluk with everything we needed. He arrived within a few hours and in among the aid he brought were the antibiotics that might save the old man. Lynne, a dab hand at fundraising and coordinating aid deliveries, was delighted that a simple phone call enabled us to save a life, and she decided to continue working with me.

On our next visit to the medical centre at Bijeli Brijeg we were introduced to some of the other members of staff. Dr Sefo, a surgeon, had heard that I was trying to rent a vehicle and offered to lend me his white Renault 4. We agreed to a rate of a hundred marks per week, and I gave him two hundred in advance. I asked Vladlena if it would be possible to get a document that would demonstrate my right to drive the car. She told me to wait and marched off down the corridor, returning a few minutes later with a man in uniform.

'Brigadier Dr Ivan Bagarić, head of the Croatian Military Health Authorities,' she announced with pride. The brigadier was only about thirty, tall and broad with thick wavy black hair, olive skin and glittering dark eyes. He couldn't speak English, so Vladlena translated, and to my surprise he beamed when she told him that I was Jewish. He spoke of his admiration for Vladlena and his affection for Zoran Mandlbaum, whom he'd obviously known for some time. When I told him about the lack of aid in their warehouse he immediately offered to arrange for Zoran to obtain whatever he needed from the priests at Medjugorje. I also mentioned Damir's grandfather, and he arranged to have him transferred to the medical centre at Bijeli Brijeg, where he'd receive better care.

I explained that we'd managed to hire a car and would need permission to enter the city; following a recent offensive the HVO controlled all roads leading into Mostar and the international aid organisations were being denied access. Within an hour we had a letter signed by him and stamped by the Ministry of Defence that would enable me to pass through all the checkpoints within Croat-controlled areas. We left Mostar shortly before the 6 p.m. curfew and our work could begin the next day.

Before my next visit to Mostar I bought some food, heaters, fans and blankets for the elderly members of the Jewish community. I drove to Damir's apartment, where I'd been invited to stay for the weekend, and as I began to unload the car, Erna leaned over the balcony, too excited to wait. She told me that since he'd been given the right medication, her father's leg was beginning to heal. Damir helped to carry two large boxes that I'd bought from a grocer in Čitluk up the stairs, and I watched with great satisfaction as Erna's eyes widened as she started unloading the supplies then happily filled her shelves with all the things they'd been denied for a very long time.

She also took pleasure in sharing some of the goods with her neighbours, especially a Muslim family who were desperately trying to keep a low profile to avoid eviction or arrest. Erna and her family did not discriminate on the grounds of race or religion, and her husband Stipe, a Croat who worked for the police administration department, had helped many people caught up in the war.

Zoran came to visit, mopping his brow as usual as he sweated in the heat. We talked for a while, and before he left he announced that he'd return the following morning to take me to his office on the front line. I wasn't sure what to say, but by the time I'd decided to decline his invitation he'd already gone.

That evening Erna cooked a delicious meal of roast meat and potatoes, served with a fresh salad. The meal tasted particularly good after the greasy fried food served at the Čitluk Hotel, and it was great to see the undernourished family eating well. Damir was a gangly teenager so it was hard to tell what his natural build would have been, but Erna was so thin that her shoulder blades jutted out and her clothes seemed to swamp her. Even Stipe seemed lost in his sweater.

While we were having dinner there was a series of loud explosions overhead. I prepared to dive for cover beneath the table but no one else moved; they just carried on eating. We learned later four RPGs had landed on the roof of the apartment block but no one was hurt.

While there was electricity we watched a news item about Operation Irma, the airlift of wounded children from Sarajevo, which had been inspired by the plight of one little girl. The evacuation, instigated by British Prime Minister John Major, resulted in an offer of hospital beds from around the world. To my surprise, this made Stipe furious.

'It's obviously just a publicity stunt for political gain,' he said, 'otherwise why would they choose Sarajevo? The city was in a terrible state for a long time but now the situation has improved. Aid is reaching the people, and they've even got electricity and water, but most importantly of all, they have the attention of the media!' He stood up and began to pace around the room. 'But what about Mostar? Nobody knows or cares about what's happening here. This incredible city's being destroyed, yet nothing's being done to prevent it. Why?'

I had no answer for him, though I understood his frustration. Around 55,000 people were trapped in east Mostar, with no one able to get in or out. They had not received any aid for months and the area was constantly targeted by heavy artillery and sniper fire.

That night I could hear the soldiers in the street below, their voices drifting through the open window, punctuated by erratic bursts of machine-gun fire and the occasional explosion of an RPG. Unable to sleep, I went to the kitchen, where I found Damir standing at the window in the dark. He stopped me thoughtlessly lighting a cigarette, which would have drawn sniper fire from across the street. As we watched the tracer fire lighting up the night sky, I shuddered as I realised that for Damir, just fifteen years old, this was the new normal. He'd witnessed two years of fighting right on his doorstep, and his school had been blasted by shells from Serbian tanks. Many of his friends had been wounded and some of them killed. He'd comforted his mother when his grandfather had been shot and he often risked his own life to visit his grandmother just a few streets away. He had no social life and there was nowhere he could go – no clubs, coffee bars or football games, none of the pleasures that most young people take for granted. For Damir, life in Mostar meant the odd snatched conversation on an empty rubble-strewn street, with friends who barely flinched as a shell exploded close by; the terrifying dash across road junctions to avoid being targeted by a sniper; the anxious wait for his mother to return from the hospital; and the knowledge that if the war continued, he'd soon be called up to fight against his former friends and neighbours.

If ever a teenager could be forgiven for getting into trouble, for using drugs or escaping into a life of crime, it was now. But he did none of these things. Instead he risked his life delivering messages for others – hardly anyone had cars or telephone lines anymore – and in between he taught himself English from old books and magazines.

I was proud that he considered me to be his friend, and as I watched him standing there in the flickering light, I was determined that somehow I'd help him escape this nightmare, something his parents wanted above all. Erna couldn't go with him because she refused to leave her parents or her husband, but she desperately wanted her son to be able to live a normal life.

Zoran came to collect me the following morning and I was surprised when Erna suddenly gave me a hug. She wasn't a particularly demonstrative person, but she knew that Zoran's office was situated in a very dangerous area. 'Take good care of her,' she called to Zoran as we left.

Following his directions, we drove across the boulevard where an overturned truck was the only defence against ground attacks. We passed HIT Square, named after a former department store, and glimpsed a machine gun that seemed to be pointed straight at the car. I tried not to panic, but Zoran just casually directed me towards Aleksa Šantića Street, which commemorates a famous Christian poet who fell in love with a Muslim woman. Ironically, this was the scene of some of the most intensive battles of the war, where the soldiers fought from room to room and could hear each other creeping around through the walls.

We stopped outside the Hotel Ero, a large concrete building blackened by smoke. Zoran explained that his office was inside, and we hurried past a group of soldiers lounging in the doorway. Part of the building had been a care home for the elderly, and some were still there, together with a number of refugees with nowhere else to go. Zoran pointed out that this was one of the few places where Serbs, Muslims and Croats lived together in peace. The hotel was also headquarters for the HVO, so it had sustained a lot of damage caused by the constant RPG rounds and sniper fire from the Bosnian side of the street. Most of the windows were shattered, and glass and shell casings littered the floor.

Each time we passed a window that faced the front line, we had to crouch down low to avoid the snipers. One or two old people muttered a greeting while others ignored us and just shuffled past. Most of them were old enough to have lived through the Second World War, some surviving atrocities that the world had vowed would never be repeated. Now, bloodshed and cruelty had returned for them towards the end of their lives.

Zoran's office was at the front of the building facing east, but as it only had one small window in the corner it was relatively safe. I glanced across the street and saw the once handsome 16th-century buildings now charred and pockmarked with shrapnel or missing their roofs and upper floors. The scene of devastation contrasted with the clear blue sky above, but when I looked down I saw the sunlight glinting on the broken glass scattered around my feet.

The shelves were piled high with books, some of them from Israel, where Zoran's wife and daughter were now living, and a large framed photograph of Tito dominated the room. We sat down and Zoran offered me a glass of schnapps, but I wanted to keep a clear head as we were so close to the fighting. Every time a mortar exploded I jumped but, like most of the residents of Mostar, Zoran didn't seem to notice.

We spent an hour sitting in the tiny room as Zoran recounted the history of his people and the city of which he was so proud. He told me that he understood the meaning of ethnic violence, his mother's family having been wiped out during the Holocaust, so he did whatever he could to help the people caught up in this conflict.

Afterwards we went down to the basement where two old women had made their home beneath the stairs. One of them had been living on the upper floor but her room was destroyed by an explosion just a few days earlier. Everything she owned was lost, so I offered to bring her some new clothes.

'It's kind of you,' she said, 'but I have no need of anything now.'

The other woman, a Serb, had been forced to leave her home and was now a refugee. She'd become separated from her family in the confusion and, obviously traumatised, wept constantly, flinching at every sound.

Zoran took me to an apartment building close by and as we climbed the stairs he warned me to keep quiet about what I was about to see. When he knocked there was the sound of panic from inside the apartment, but eventually the door was opened by a middle-aged woman. The fear in her eyes turned to relief when she saw that it was Zoran, and she quickly ushered us inside. The walls of the sitting room were lined with books and there were antiques displayed in a handsome oak cabinet. A small boy was sitting on the couch between his mother and grand-mother. When the woman left the room to bring us some water, Zoran explained that she was a Croatian high court judge who'd been forced to resign her position because her husband was a Muslim. He'd recently escaped to Austria and she planned to join him shortly, leaving behind her spacious apartment and most of her belongings.

I sipped the water while the women talked with Zoran, occasionally glancing in my direction. He must have convinced them that I could be trusted for they soon revealed that the boy's father was living in the apartment, hidden in a concealed cupboard in the hallway. Every time somebody knocked at the door they were thrown into a panic, afraid that he might be discovered. I was immediately reminded of *The Diary of a Young Girl* by Anne Frank.

The reason for our visit soon became clear. The man was a civil engineer who'd worked alongside Zoran for many years. As a Muslim he was listed for internment, and in order to flee the country he'd have to be smuggled across the border. I wasn't expected to risk the journey with him, as if we were caught I'd be arrested and deported, forced to abandon those I'd come to help. Instead, they wanted me to take his mother to Makarska in Croatia, where her other two sons would be waiting. From there, they'd all travel to Austria. Without a visa she'd be unable to cross the border at Metković, but I told them I'd try to think of some way to help. Before we left, the man came out of his hiding place to meet me. As he clasped my hand, I noticed how pale and drawn he looked from the months spent in hiding.

The next day I went to see Ivan Bagarić and asked him tentatively for his advice. I gave him no details, saying only that I knew an old Muslim woman who wanted to leave the country. He said that a visa would be difficult to obtain because thousands of refugees, mainly the elderly and the very young, had been fleeing from Bosnia into Croatia, putting enormous strain on the country's resources. The government had therefore decided to refuse all requests for visas except from those who could prove they were going abroad or were already self-sufficient. I assured him that she really was leaving the country and asked him to consider her case.

He looked thoughtful for a while and then asked me for the woman's name. I hesitated until he took my hand and looked into my eyes. 'Do not worry,' he said and I knew he meant it. When he returned with the transit visa, he warned me that it mightn't be enough, that if it were discovered that she was a Muslim she might be sent back and I'd be in a great deal of trouble, as would he. But I only had to think of the man living in a twilight world of terror while his mother looked on, and I knew that the risk was worth taking. I arranged to meet Zoran later in the week when we'd come to collect her.

When the day came, I waited outside the apartment block while Zoran went upstairs. I didn't want to intrude as she said goodbye to her loved ones. I thought of her grandson, who'd be left there to continuing living with the fear that his father might be discovered. I carried a few items in a holdall given to me by one of the soldiers at the hotel. The bag was standard HVO issue, which I hoped might indicate a connection to the Croats.

The old woman shuffled across the street carrying two small carrier bags. Tears pricked my eyes as I wondered how she'd chosen the few possessions she was going to take. She hesitated before getting in the car, obviously reluctant to leave, but Zoran hurried her up. I could see that he was worried, his usual broad smile replaced by an anxious frown.

I drove along Mostar's deserted avenues, lined with splintered trees and bombed-out buildings, towards the mountain road that led to the first military checkpoint. To our surprise we weren't even stopped; perhaps the soldiers had grown used to seeing the Renault travelling back and forth from Čitluk.

It took about an hour to reach Metković. We'd then have to pass through another two checkpoints before reaching the border. The tension in the car was palpable but the policeman on duty at the first barrier barely glanced our way as he waved us through. The second checkpoint was manned by the Croatian police, and it was here that I'd been warned to expect trouble. As I was directed to pull over I could feel Zoran tensing beside me, and glancing in the rear-view mirror I saw fear in the old lady's eyes.

'Is she all right?' I asked Zoran, as she didn't speak English.

He said something to her but she didn't answer. A policeman approached and I gave him my documents, including Ivan's letter of authorisation allowing me to travel freely throughout Herzegovina. He waved us on without even asking for the woman's papers and as I pulled away she leaned forward and squeezed my shoulder. This time when I looked in the mirror, she was smiling.

We sped along the Croatian coast in high spirits and finally reached the once-popular resort of Makarska. On Zoran's instructions I parked outside a small guesthouse on the sea front where three large men were anxiously awaiting our arrival. One of them opened the back door, shouted 'Mama!' and half lifted her out of her seat. As he gently put her down on the pavement the others gathered round her and I could see she was crying. Zoran got out of the car but I stayed where I was, content just to watch.

Suddenly they descended on the car and hauled me out, kissing and hugging me before marching me into the bar for a drink.

The judge was waiting inside. 'You've given them back their mother,' she said smiling. 'Thank you so much.'

Before we left, the old lady took my face in her hands and kissed me, tears streaming down her wrinkled cheeks. I didn't feel that I deserved her thanks. Her son was still trapped in Mostar, living in a cupboard in fear of his life and my country was letting it happen.

4

Lynne was very relieved when I returned to the hotel. Thierry had been told by his commander that due to my 'interference' with the distribution of aid from the Medjugorje Appeal, I was going to be deported. Having discovered that the aid we brought from the UK was destined for Croat refugees, we had intervened and insisted it go to the Muslim camps too. We found out later that the order had been countermanded due to my 'connections'. I could only assume that the baby brigadier had somehow intervened.

The doctors indulged in much banter and teasing with Ivan, but it was clear that they held him in great esteem. Although he was still single, he'd adopted his niece and nephew when their father had been killed during an attack by Serb tanks. Bagarić, a staunch Catholic who blamed the war, not the Serbs, for his brother's death, was devoted to his 'little family'.

There were three main hospitals in Bosnia: Sarajevo, Tuzla and Banja Luka. The first two were in Muslim-held territory and the third was under Serb control. The only other hospital was at Bijeli Brijeg in Mostar. Bagarić and his colleagues had established a network of military hospitals, including ones in a Franciscan monastery in Nova Bila, a chapel in Orašje, a school in Žepče, a tobacco factory in Grude, a hotel in Neum and a computer company in Rama. These makeshift hospitals treated about 40,000 wounded people, mostly Croats, but also many Muslims and Serbs. They were trying to include the hospitals in east

Mostar and other Muslim enclaves but getting messages through the front lines was almost impossible. Ivan had written to the UNPROFOR (United Nations Protection Force) battalion in Medjugorje to request their support and his letter was published in the *Lancet*. It outlined the need to help all the people of Mostar. UNPROFOR didn't reply.

One afternoon Ivan showed me a fax headed 'Top Secret' that he'd received from his colleagues in the enclave of Nova Bila, an area approximately twelve kilometres long and up to six kilometres wide. Of the 70,000 residents, over half were women and children. The enclave was besieged by Muslim fighters who controlled the mountains surrounding the valley of Lašva. Within this area were two small Muslim enclaves, the old town of Vitez and the village of Kruščica. Food and medicines were short and there were dozens of wounded, including many children. The local authorities made numerous appeals to Croatia and the international community, but these went ignored.

The fax contained an urgent request for help because no aid had reached the area for months. When I asked whether the UN had been informed, he replied, 'They're aware of the situation, but they do nothing. They have a base in that area, but they've no interest in helping the Bosnian Croats.'

It was the same criticism I'd heard from Vladlena and the other doctors, and I was somewhat sympathetic. After a particularly brutal massacre of civilians by local Muslim forces, a human rights organisation had called a press conference, but few had attended and even fewer reported it. I offered to take the fax to the UN base in Medjugorje, but it was only after I told him that Albert Benabou, the UN civil affairs officer, was Israeli that he agreed to let me try.

As I drove towards the base I kept a close eye on my rear-view mirror. The UN was so unpopular within Herzegovina that I feared my visit might be regarded as suspicious, especially as I lived in a military hotel. The gates were manned by a couple of

Spanish soldiers from UNPROFOR who were watching the road from behind a pile of sandbags. I gave them my name and asked for Benabou, but he was not there. I was taken to see a Spanish captain, who offered me some coffee and asked how he could help.

I told him of the problems the doctors were facing in Nova Bila and that children as well as adults were dying for lack of medical supplies. The officer rested his chin on his hands and looked at me coldly. 'What, may I ask, is your interest in the matter?'

'I just want to try and help them,' I said, surprised by his question.

'Miss Becker,' he said, sitting up straight, 'Nova Bila is close to Vitez, where the British Army is based, so I'm sure that they can survive without your help.'

Irritated by his patronising tone, I was tempted to show him the fax but I remembered that it was marked 'Top Secret' owing to the detailed statistics it contained.

'They really seem desperate,' I said. 'The hospital is responsible for the health of thousands. The letter was marked for the attention of the Health Authorities in Mostar. I just want to help.'

He smiled condescendingly. 'The Croats produce propaganda like this all the time. Take no notice.'

I was confused. Could he be right? Was I just being used? I decided that the only way to find out was to go there and see for myself.

'Would it be possible for me to tag on to one of your convoys?' He looked at me as though I were deranged.

'We cannot allow you to travel with a UN convoy. You have no authorisation and anyway there are no convoys planned at present. We use helicopters to access central Bosnia.'

'Would there be room for me on a flight?' I asked, but the captain just laughed.

'Believe me, all the Croats want is an aerial view of the Bosnian and Serb positions in order to assist their military operations.'

I tried another tack. 'I could take the supplies in myself but I only have a small car that isn't armoured, and of course it can't carry much. Would it be possible to borrow one of your armoured trucks?'

He stood up, indicating that I should leave. 'I've told you,' he said, ushering me towards the door, 'it's all propaganda, they don't need a thing. Stick to helping the Jews.'

Parked at the entrance to the compound was a Land Rover marked UNICEF (United Nations Children's Fund). On impulse I approached the vehicle and spoke to a glamorous French woman called Danielle who was sitting in the passenger seat. I told her that I'd been tasked with getting medical aid sent to Nova Bila hospital in central Bosnia. She suggested we have a chat somewhere more private and she would try to arrange a meeting with her boss. I followed her to a large apartment block on the main street and she invited me inside.

Over drinks she talked about her work on behalf of UNICEF and how her mission in life was to help children in need. She was interested in the fact that I was able to travel freely in and around west Mostar; and she told me I was the only foreign aid worker to be given this privilege.

She said that the UN were planning to take a convoy into east Mostar, the first to enter the area since the siege began. As we chatted, she suddenly let out an ear-piercing scream.

'Mon Dieu!' she cried. 'Get eet out of ere, kill eet!'

I had to laugh. Here was an extraordinarily courageous woman, seemingly unfazed by shot and shell, yet screaming at the sight of a spider meandering across the floor.

One evening we were sitting with the boys in the room shared by Sean and Collette, and Thierry asked me to read his Tarot cards. The cards indicated a bright future with love on the horizon, and when I finished, Dommie and Paul wanted readings too. Each spread produced similar readings, with nothing untoward revealed.

'Well, you may as well read my cards 'n' all,' said Paddy, shuffling the deck. I lay them face down on the table and asked him to pick ten. One by one I turned them over, explaining the meaning behind each symbol. The final card, which depicts the outcome of the question, was the ten of swords, an ominous card that foretells painful endings, deep wounds, betrayal, loss and crisis.

I asked him what had been on his mind when he chose the cards, and he said that he had asked about a mission that would take place the following day. He was due to return home to Ireland very soon and, although I remained sceptical about such things, I warned him not to go on the mission. He laughed, insisting that this would be his last one with the boys, so he didn't want to let them down. There was nothing I could do to convince him otherwise, and by the time we came downstairs the next morning they'd already gone.

Upon our return to the hotel later that morning Collette appeared looking terribly upset. In hushed tones she explained that Paddy was with his unit in Gornji Vakuf when he stepped on a mine. Despite losing both of his legs in the explosion, he'd managed to survive long enough for his colleagues to get him out. He was now in Split undergoing an emergency operation.

Trying hard to contain our emotions, we entered the hotel and saw Thierry and the others sitting around a table, mute with shock. Paddy was a very special person, kind, considerate and very funny, someone who could always be relied upon to lighten the atmosphere when things were going badly. To make matters worse, he wasn't even a professional soldier, having come to the Balkans in search of adventure. When he left Ireland, he hadn't told his mother where he was going.

When Lynne and the others went to visit him in hospital, I remained behind. Although the reading was probably just a tragic coincidence, I felt guilty for not having tried harder to stop him. To my surprise they all seemed much brighter when they returned, and I was amazed to hear how resilient he was. The loss of a limb was one of my greatest fears, yet Paddy was apparently laughing and joking despite losing both of his legs. 'Well, look on the bright side,' he told them, looking round at the sombre faces of his friends. 'You know I've always hated being short; now the doctors tell me they can add a few inches to my prosthetic limbs!'

The squad commander was arranging for Paddy to be flown home once he was fit enough to travel, and as we helped to pack his things I was very aware of how fragile we all were in this war-torn country.

During my next visit to west Mostar Zoran took me to meet Vinko Martinović, a Bosnian Croat known as 'Štela'. Vinko acquired Croatian citizenship and became a commander of HOS, the Croatian Defence Force militia that operated in Mostar in 1992. He then joined the KB – the Kažnjenička Bojna, or Convicts' Battalion – where he became the commander of the sub-unit ATG 'Mrmak', later named 'Vinko Skrobo'. It was rumoured that Stela operated a black van with tinted windows that was used to round up Muslim men of fighting age. He'd later be tried for war crimes at The Hague and would serve fifteen years in prison.

Zoran hoped the introduction might afford me some protection as I carried out my work in west Mostar, although for some reason he told Štela I was a journalist rather than an aid worker. Damir came with us to translate, and he and I were both nervous as we were shown into Štela's office.

Štela asked Zoran a couple of questions and then proceeded to stare at me in silence as he played with a small model of a tank displayed on his desk. Slowly he twisted the turret around towards me until it was pointing at my chest. In order to avoid his eyes, I glanced around the room and noticed some bullet holes in the door.

'Have you been attacked?' I asked, hoping to dispel some of the tension in the air. There was silence as he looked at me coldly, and then with a slight sneer on his face he pulled out a pistol from the drawer in his desk.

'No. When I'm bored I like to practise my shooting skills,' he replied.

A few days later Thierry asked if I would consider talking to a journalist he knew. From an initial interview with a local news-paper, interest in our work had grown and I'd already been contacted by the BBC. Several journalists and television crews had begun to descend upon the area, so I wasn't surprised to be asked. Mostar was becoming 'hot' news and the fact that there we were the only aid workers with direct access to the city had attracted the attention of the press. I agreed to the interview that Thierry proposed as I wanted to highlight the worsening situa-tion in Mostar, but I was also slightly nervous, knowing that the broadcast would be monitored by all sides.

When we were introduced to the tall, sun-tanned stranger from Denmark I suggested that Lynne spoke to him first. She'd been the unsung heroine in the back room and much of her hard work had gone unnoticed. He began to ask a series of questions but after a few minutes I got the feeling that something was awry. It was more like an interrogation than a press interview, so I challenged him.

'You're not really a journalist, are you?'

He looked a little shame-faced and seemed to blush beneath his tan.

'Actually, I'm with UNCIPOL, the UN civil police.' He explained that the interview had been a device to gain an insight into my character.

'My name is Leo Bang Sorensen. And I need your help.'

We both stared in amazement.

'What kind of help?' I asked. 'And why me?'

He stood up. 'I'm afraid I don't have time to explain but I'll return this evening. And if you don't mind,' he said, glancing at Lynne, 'I'd prefer to speak with Sally on her own.'

I shrugged. 'I'll be here,' I said, 'but I want Lynne to hear what you have to say.'

As he hurried from the room, Lynne gave me a rueful smile.

'Isn't that typical?' she said. 'The first time I get asked to do an interview and the reporter turns out to be a policeman.'

Leo returned that evening wearing his uniform, which made me a little concerned. These were tense times and the sight of a UN officer in what was in effect, Croat military headquarters, could lead to trouble. There was also a soldier staying in a room just along the corridor who had a pathological hatred of the UN. He was convinced that they were directly responsible for the death of his wife and child, and he was fixated upon vengeance. I quickly ushered Leo inside and closed the door, motioning him to sit on the small couch. He removed his blue helmet and placed it on the table, and as he began to talk, Lynne discreetly pressed a button on my tape recorder.

'There's a three-year-old Muslim boy called Droce Azem living in east Mostar,' he said. 'He has a serious heart problem and is in desperate need of an operation. As you know, the area has been sealed off for months, but if this child remains there any longer he'll probably die.'

I glanced at Lynne who shook her head in wonderment. 'Sorry if I appear a little ignorant,' I said, 'but what exactly does this have to do with me?'

He shifted slightly before answering. 'As the only aid worker with free access to west Mostar, you obviously have some influence with the Croats. I'm therefore hoping that you'll agree to use your connections to get permission for an evacuation from the east side of the city.'

'I suppose there's no harm in asking Ivan,' I said, but east Mostar was probably one of the most dangerous areas in Bosnia at that time so I didn't really think he would agree.

'I saw him earlier,' said Lynne, 'so he may still be in his room.'

Excusing myself, I went along the corridor and knocked on Ivan's door. I was nervous, having only ever met him at the hospital.

The door was opened by a soldier, who invited me inside. Ivan was lying on a bed, his hair tousled, and I had to stifle a smile as he was dressed in army issue camouflage pyjamas.

'Would it be possible,' I ventured, deciding to get straight to the point, 'to arrange for the evacuation of a sick Muslim child from east Mostar?'

My question was greeted with a long silence before Ivan launched into a history of the Balkans. He was a skilled politician who could see beyond the day-to-day crises, but he unfortunately also had a politician's knack of skirting around an issue.

With the soldier translating, he gave me a lecture on the war and described the massacres that had been ignored by the international community. He reminded me of the terrible conditions at the hospital in Nova Bila, and though I assured him that I'd do my best to draw attention to the area, it seemed highly unlikely that he'd agree to help. About ten minutes passed while he and his colleague discussed the matter between them, and at last they both turned to me.

'How do you intend to rescue this child?' he asked.

I told him about Leo and suggested that he arrange something through the UN, who were planning on running a convoy to the area within a few days. His eyes darkened.

'We do not trust the United Nations,' said Ivan. 'They are biased against the Croats and choose to ignore the suffering of our people.'

I was disappointed, convinced that he was about to tell me to leave, but instead he said something that would influence the rest of my life.

'Sally Becker,' he said, 'we will give you permission to carry out the evacuation. Not for one child but for all the sick and wounded children and their mothers. You must travel with the convoy, of course, for it would be too dangerous for you to go there alone.'

I was astounded, knowing that his words marked a significant development in the war. If successful, the evacuation would be the first to happen in this area since the siege began. For a moment I was speechless.

'Thank you, thank you very much,' I said, then turned and hurried back to my room, where Leo and Lynne were anxiously waiting. When I told them the news Leo seemed surprised, but he said he'd speak to his colleagues and make arrangements.

'I assume we'll go in with UNPROFOR?' I said, as he stood up to leave.

'Oh, I don't think that UNPROFOR needs to be involved,' he replied while securing his helmet.

'But we can't drive across the front line without protection. We have to have an escort, if only for the sake of the children.'

Leo was now becoming impatient and simply replied, 'The Croats will arrange a ceasefire, so I'm sure it'll be fine.'

When he'd gone, I thought about what had just taken place and I wondered why Ivan had agreed to my request. Many years later when he was asked that very question by a BBC reporter, he replied, 'We were both there for the same reason – to help people.'

I was filled with apprehension about crossing the front line, but I would have risked my life to save just one child. Ivan was giving me a chance to save them all.

5

When I met with Leo the following day he told me he'd be travelling to east Mostar with the UN aid convoy. The evacuation couldn't take place at that stage but he'd make all the necessary arrangements while he was there. I couldn't see the sense in this, especially as he had told me how desperate the situation was. Why couldn't I simply join the convoy as Ivan suggested and evacuate the children under UN protection?

I decided to call the base and found myself speaking to the Spanish captain I'd met on my previous visit. He was no more helpful than before, saying that I'd need special permission to join their convoy. I asked whether he could arrange protection for me to carry out the mission alone but he repeated what Leo had already said. 'If you have official permission for the evacuation, then there will also be a ceasefire arranged, so you need not fear an attack.'

I was surprised and disappointed by his response. The UN was a multi-billion-dollar organisation with thousands of soldiers, yet they were not prepared to support the evacuation of wounded children from an area that had been under siege for months. It was my first real experience of UN intransigence, and it wouldn't be the last.

I had another major problem: we were almost out of Deutschmarks. I'd sold a piece of jewellery left to me by my grandma but the proceeds from that were long gone, and we'd been promised funds from a British charity but so far nothing had been forthcoming. Without money to pay for our food and accommodation we'd have to go home; the prospect of leaving when so many people were still in need of help was unbearable.

Hearing that the representative from the charity had arrived at the Pax hotel in Medjugorje, we drove there to see what was happening. Their press officer was in the middle of a photo shoot with a little boy who suffered from asthma. After watching her record the children singing the Pax 'Song of Peace' for her local radio station, I managed to get her attention and showed her the permit that had been issued for the evacuation of wounded children. She told me that the charity had raised £1,000 for the refugees, but it was to be given to the local priest.

We were in despair, but as was often to be the case, whenever it seemed there was no way forward, a helping hand would be offered from the most unlikely source. A woman who'd overheard the exchange invited us to meet a friend of hers, Peter Kates, a quiet, unassuming man who'd come to Medjugorje on a pilgrimage with his wife and daughter. We told him about the lack of funds to continue our work and give us time to arrange the evacuation of wounded children. His daughter had also been listening to the conversation and she suddenly spoke up; we could have the savings that she'd brought with her. Peter told her that wouldn't be necessary; he'd give us the money himself.

We calculated that we'd need around £400 in order to survive a few more weeks, and that's exactly what he gave us. I thanked them both and assured him that he'd be reimbursed as soon as I got home. Peter Kates wasn't a rich man by any means; he'd used his savings to pay for the pilgrimage of his family and for others to come along with them. That evening we returned to Čitluk with a renewed faith in human nature.

Waiting at the hotel was a film crew from ITN. They wanted to film us delivering aid to west Mostar and we agreed, knowing it would provide another opportunity to highlight the situation.

I had to get special permission for them to accompany us but Ivan came through as usual. Sean and a friend of his who worked with the Croatian Army had offered to act as an escort. They were both in uniform and carried guns, which I hoped might serve as a deterrent should anyone be tempted to harm the journalists. The British press were extremely unpopular with the Croats and therefore prone to attack from angry individuals convinced of their bias.

Damir's grandfather had refused to be transferred to the medical centre at Bijeli Brijeg, wishing to remain close to his family instead. He'd agreed to be filmed so we arranged to meet Damir and Erna at the old hospital. As the reporter questioned him beneath the bright lights, I could see he was getting upset and I asked them to stop filming. They insisted it was necessary to emphasise the situation, but I felt he was being exploited and was relieved when they agreed to talk to a member of staff instead.

The surgeon told them that the hospital's policy was to treat all patients equally. The war ceased for them, he said, the moment they entered the ward regardless of whether they were Muslim, Croat or Serb. Lying in one of the beds was a young Bosnian soldier who had been taken prisoner by the HVO. He told the reporter that when he was forced to build trenches for the Croats, he'd been shot in the leg by a sniper from his own side. Damir explained that it was common practice for all sides to use their prisoners in this way, but I was surprised that the Croats would allow him to discuss it openly and on camera.

As we were leaving Mostar, I stopped off at the main hospital to pay Dr Sefo for the Renault, but Vladlena told me that he was no longer there. She believed that he may have saved the Deutschmarks I'd been paying him in order to escape. He was a Muslim and either through fear or because he no longer wished to work with the Croats, he'd fled with his wife and children during his weekend leave. Whatever the reason, he'd left me with the papers for his car.

That evening we were watching the news on satellite television and saw the piece by ITN. Lynne was not included in the broadcast, which seemed unfair as she'd been a tower of strength over the past two months. Where I was impulsive, she was practical, and she was always supportive, sympathetic and kind. While I was dashing around, she'd beaver away back at the hotel, not only struggling with endless faxes and phone calls but also having to deal with some of the dangerous characters who hung around the place.

There was a particularly strange individual called Eddo who'd hassle her every time I was away. He was a German mercenary, a psychopath who'd joined the HVO for the sheer pleasure of killing. Tall and thin, with greasy blond hair and very few teeth, he carried a knife as well as two guns. He was nearly always drunk, which exacerbated his aggression.

We first met when he lurched towards our table during dinner one evening and began spouting insults against Muslims. As we attempted to eat our greasy eggs and chips, he described in guttural German the vile ways he used to kill his victims. We were both disgusted and hastily pushed our plates away, having lost our appetites. We didn't dare leave yet, for fear of provoking him, but he soon got around to the subject of Jews; how Hitler was right and they all should have died in the gas chambers.

Staring at me with cold blue eyes, he ran his forefinger along the edge of the long, thin blade of his knife. It glinted menacingly as he described in detail what it was used for, but I met his gaze steadily, though I was trembling inside.

'I'm Jewish,' I said slowly. 'So what do you intend to do about that? Kill me?'

I heard Lynne's intake of breath but to my surprise Eddo just seemed shocked. 'But you can't possibly be Jewish,' he said. 'You're good-looking.'

I shook my head in disbelief as he continued. 'Anyway, I've got nothing against the Jews, so long as they stay in Israel.'

Unable to stand his psychotic ramblings any longer, I pushed back my chair and stood up, aware that the rest of the diners were watching. 'Come on, Lynne,' I said. 'We've got work to do.'

As far as I was concerned, Eddo was an ignorant fool, but he terrified Lynne and it didn't help that his room was very close to ours. I was given a small can of tear gas by one of the boys and we decided Lynne should keep it with her whenever I wasn't around.

On 25 August 1993 the UN convoy was finally assembled, and nineteen ODA (Official Development Assistance) trucks were lined up on the main street in Medjugorje. Behind them were the representatives of the major aid organisations including UNICEF and the International Red Cross, their 4×4s slowly baking in the midday sun. There were twelve armoured personnel carriers (APCs) belonging to the Spanish contingent of UNPROFOR (Tactical Group Canarias), plus several vehicles belonging to the press.

We approached some of the aid personnel and showed them the documents, one of which was signed by General Slobodan Praljak, commander of the HVO. I also had a letter from Dr Sarić, the minister of health, but no one seemed willing to get involved. An official from the Red Cross told me that they had no evacuation policy in place outside of Sarajevo.

The heat was intolerable, so eventually we gave up and returned to our hotel feeling despondent. It seemed that nobody was interested in what we were trying to do and we were both growing increasingly frustrated. As time went by, however, we discovered that this attitude was commonplace for most of the major organisations. They all had their own well-established way of doing things and resented outsiders rocking the boat. Apparently strangled by bureaucracy, they were incapable of swift and decisive action in emergencies. Everything had to be done through the 'proper channels', regardless of the desperation of those in urgent need. I was frustrated that we were so dependent on Leo and concerned that any delay could jeopardise the mission, but I could hardly carry out an evacuation of the sick and injured in a Renault 4.

The convoy arrived in Čitluk that afternoon and Leo was standing on an APC directly outside our hotel. Waving the documents at him, I asked what we should do.

'Wait until I get back,' he shouted, leaving me standing by the roadside. I threw up my hands in despair and returned to the hotel. The convoy remained there for hours, surrounded by a menacing crowd of people, most of them refugees. They were angry, as they felt they'd been forgotten. All the recent press reports had focused on the Muslims: the conditions of the camps, the siege of east Mostar and the desperation of those who were trapped there. But these people were victims too. They'd been separated from their loved ones, driven from their homes with nothing but the clothes on their backs, and they too were suffering from a shortage of food and other essentials. Their plight was not nearly as desperate as those under siege, but they also needed help. Eventually the UN agreed to make a separate delivery to a local warehouse.

A deal had also been struck whereby both sides could exchange their dead, for one of the dreadful aspects of this war was the number of bodies, civilian and military, which had been left where they fell. Sometimes the bodies would remain there for weeks, until an exchange could be negotiated and the dead laid to rest among their own kind.

A few hours later the convoy still hadn't moved. I found one of Ivan's colleagues and asked what was happening. He told me that BBC journalist Jeremy Bowen had managed to reach east Mostar and was broadcasting shocking images of the wounded children. The Croats were concerned about the effects of further broadcasts once the rest of the media entered Mostar with the convoy. I explained that I was intending to carry out an evacuation of those very same children in co-ordination with the Croat health authorities.

'In that case,' he said, lowering his voice, 'it might be better if we prevent the convoy from leaving until they agree to take you with them.' It seemed incredible that a UN convoy could be detained on my say-so.

'Nothing can justify withholding the aid,' I said firmly. 'Media attention is already focused on this convoy – if it's delayed any longer, you'll make matters even worse.'

He seemed to give this some thought, then hurried away. Half an hour later General Praljak arrived and gave a speech, following which the crowd was dispersed, the convoy prepared to depart and I breathed a great sigh of relief. Although the Croats had allowed the mission to continue, they'd confiscated some of the mobile satellite dishes carried by the television crews, hoping this would limit the information coming out of the area.

The following day we were in the dining room watching a report by Brent Sadler on CNN. The convoy had finally reached east Mostar at 3 a.m., but once the aid had been unloaded, they were prevented from leaving. A few Bosnian soldiers had surrounded the convoy, and they were soon joined by a crowd of women and children. Brent Sadler was giving a live report:

Following the delivery of aid to east Mostar last night, the convoy is unable to leave as desperate Muslims fear an attack by their enemies, the Croats. Apart from the danger and discomfort faced by nearly two hundred Spanish UN peacekeepers, truck drivers and aid workers, they also have to deal with the embarrassment of being held hostage by women and children.

The image of a tall grey-haired man wearing a blue UN helmet appeared on the screen. Beneath his image were the words:

CEDRIC THORNBERRY, DEPUTY CHIEF OF MISSION
IN BOSNIA

'Unfortunately ... those whom we came to help have been holding us hostage here,' he said. The camera then focused on Colonel Ángel Morales, commander of the Spanish Battalion, Agrupación Táctica Canarias, who began to shout at the camera from beneath his blue helmet: 'Not hostage – prisoner!' he cried.

His image was then replaced by a shot of the interior of a hospital. A child called Selma was lying on blood-stained sheets, her head swathed in bandages and her face badly burned. I stared at Lynne in horror. The situation meant further delays, for without Leo Sorensen I could not proceed. I chain-smoked and drank endless cups of coffee as we waited for further news. Ivan appeared and told me that he'd arranged for me to borrow an ambulance from the hospital, but he still couldn't authorise my departure until we had confirmation from the other side.

All we could do was wait. When the electricity was off there was no television, but I kept one ear to my radio, listening intently to the BBC World Service. Despite pressure from the international community, the position remained unchanged. The presence of the UN convoy had brought a ceasefire, and the Bosnians were terrified that as soon as it left, the shelling would recommence.

The following afternoon we sat at a table in reception that was littered with empty coffee cups and overflowing ashtrays. Lynne was called to the phone and I saw by her face that she had good news. Leo had managed to send a message through his colleagues in Medjugorje using a satellite phone, so it was now safe for me to enter east Mostar and carry out the evacuation. The mission had been approved by the Bosnian authorities, but I'd have to leave at once.

We were immediately plunged into a frenzy of activity. A slightly built fellow called Paul had been hanging around the hotel lobby, and when he heard that I was about to enter east Mostar he offered to come along too, claiming that he spoke the language and knew the route well.

Ivan had come to see me off, and as we were leaving he took my hand and said in English, 'I will pray for you.' I could see both fear and concern in his eyes; he was worried about my safety but also fearful for his own reputation. He'd authorised a rescue mission from enemy territory – and in the bitter battle for Mostar, a city emotionally and strategically important to both sides, there were many who failed to distinguish between combatants and civilians.

6

26 AUGUST 1993

This was as far as the police escort would go, and I stared anxiously across the disused airfield that crossed no man's land. Having previously been confined to driving on the west side of Mostar, the route was unfamiliar to me and I was alarmed when Paul announced that he'd never been this way before either. One of the policemen scrawled the directions on a scrap of paper but he couldn't guarantee their accuracy as he'd not been beyond this point since hostilities began.

I carried spare clothing and a torch in case we were forced to remain in the area like the UN convoy. The rear of the vehicle was filled with antibiotics, dressings and some medical equipment. I'd also brought coffee, cigarettes and cheese for the hospital staff – items that were impossible to obtain on the besieged side of the city. According to Ivan, the ceasefire would last until 1 p.m. the following day. There remained, however, the question of snipers positioned within a four-mile radius around the city. The thought that some of these maverick marksmen might not have heard of the arrangement did little for my confidence.

I drove as fast as I could across the deserted runway. It was late afternoon and the air was still hot and humid, so I slid back the door. We were the only thing moving for miles around and I knew that we were within sight of both sides. I cringed at the thought of how many eyes might be watching us but hoped that an ambulance would not be targeted by snipers. As we passed the main road that led to Sarajevo I wondered what it must have been like before the war, when the road was teeming with traffic.

The area was eerily quiet apart from the distant thump of shells and the road was empty except for the mines, whose deadly spikes protruded from the tarmac. Steering carefully around them, I followed the directions drawn on the crude map and drove towards the first checkpoint, where three soldiers stood watching us approach. They were dressed in shabby uniforms displaying the insignia of the Bosnian Army and wore sneakers instead of boots; each of them carried an AK-47 rifle.

'It seems they weren't expecting you,' said Paul.

Reaching beneath my seat I handed the soldiers a carton of cigarettes, which immediately brought a smile to their faces.

'Ask them how we get to the hospital.'

Without waiting for a translation one of the men pointed towards some buildings in the distance.

'Follow the road,' he said in English. I glanced across at Paul.

'Toto, we're not in Kansas anymore,' I said, but Paul just looked at me blankly.

When we passed through a village on the outskirts of the city, people began to appear on the roadside asking for food. We stopped to hand out some packages but were immediately surrounded, so I decided we'd better press on.

The road soon narrowed into a track filled with potholes and as we drove towards the divided city I caught a glimpse of our destination. Nestling at the foot of the mountains were small, quaint houses with terracotta roofs and moss-covered grey stone walls leading down to the River Neretva. The city looked relatively peaceful beneath the setting sun, with only the odd puff of smoke in the distance to remind us of the war.

Mostar had once been regarded as one of the jewels of central Europe and was a favourite haunt of tourists, who'd pay the local children to dive off the old 16th-century bridge. Originally commissioned by Suleiman the Magnificent, construction began in 1557 and took nine years. The architect Mimar Hayruddin was ordered – under pain of death – to construct a bridge of such unprecedented dimensions that he is supposed to have prepared for his own funeral on the day the scaffolding was finally removed from the finished structure. Upon its completion it was the widest man-made arch in the world and certain associated technical issues remain a mystery: how the scaffolding was erected, how the stone was transported from one bank to the other, how the scaffolding remained sound during the long building period. As a result, the bridge is considered one of the greatest architectural works of its time.

Suddenly there was a loud crack as a shot was fired across the roof of the ambulance, and when I realised what it was, I wondered what had happened to the promise of a ceasefire.

'Sniper!' shouted Paul as he dived into the back and buried himself beneath a pile of boxes. I slid down in my seat while trying to pull the door closed and change gear, all at the same time.

'This is a nightmare!' I cried. 'I don't know what to do!'

'Just keep driving,' he shouted. 'We need to reach the cover of the buildings.'

'Thanks for the tip,' I called, unable to see where I was going. 'You just stay there nice and safe, back-seat bloody driver.'

I desperately tried to stem the panic that threatened to engulf me but my heart seemed to be somewhere in my throat and I debated leaping from the vehicle and running for my life. Instead, I jammed the accelerator to the floor and with the engine roaring in protest, I weaved the lumbering vehicle to and fro, hoping to confuse the snipers.

The shots came one after the other and I was convinced that we would both be killed. I was sure that the gunman would not be shooting if he knew we'd come to help the children, but I had no way of letting him know. I'd never stared death right in the face before and it was the most terrifying experience of my life.

I kept my head down most of the way, only popping up when I needed to see where I was going. My heart thumped loudly in my chest, the sound reverberating in my ears, and in the background I could hear Paul's muffled voice issuing instructions. It must have taken about ten or fifteen minutes to reach the cover of the buildings, but each of those minutes felt like an hour.

I'm often asked whether I get a 'buzz' from such experiences and the answer is no – not for one moment. I was filled with dread, believing that my life was about to end on that dusty road. The fear never left me, and in fact it just got worse.

As we approached the main street, I saw that the way ahead was blocked by an overturned vehicle. This was Marshal Tito Street, which runs the full length of the city. Behind the makeshift barrier stood the nineteen ODA trucks that brought in the first consignment of aid to reach the city since the siege had begun. Alongside them were the UNPROFOR armoured vehicles, there to protect the truck drivers, the representatives of the international aid organisations and members of the press. The position of the convoy was precarious, constantly exposed to the threat of shelling or sniper fire, and some of the soldiers looked worried, having already lost half a dozen members of their battalion since their deployment in Bosnia.

I parked the ambulance and climbed out, my hands and legs shaking from the tension of the journey. Paul announced that he was going to visit some friends, so I locked the vehicle, as once again I was surrounded by desperate-looking people. They were quite thin but didn't seem to be starving, as we'd feared, though the children were pale and sickly.

UN soldiers with their heavy flak jackets and steel blue helmets stared in surprise as I strolled passed them dressed in my white T-shirt and jeans. Albert Benabou and Leo Bang Sorensen appeared, and to my surprise Albert clapped me on the back.

'I knew you'd come,' he said, smiling. Unable to think of a suitable response I ignored him and turned to confront Leo.

'You assured me that everything had been arranged, but we were almost killed!'

He looked a little shamefaced. 'Sorry but I couldn't tell them you were coming. I wasn't able to leave my APC.'

'Well, what about Droce Azem, the child in need of surgery?' I asked.

'I'm afraid he died about three weeks ago.'

I was shocked and saddened by the news, as well as a little confused – but I'd been granted permission to evacuate all the children in need of medical treatment, so I decided to get moving.

A Spanish officer accompanied me back to my vehicle and offered to drive me to Higijenski in the centre of Mostar, where the wounded were being treated. The walls of this makeshift hospital were painted red and pockmarked by shrapnel and bullets, the windows blocked with sandbags and wood. The building had suffered constant shelling and artillery fire, and part of the upper floor was missing. I had to use a torch to negotiate my way down the stairs, and as soon as I entered the basement I became aware of a terrible smell; sweet and cloying and overwhelming, the stench of blood and putrefaction. I had never smelt anything like it before, but I knew that it was the smell of death.

7

The floor was slippery with blood, which squelched beneath my feet as I picked my way along the dimly lit corridor. The building had once been a public health laboratory in a thriving city but was now a makeshift hospital in a devastated war zone. Around me there was a frenzy of movement and noise as doctors and nurses, their eyes red and their faces slack with exhaustion, struggled to deal with the constant flow of sick and wounded. Patients were lined up on stretchers, trolleys and tables, anything that could be pressed into service as they awaited emergency surgery. Drip lines dangled from hat stands and some of the patients were moaning or crying out in pain, while others lay still in grim resignation. It was a production line in hell.

A reporter from ITN approached me and told me she had permission to film me with the evacuees. 'It's a wonderful story,' she enthused. 'A UN convoy trapped in a war zone and you come in to rescue the children.'

Following her into a small room, I was met by a sight that would forever haunt me. This was the children's ward, crowded with the innocent victims of a conflict beyond their comprehension. They'd been wounded by shrapnel or sniper fire, mines or RPGs, either in their own homes or while running a desperate errand for their families. The oldest was sixteen, the youngest a toddler.

Lying in one of the beds was Selma Handzar, the ten-year-old girl I'd seen on TV. Her face was burned and pitted with shrapnel, and beside her on the blood-stained pillow was a yellow teddy bear with a large pink nose. Next to her was Mirza, her brother, who was also wounded, an enormous bandage covered his right leg. Their mother had tears streaming down her face as she spoke to me.

'My Selma was so beautiful. Why her?'

'The doctors will make her beautiful again,' I said, wanting to give her some hope.

I sat down carefully beside the little girl. 'I've come to take you away from here, to somewhere safe and quiet. There will be no more bullets, no more shelling, just a peaceful place where doctors can make you well again.'

The nurse translated my words and Selma smiled. She then threw back the sheet to reveal a small stump where her right arm used to be. The horror must have shown on my face for she tried to reassure me.

'Don't worry,' she said, 'it's nothing.'

A nurse explained that when the children were brought in to the hospital there was only enough anaesthetic for one operation and Selma insisted that her brother should have it. Her arm was then amputated, with only the teddy to bite on for relief from the pain.

I recalled all the times I had moaned about a toothache, headache or some other trivial complaint and was filled with shame. I realised that for her, this tragedy was part of her normal life; she'd seen friends suffer similar trauma and probably worse. To me, this was a living nightmare but for her it had become an everyday reality. Her brother called out 'Kiki-riki' and a nurse translated.

'He's asking for peanuts. They're his favourite.'

'Tell him he'll have peanuts, chocolate and anything else he wants,' I said, fighting back the tears.

Nermina Omeragić, who was just thirteen, had been preparing medical supplies for distribution to the wounded in Mostar when she was hit by mortar shrapnel. Her lower right leg was shattered and several inches of the tibia destroyed. The wound was badly infected and she'd need extensive treatment if she were to survive.

A sixteen-year-old girl called Maja Kazazić was lying on a bed close by. She was wearing a red baseball cap and in spite of her pain she was smiling. She'd been wounded several weeks earlier when a mortar exploded outside her apartment, killing five of her friends. Due to the heat and lack of antibiotics, she'd developed infections in both of her legs and one of them had to be amputated without anesthetic. Her father, who'd also been wounded, was sitting beside her. He told his daughter what was happening and explained that she'd be leaving with her aunt.

The doctors were grateful for the supplies we'd brought, as even the simplest items were scarce. Before this latest convoy there had only been one delivery of humanitarian aid, and that had been sixty-seven days ago, with even the two hundred tonnes brought in by the ODA only relieving the situation for a very short time.

Word of my arrival spread quickly, and upon my return to the main street, Albert drew me to one side: 'We're trying to arrange the release of the convoy in return for the evacuation of the children.'

Still shaken by the scenes at the hospital, I rounded on him. 'When I requested UN assistance for this mission. no one wanted to know. Yet now that you're in trouble you're prepared to use me to get you out!'

'Don't you understand!' he said, beginning to get angry. 'We're all in danger here. There's been a great deal of shelling and there's no food or water. The locals are desperate and could turn on us at any time. Your evacuation may be the only chance we have of getting out.'

He then tried another tack. 'In any case it would be impossible to take all the children and their mothers in your own vehicle, but we can lend you an ambulance. We also have helicopters on standby in Medjugorje to fly patients to the field hospital in Zagreb.'

I thought for a moment. He was right about the lack of space in my ambulance, and in any case it was too dark to move the patients now. If we had to leave without the protection of the convoy, it would certainly be better to wait until daylight.

'OK,' I said finally. 'Go ahead and negotiate, but we'll have to leave tomorrow morning, regardless.'

I went to sit in the ambulance, and was joined by Brent Sadler and his camerawoman. They'd entered Mostar by trekking through the mountains from Sarajevo, carrying their equipment on the back of a donkey. Brent stretched out on the floor, oblivious to the thuds and bangs around us, not even waking when a shell exploded in the car park.

After a while I returned to the basement where the doctors sat talking and smoking their precious cigarettes. Hafid Konjhodžić, a neurosurgeon, was a slightly built man in his forties, serious and sad, with intense dark eyes and a nervous manner. He'd come to work as usual one night and became trapped when the Croats began their offensive against the eastern side of the city. He and his colleague Jovan Rajkov, a Bosnian Serb, were averaging twenty to thirty operations per day in the appalling conditions. They often worked stripped to the waist because there were only two sets of surgical clothes between the two teams.

Many of the patients had come from west Mostar, evicted from their homes by the Croats and forced across the front line at gunpoint, putting extra strain on the scant resources. The city lay in ruins and of the seventeen mosques only two remained standing. There was no running water or electricity, and people were using their furniture for fuel to cook and boil water. The front lines were no more than ten metres apart in some places, so the enemy was half a street away. Fortunately, the houses were built very close together so those people brave enough to venture out would use each other's kitchens and living rooms as cut-through routes to avoid the snipers.

Hafid's wife, who was still living in west Mostar, was pregnant with their first child. He believed she was in danger as a Muslim, and he was desperately worried. She also had endometriosis, hazardous in childbirth when it can cause complications such as abscess or rupture. He asked me to deliver a letter to her, and some of the other doctors overheard and wanted me to do the same for them. One doctor asked me to phone his brother in Germany and tell him that his wife had been killed.

I asked them if it would be possible for the UN convoy to leave with me, and Hafid suggested I talk to the hospital director Dr Dragan Milavić, a tall, muscular man with dark hair and a beard, dressed in surgical greens. Milavić, an anaesthetist, had founded this makeshift hospital at the start of the conflict between Croats and Muslims.

He looked annoyed and said, 'It's clear that you've entered the city independently. If you want to help the children you can do so, but don't bring politics into this.'

Most of the journalists who were trapped with the convoy were also desperate to get out. Some had urgent stories to file, others were simply afraid, but they too had been refused permission to leave. I asked him if it would be possible for them to follow us out so they could highlight the situation in Mostar. To my surprise, he agreed.

The Spanish officer joined me at the entrance to the hospital and offered me a cigarette. We talked against the background hum of the oil-fired generator, the building's only source of power. I explained that I wasn't able to get permission for the convoy to leave.

'My ceasefire ends at lunchtime,' I said, 'so I can wait until mid-morning to give you more time to try and convince the Bosnian Army, but then we really must go.'

As dawn broke, Jeremy Bowen sent a report to the BBC's *Today* programme on Radio 4. 'There's been an amazing turn of events,' he announced. 'Sally Becker, an independent aid worker from Britain, has entered east Mostar to rescue wounded children and the UN is planning to use the evacuation to come out on her tail.'

At 11 a.m. there was still no sign of movement from the convoy, so we began to bring the children up the stairs. As they were lifted into the vehicles, Selma's mother wept as she kissed her husband goodbye.

Suddenly a car screeched into the compound. There was no glass in its windows, the bodywork was scarred with bullet holes and a crude red cross was daubed on the side. I watched in horror as two little boys aged three and five were carried from the back of the vehicle. Their small bodies were covered in blood and they writhed and screamed in agony. Behind them their mother was led from the car in a state of shock. She was carrying a new-born baby girl with shrapnel wounds to her legs and face.

The scenes in the basement were bad enough, but the sight of those small bodies with their appalling injuries was even worse. A doctor grabbed my arm and asked me to help them. He told me that the older boy was critically injured, and the younger child had shrapnel in his eyes and damage to his kidneys. He told me that they'd need to be stabilised before they could be moved, but he hoped I'd come back in two or three days to get them. I promised that I would.

'Of course,' I said, knowing that I might regret it.

Outside the hospital the young father was leaning against the vehicle with his head in his hands. To see a child in pain is hard for any parent, but he had three injured children, two of them with horrifying wounds.

We tried to make the patients as comfortable as possible in the back of my ambulance, while Brent Sadler and his camerawoman squeezed into the passenger seat beside me. Paul turned up just as we were leaving, and he climbed in the back.

I pulled out of the hospital compound and waited on the main street for the other vehicle to join us. Five, ten minutes ticked by, and still there was no sign of them. Brent offered to find out what was happening, and we stayed put, with the sun beating down on the roof. The intense heat was causing the children to moan in discomfort, but I'd brought some water along and handed it around. At last Brent reappeared with Albert and Leo.

'We can't allow you to leave without the convoy,' said Albert.

'What do you intend to do?' I asked. 'Hold us hostage?'

It seemed incredible that the United Nations should consider delaying the evacuation of seriously injured children as a means of solving their own problem. I was outraged and told him so.

'You have to have co-ordination,' he insisted.

The second vehicle pulled up behind us but Albert said that it might now be needed by the UN soldiers. We'd either have to carry all the patients inside my ambulance or return some of them to the hospital. I couldn't decide which was worse: to endanger the children by crowding them together or to tell them that they couldn't leave at all. He alarmed me still further when he announced that the UN helicopters would no longer be waiting to transport the patients to Zagreb. They'd been cancelled.

My head was spinning. The ambulances were parked in the blazing heat filled with wounded children and the ceasefire would end in forty minutes. I couldn't believe that UN personnel were prepared to endanger lives in this way. The local people were equally desperate, knowing that as soon as the UN convoy left the area, they would be bombarded with RPGs and shells. They wanted the UN to establish a permanent presence in Mostar, and this was the only way they believed they could get it. My own mission was a separate issue: I had entered the city alone and it was clear that the army would not release the convoy in return for the lives of five children. Fifty-five thousand people were trapped in east Mostar, all of whom would be at risk from the moment the UN departed, the shelling and sniper fire providing a never-ending staccato accompaniment to relentless hunger and deprivation.

Cedric Thornberry appeared with Colonel Morales, and as I got back behind the wheel I was accosted by the UNPROFOR commander. He demanded that I hand over the keys to the ambulance, and I tried to explain that it didn't belong to the UN but was in fact on loan from the hospital in west Mostar. He ignored me and started shouting as he tried to drag me from my seat. The children looked frightened, and I told Paul to reassure them, though I felt far from reassured myself.

As I left the vehicle, prepared for a confrontation with Thornberry, the TV cameras began closing in. But before I could say anything, Albert took me aside.

'It's OK, you can take the other vehicle after all. There's been a misunderstanding.'

I received no explanation for the sudden change of plan, but at that moment I didn't care. As soon as the second vehicle joined us we made our way through the ruined streets, followed by some of the press. Ahead of us, hobbling along on crutches, was Selma's father Mirsad Handzar, determined to ensure that nothing else would impede our departure.

8

27 AUGUST 1993

I was feeling euphoric as, mission accomplished, I headed towards Medjugorje with my precious cargo. When we reached the UN base a crowd of photographers and film cameramen were waiting at the gates. We drove into the compound, and while the children were carried from my ambulance the press began to clamber onto the gates in order to get pictures.

An officer suggested I should leave, but first I asked to see the patients. He refused my request, and as I turned towards the gates and the flashing cameras, Christopher Morris from Sky News suddenly intervened. He'd overheard the exchange and began talking to the officer in Spanish. To my delight I was suddenly called back. I rushed into the clinic where each child had been allocated a bed, and those that were able were sitting up and eating. I just had time to kiss each of them goodbye before being hurried from the room.

Once outside the compound, Brent Sadler asked if I'd agree to an interview. I'd never been on live television before and was feeling nervous, but he stood beside me and looking directly into the camera he declared, 'This woman got us out!' Between various interviews, Lynne and Ivan arrived, both of them having waited anxiously for my return. I gave Lynne a hug and clasped Ivan's hand in mine and thanked him for making it possible.

The mission made headlines around the world and appeared on the front page of the *Independent*, *The Times* and the *Daily Telegraph*. Silvana Foa, spokesperson for the UN, issued a statement to the press saying: 'Becker has helped to raise the profile of medical evacuations but we don't want every granny with a bus turning up in Bosnia.' I was only 33 at the time – perhaps the war had aged me.

I was dubbed the 'Angel of Mostar' but with my short black hair I was an unlikely looking angel. I've never felt I warranted such attention, especially when there were people throughout the region risking their lives daily. The name seemed to stick, though, and other versions developed over time: 'Angel of Mercy', 'Angel of Bosnia' and even 'Angel in Blue Jeans'.

A few days later I prepared to return to east Mostar to evacuate the children who'd been injured during our departure. I had no desire to make the journey again but I'd given my word, and the image of the two blood-stained little boys had haunted me ever since.

Before setting off, I visited the UN base to inform them of my intentions and to make sure they'd be ready to receive the children. Following negotiations between Boutros Boutros-Ghali and President Izetbegović, the UN aid convoy was finally being released. It had been agreed that two APCs would remain behind as insurance, and I asked the Spanish captain to send a message to his colleagues to ensure that the Bosnian Army would be expecting me. In the meantime, Lynne had been visiting various organisations in the area to request help for the children once they were out.

Sky had set up a live link through a satellite dish and I was able to speak to my mother and father on television. It had been several weeks since they'd seen me, and my mother was thrilled. Even my father, not given to emotional outbursts, declared how proud and pleased he was with what I had achieved. The television crew had a whip round and gave me £50 to buy cigarettes for the doctors in east Mostar.

Unfortunately, Lynne had not had much success. None of the aid agencies, including the Red Cross, would agree to take responsibility for the children. I wasn't overly concerned, though, as these children were wounded during the original evacuation, so I assumed the UN would transfer them to the US field hospital in Zagreb with the others.

Ivan turned up with the new documents authorising the mission, and once again he agreed that I could take along a colleague. This time I chose Tim Clancy, an American Suncokret volunteer with strawberry blond hair who spoke a little Serbo-Croat.

Helping us load the aid into the back of the ambulance was Vladimir Mikulić, a thirty-seven-year-old Bosnian Croat known as Vava. Tall and lean, with fair skin and an open, friendly face, Vava was a teacher, a painter and a poet. His hair was cut short and sprang up in cartoon tufts. Although born in Široki Brijeg, just a few kilometres away, he was based in Sarajevo until a year into the war, when he managed to escape. Ivan had appointed him to be our interpreter, and he'd soon become my great friend and protector.

Our departure was filmed by a local television crew, and it occurred to me that unlike the last time, millions of people would know about this mission, which might help ensure our safety.

Once again we were escorted to the front line by the Bosnian Croat police. The airport was bathed in sunshine, and it all seemed very quiet as we crossed no man's land. The first check-point seemed to be abandoned, so Tim climbed out and was about to lift the barrier when a group of Bosnian soldiers suddenly appeared.

Tim did his best to explain who we were, but the soldiers kept shaking their heads, unable to comprehend what he was saying. One of them spoke German and I understood that he wanted to take us to his commander. They'd obviously not been informed of our mission, and I cursed the UN for their intransigence. I refused to leave the ambulance, though, afraid they might take it, and to their annoyance I clung stubbornly to the keys. Eventually they agreed to let us follow behind with the vehicle.

We began to make our way down an old railway siding, but halfway down I stopped, afraid that we might get stuck. The soldiers insisted we press on, yet a few minutes later my fears were realised; the wheels were buried in the shingle and we were unable to move.

I was startled by a burst of machine-gun fire that sounded close by, and the soldiers immediately ran to take cover behind an old railway carriage. They gestured for us to join them, and as bullets ricocheted against the sides of the train we crouched behind the rusting wheels for what seemed like an eternity.

'Why are they doing this? There's supposed to be a ceasefire!' I cried, but Tim shrugged and shook his head, no wiser than me. We had no idea who was shooting at us. After a while one of the soldiers raced off down the hill, returning a few minutes later with an older man, who seemed to be in charge.

He couldn't speak English but I handed him my documents, which were written in Croatian. As he read Ivan's letter, he nodded and pointed towards the ambulance, then mimed the rocking of a baby.

'Yes, yes,' I said, relieved that at last someone understood the purpose of our mission.

Ducking and weaving to avoid the bullets, he ran over to the ambulance and started the engine. His head was in full view and I feared he might be shot at any moment. The engine roared, as he was unfamiliar with the vehicle, and I had no choice but to leave the cover of the train.

Fearful that a bullet could penetrate the windscreen, I leaned inside and pulled the gear stick into reverse, but the vehicle was still well and truly stuck. The officer shouted to one of his men, who disappeared into a small outbuilding then returned a few moments later carrying a spade, and I watched anxiously as he courageously began to dig away the gravel from beneath each of the wheels. The officer released the handbrake and gunned the engine while the other two soldiers pushed us from behind. It was a very tense few minutes as we were all directly in the line of fire, but at last the vehicle was free.

I shouted my thanks as the soldiers left, but the officer remained in the driver's seat. Tim ran over and climbed into the back while the officer manoeuvred the ambulance back onto the road. He insisted on driving us into the city and I readily agreed, glad to put our lives in someone else's hands. As we headed back onto the road, he pushed my head beneath the dashboard and put his foot down. He was an excellent driver, fast and skilful, and when we reached the relative safety of the main street he insisted on taking us right to the hospital, offering to wait outside and drive us back.

The doctors were surprised to see us when we entered the hospital. Tim went off to find August and Erna Cipra, a Jewish couple who'd been trapped in the area since the siege began. August was very sick and his wife was desperate to get him treatment. Their grandson had been killed while playing in the school yard and his death had affected them both deeply. Erna Cipra had spent part of her own childhood in a concentration camp, but she felt that was nothing compared with the pain of losing her beloved grandchild. Ivan knew them well and had added their names to my list. They'd packed a small bag, leaving almost everything they owned behind.

Three-year-old Elmir and his baby sister Lela were waiting with their mother Sendzana in the ward, but I was devastated to learn that five-year-old Damir Greljo had not survived. Their mother was still in shock and sat staring ahead, seemingly oblivious to everything around her.

When I returned to the ambulance I found Mirsad, Selma's father, had climbed into the back. He was refusing to budge, insisting that he should leave with us. Tim explained how dangerous it would be for us to take him, a Muslim man of fighting age.

He eventually got out but only after I promised to try and get him a visa.

We left Mostar as dusk was falling, and once again I was in the passenger seat while the officer drove us to the outskirts of the city. Elmir lay on a stretcher in the back of the ambulance attended by Tim. With him were his mother and grandmother, who was holding the baby. August and Erna sat opposite them. Thankfully the ceasefire held, and once we reached the last Bosnian checkpoint the officer got out. I gave him some chocolate and two cartons of cigarettes; it didn't seem much, considering he'd just saved our lives.

After crossing the airfield, I became confused in the dark and missed our escort. To my horror, a group of HVO soldiers appeared and signalled for me to stop the vehicle. They were dirty and scruffy, their appearance suggesting they'd returned from a long stint on the front line. I was immediately concerned for the safety of my passengers, some of whom were Muslim, and I held my breath as they tried to peer inside. Sendzana was too traumatised to know what was happening. She stared blankly at the fearsome faces of the men while her mother-in-law stroked her hand; August and Erna remained relatively calm, even when the soldiers ordered everyone out of the vehicle. I was about to intervene when I spotted a familiar face in the crowd. It was one of the policemen sent to escort us, and he ordered the soldiers to move away.

Lynne was waiting for us at the UN base in Medjugorje; when she asked the soldier on guard to open the gate, he refused. I looked around for someone to help us but there was only a dark, empty road.

The Spanish captain came to tell me that they were forbidden to assist us in any way. I asked if we could at least have some food and water for the evacuees, and eventually a soldier brought some yoghurt and water. Jonathan Morris and Simon Dack, two journalists from the *Evening Argus*, had been awaiting our arrival, and Simon asked if it would be all right to photograph me with Elmir. Headlights came down the road and a Sky news van pulled up. To my surprise, Chris Morris stepped out of the vehicle, followed by his film crew. I told him what was happening and one of the crew turned to the captain.

'This is an ambulance,' she said slowly, 'an ambulance with sick children inside.'

'I don't understand,' said the captain, then turned away.

When Elmir started to cry, my frustration turned to anger. I railed against the UN and all the major aid organisations whose policies were so rigid that they couldn't respond in an emergency, even when wounded children were involved.

'They're funded by the taxpayers and charitable donations, and I'm sure that people would prefer it to be spent on saving lives, rather than on bureaucracy!'

To the huge embarrassment of the United Nations the scene was flashed around the world. To be caught on camera ignoring the cries of children in need was very bad PR. Inevitably, they denied all knowledge of the mission, insisting that they hadn't been informed and they were therefore unprepared. Lynne and I, of course, knew that this simply wasn't true.

Lynne managed to send a message to Ivan, and he and his colleagues arrived at the base and carefully transferred our patients into a fully equipped ambulance and drove them to the main hospital in Split. The whole incident was filmed by Sky News; Bosnian Croats helping Bosnian Muslims while the UN turned their backs.

When I returned to the Čitluk hotel, Thierry took me to one side.

'Sally,' he whispered, 'you weren't expected to make it out of there.'

I was puzzled by his words, but he refused to say anything more on the subject and when I pressed him he said that he couldn't discuss it.

All the phone lines to reception were blocked as the media tried to get through. It had become a massive story – the human face of war – and we did our best to highlight the suffering on all sides of the conflict. I was going back to Britain to arrange for more aid to be sent out, and on the way to the airport we visited the hospital in Split. Against all my expectations, Elmir was sitting up and smiling. The shrapnel had been removed, his sight had been saved and as I approached his bed he muttered something to me. The doctor seemed a little uncomfortable, but I persuaded him to translate.

'He says he wants you to move aside because you're blocking the view of his mother.'

The hospital staff gave me some flowers and a book about Croatia. As I stepped outside there were crowds of people pointing and waving. It was quite extraordinary. I'd become a local celebrity, even though the people I helped were from the opposite side.

I boarded the plane with Alan Little, a BBC reporter I'd first met through my cousin Jonathan Silverman, political correspondent for the BBC. He warned me that there would be trouble ahead because of a statement that had been issued by the UN. There were so many journalists waiting at the airport that I had to be escorted through customs by the police – and I soon understood why. The UN had accused me of spying.

At first I was amused as it seemed so ridiculous, especially since the UN implied that I was spying for them. The headline on the front page of the *Daily Mirror* wasn't funny, though: 'UN SIGNS SALLY'S DEATH WARRANT'. If this was taken seriously it could endanger me personally and threaten any future operations. Of course, I hadn't learned any secrets as I'd never been interested in political power plays or military strategies, but the situation in Bosnia-Herzegovina was so tense that I couldn't allow the allegations to go unchallenged. I was invited to take part in a televised political debate with two politicians from the leading parties in Britain. I was expecting a fight, but within a few minutes it was clear they both supported my work.

Chris Morris was interviewed around the same time and insisted that the accusations were rubbish. When he was asked why he thought the UN would make such an accusation, he said that it might be a case of sour grapes. I was given a chance to speak out on *Talkback*, a live phone-in show on Sky. Calls came in from around the world, and I found the questions interesting and challenging. Almost every caller began by congratulating me and expressing their support, but one woman complained that I hadn't helped Serbian children. I explained that the children's ethnic background was never an issue; I was working on the basis of need, not creed. Another caller, speaking from Rome, suggested that we should leave the Balkans to its fate, and he remained unmoved when I argued that innocent people would die if the aid agencies pulled out. The last question was from Laurie Mayer, the programme's presenter, who asked how I felt about being called a publicity seeker.

'Anyone who believes that I'd risk my life for the sake of publicity,' I replied, 'has a serious problem. If publicity was my aim, I could have climbed the Post Office Tower naked. It would certainly have been a lot easier!'

With the proceeds from an exclusive interview with the *Daily Mirror* I was able to buy blankets and shawls for the elderly, as it wouldn't be long before their problems were magnified a thousandfold by the bitter cold of a Balkan winter.

9

When I landed back in Croatia I was met by Roger, a South African cameraman who'd been commissioned by ABC News to cover my next mission. I was hoping to get a transit visa for Selma's father Mirsad so he could be reunited with his family in the States, but this wouldn't be an easy task because he was a Muslim adult male. I'd agreed that Roger could cover the story in the hope that the presence of a journalist might help to keep Mirsad safe.

Roger's fixer was a young Bosnian with the unlikely name of Elvis. They'd rented an armoured vehicle, but when I asked if Mirsad could travel with them I was told it wouldn't be possible. Apparently, it would be 'unethical' for a news crew to assist the operation in any way.

I arrived at the Čitluk hotel to find Lynne in a heightened state of anxiety as she'd spent the last few days trying to avoid Eddo the Psycho. Before leaving I'd asked Ivan to keep an eye on him, but unfortunately he'd taken my request to the extreme. Eddo was arrested for being drunk and suspended from duty. Collette and the boys were away, so poor Lynne was subjected to his constant presence at the hotel, and she had spent most of the time locked in her room.

Ivan was in Zagreb so he sent his close friend Vava to help us with the paperwork. Vava could do a great impression of Ivan, whom he teased unmercifully, insisting he looked like Colonel

Gaddafi. Throughout those few tense days, he remained at the Čitluk hotel, keeping us amused and insisting I remain optimistic when it seemed that the mission might not happen.

Tim Clancy had heard about our plans, so he called me from Zagreb and asked to be included. Roger was delighted as this meant he'd have a real American hero for his news piece. A friend of Tim's was also hoping to join us. Tall and slim with neat blond hair, Tim Higham was an unassuming man. He was working for a charity called War Child, who were operating a mobile bakery from the back of a truck in Medjugorje. They were hoping it could be moved to the east side of Mostar, and he'd been asked to do a recce.

The conflict had escalated, with both sides pushing harder in a desperate attempt to gain territory. The Bosnian Army had managed to take Hum, the mountain that dominates the valley and overlooks the whole of the city, so emotions were running high. Locals were directing their anger at foreigners like Lynne and me, and it was going to be difficult to secure the documents necessary for our forthcoming mission.

Although the Bosnian Croats had supported my rescue operations, the local people had very little access to the media and knew only that we'd helped the 'other side'. They were unaware, for example, that I'd also managed to highlight the problems in Nova Bila, and that as a result an evacuation had already taken place.

When the transit visas finally arrived they caused some problems. Vinko, a young soldier who'd become friendly with Lynne, was hanging around reception while we were checking the papers, and when he saw Mirsad Handzar's name on the list he immediately launched into a torrent of abuse. Lynne tried to talk to him about it but he spat on the floor and muttered, 'You help Muslims!'

'I'm sorry for his behaviour,' said Vava. He knew Lynne liked Vinko and considered him a friend.

To his surprise, Lynne merely smiled wryly and shrugged. 'Life's a bitch and then you die!' she said.

For a moment Vava looked quite shocked as he'd obviously never heard the saying before, but he started laughing and kept repeating it to himself.

When Lynne and I were alone she admitted that in actual fact she was extremely upset. The situation was really starting to get her down and she didn't know how much more she could tolerate. Rather than make a decision she might regret, she agreed to wait until after I returned from east Mostar before deciding what to do.

We'd been waiting for several days but still had no promise of a ceasefire, then one morning I was told that permission for the operation had been cancelled. I'd just informed Roger, who couldn't hang around much longer, when to our surprise there was another phone call, this time from the minister of health informing me that the mission could go ahead after all. I was sceptical. It seemed a little odd, to say the least.

Roger wanted to proceed immediately, but I knew that the UN wouldn't support us. This also meant that it was unlikely the Bosnian Army would be forewarned of our arrival. Despite this, he was keen to get going. I insisted that we at least wait until the following day, giving me time to buy supplies for the hospital.

Tim Higham had borrowed two flak jackets and helmets from War Child, which he threw in the back of the ambulance. As we prepared to leave, Eddo suddenly appeared, having come to see us off. His suspension from the army was now over and he was off to the front to join his brigade. He was wearing his full kit and carried his weapons on his back; for some strange reason he presented me with a stack of personal photographs and his wedding ring, which he asked me to take care of until he returned. I handed them to Lynne, as I didn't want to carry them through a war zone, and I tried hard not to grimace as he gave me a hug and wished me luck, telling me that he liked me very much despite my being a Jew. Saluting dramatically, and giving us a toothless smile, Eddo the Psycho then marched off into the distance, never to be seen again.

We crossed the front line without any problems and proceeded towards the main street. Tim Clancy was attempting to give me directions, but we took a wrong turning and ended up on a hill that overlooked the city. There was a loud burst of gunfire, so I drove behind an apartment block for protection.

Within a few moments people started to venture onto the street and stood staring at our vehicle. We explained that we were lost and a man offered to show us the way to the hospital. As we headed back down the hill I could hear sporadic shooting and the blue light on the roof of the ambulance was shattered. I realised to my dismay that once again we were being targeted by a sniper. Ahead of us was a small, narrow tunnel, so I quickly drove inside. The ceiling was low, scraping the roof of the ambulance with a grinding screech of metal. Unable to go forwards, I would have to reverse into the path of the bullets.

Our lives depended upon what happened next, and I was consumed with fear. Taking a deep breath, I put the vehicle into reverse and pressed the accelerator to the floor and as we came out of the tunnel, I shunted the ambulance back and forth in an attempt to turn around on the narrow track. Bullets whistled past in quick succession and my heart was thumping so hard I could barely think straight. At last, we were facing back the way we came, and I quickly drove around the corner, where Roger and Elvis were waiting in their armoured vehicle.

Our guide showed me the way to the hospital, and when we pulled up outside I thanked him for his help and offered him some cigarettes and coffee. To my surprise he shook his head and grasped my hand.

'No need to thank me,' he said. 'You are the angel who comes to save our children.'

When we entered the hospital I was confronted by Dr Milavić. He accused me of being a traitor, and at first I assumed he was referring to the UN allegations. Hafid took me to one side and explained. Croatian television had shown the Croat doctors transporting my patients from the UN base to the hospital in Split, and Sendzana, Elmir's mother, had appeared on television thanking them for their help.

The local commander of the Bosnian Army's 4th Corps, Arif Pasalić, was enraged by the film and insisted that the woman had been forced to say the words at gunpoint. Milavić had received a dressing down for allowing the mission to take place and he was ordered to prevent any further medical evacuations.

I spent a long time trying to persuade him that my actions were justified. Children who otherwise might have died were now safe and well. He understood, but insisted that only the Bosnian Army could authorise any further evacuations. Before setting off to the army HQ, I went to see the children and made a note of all their details.

Elvis offered to accompany me to the Bosnian Army headquarters, and just as we were leaving, Selma's father arrived at the hospital. He'd heard from the Red Cross that his family was safe in America and the relief on his careworn face was clearly visible. He was desperate to join them, although he doubted whether the Bosnian Army would agree to let him go. Nevertheless, he insisted that he'd be leaving with me 'whether or not they gave him permission'. He led us along the main street past three APCs manned by the unfortunate UNPROFOR soldiers who'd been forced to remain behind. Once we reached the main junction, I saw a sign that read, 'Warning, Snipers'. There was a nerve-racking wait while we prepared to dash across the exposed area, targeted by snipers who'd taken over the upper storey of a bank that overlooked the square.

We arrived at the command headquarters of the 4th Army Corps only to find that the commander would not be available for at least another two hours. Not wanting to risk the snipers any more than necessary, we decided to wait. Sitting side by side on the front porch, we surveyed the damage caused by two years' fighting. The Serbs had bombarded the city from the mountains to the east, and since May their job had been taken over by the HVO attacks from the west. Few buildings had escaped entirely, and many were blackened shells.

As evening drew near, Elvis became anxious. 'I'm not spending the night here. If we haven't sorted this out by eight o'clock we'll have to go.'

'I don't want to leave without the children,' I said. 'I'll wait until tomorrow if necessary.'

After a while the commander pulled up outside the building in a gleaming black Suzuki 4×4. He was a good-looking man of fifty, and after pausing in front of me for a moment he strode past without a word.

A short time later Elvis was summoned to see him, but he was only gone five minutes before he returned looking annoyed. Mirsad was refused permission to leave unless he had a visa issued by the United States. As for the children, they weren't his concern; I'd have to get permission from the War Office.

To the people of this besieged section of the city, Arif Pasalić was a hero for holding off the enemy for such a long time, and although frustrated by his attitude, I understood his antipathy towards me; the sight of a mother thanking the enemy for saving her child was damaging to morale. Nevertheless, I was surprised that he'd be prepared to delay the children getting the medical help they so desperately needed.

Elvis thought we should leave, but I was damned if I was going to abandon the children after we'd risked our lives to get here.

Hafid had just removed a part of a young boy's brain by torch-light. The boy, called Amel Demić, had been blasted against a wall when a mortar exploded near his front door. His mother had been calling him to come inside and she was also wounded, with pieces of shrapnel embedded in her stomach. Amel, whose skull had been shattered, was now in a coma and Hafid told me that it would be a miracle if he survived. His colleague hadn't wanted to waste the anaesthetic, which was in such short supply, but Hafid pointed out that had it been his own child, he would want him to try.

There was no normal oxygen supply; instead they relied upon the industrial variety, and amputations were performed where in other circumstances the limbs might have been saved. He told me that they were forced to play God, keeping back vital medicines for those who might have a chance.

Later that night Hafid showed me to a room upstairs where there were a few empty beds awaiting a new team of doctors who were travelling across the mountains from Sarajevo. The two Tims chose to sleep in the ambulance parked in the hospital compound, and Roger and Elvis slept in their jeep. I was kept awake by worry and the constant thump of explosions. By the morning I was desperate to be on my way.

Meanwhile, at Bijeli Brijeg Hospital in west Mostar, Vava was having a few beers as he anxiously awaited my return. He told me later that he was sitting in Ivan's office when a phone call was put through from my mother.

'Have you heard from Sally?' she asked.

'She's fine, Mrs Becker, she should be here in the morning,' said Vava, crossing his fingers.

'Please send her my love when you see her.'

'Of course I will,' he replied, as he hastily reached for another bottle.

I arrived at the War Office on the stroke of eight – I had one other card up my sleeve. I had a letter of introduction from Stipe Rozić to an old schoolfriend who worked there. Stipe had told me to ask him a question before handing over the letter. If the man answered correctly, then I would know he could be trusted. After all, the letter was in effect written by the enemy: a Croat.

I found Stipe's friend and promptly asked him the question, which was about a place where they had played as children. He gave the right answer and I handed him the letter, but his response was all too familiar.

'First,' he said, 'it's impossible to help Mr Handzar without a visa from the US. He's of fighting age and although he's been wounded, he must remain here.'

'But what about the others?' I persisted, handing him my list. 'There are six children in need of medical treatment and a woman with a severe head wound whose son might lose his arm.'

The man lowered his voice so as not to be heard outside the office. 'Maybe if you wait two, perhaps three days, we can make sure that the children have the necessary documents that would enable them to leave.'

'But there wasn't any need for documents last time,' I said, struggling to control my anger. 'I've got permission from the Croats to bring them all out.'

'Either you can wait and try to help the children, or you'll have to leave without them,' he replied.

As he began to usher me from his office I asked whether there was anywhere that I could get some cigarettes as I'd given mine away. It was rumoured that there were vast quantities of hashish available in east Mostar but hardly any tobacco.

He took me to a small room and unlocked the door. Cigarette cartons filled the space from floor to ceiling. There had been an attempt to obscure the brand name, but I could just about read it: 'Yugoslavia'. They had no filters and when I tried one it tasted very stale, but I realised they'd have to do – this wasn't the time to try and give up smoking.

Back at the hospital I broke the news to the others. Elvis wanted to leave but Roger preferred to wait a little longer. I left them and entered the reception area where the staff ate and slept. Behind a curtain were four beds, one of them Hafid's. A small team of doctors had arrived from Sarajevo and the dormitory upstairs was now full. Hafid insisted that I use the bed whenever he was on shift, which was basically all the time. He looked exhausted, but I told him that his wife was in good health and being well looked after, which cheered him immensely. The pillows were soft and I closed my eyes, hoping to catch some sleep, but suddenly there was a screaming whine followed by a loud explosion – an RPG had blasted the window just a few feet away from my bed. Although we were in the basement, the windows were level with the pavement outside, and dust and debris were hurled into the room, covering every surface. My ears were ringing from the noise as I sat up, pulling slivers of glass from my hair. I pulled out a small mirror from my overnight bag and saw blood was trickling down my face, tracing fine red lines through the dust.

There was no one around, so I tentatively stepped into the corridor, where I found Dr Milavić's three-year-old son sitting on the floor. I crouched down beside him just as another explosion rocked the building, causing me to jump. He giggled with delight. He hadn't seen anyone react to the bangs before; here they were just a part of everyday life.

A young woman was carried in on a stretcher and laid beside the injured from the previous night. I could hear her screams and cries echoing in the space between us. After a while the noise stopped, and I asked a nurse if she had been given morphine for the pain.

'We don't have any morphine. Anyway, she doesn't need it now because she's dead.'

10

Sixty-five shells hit the area in the first twenty-four hours, and the stream of casualties seemed endless: men and women, boys and girls, babies. Many died while they were waiting for treatment. The HVO didn't have direct line of sight to the hospital from Hum mountain, but their artillery was aimed in our direction and shells often exploded above or in front of the building. It was rumoured that the Bosnian Army kept their ammunition stores in the basement and that the doctors had been struggling to get them to move it.

Hafid ran from one operation to another like a man possessed, his hands bloodied and his eyes frantic. Milavić assessed each patient as they arrived, carried in on stretchers by two brave men. He looked at me and murmured, 'Your friends did this.' I knew that in a way he was right.

Roger had left to film some soldiers, but he returned a short while later unscathed. Elvis wasn't so lucky. He was wounded while anxiously waiting at the hospital entrance for his colleague to return. I watched the doctor extracting the jagged pieces of shrapnel from his back and realised that this young man represented the internecine mess that was Bosnia. His father's people were attacking his mother's people, and he was one of the victims caught in between. He and Roger left the following morning during a lull in the fighting, and after giving blood the Tims arranged to leave with UNPROFOR when they changed shift the following day.

The conditions inside the hospital were appalling. There were only three makeshift water tanks but no purification system, and the electricity supply was almost non-existent as the kerosene-powered generator was generally only used for surgical procedures. Most of the time the surgeons worked using head-torches. What equipment they had was sterilised in an old autoclave heated with wood.

The food consisted of dry bread for breakfast, a bowl of rice or beans cooked in salt water for lunch and the same in the evening. That's all they had. When I received my first ration of rice and 'gravy', I attempted to pick out the weevils but soon gave up. The woman in charge of the kitchen made 'coffee' from a type of green bean; although it tasted nothing like coffee, it was brown and hot, and much better than cold water from the river, which was contaminated with the decomposing bodies.

Milavić asked me if I'd like to speak on Mostar radio. I initially declined the offer, not wanting to become any further embroiled in the propaganda war. He thought that if they announced that I was staying at the hospital, this might deter the Croats from shelling the building. Unable to convince him that it wouldn't make any difference, in the end I agreed.

He took me to the bedside of a young HVO soldier who'd been captured and put to work on the front line. The soldier was wounded in the stomach and urgently needed a transfusion, but he had a rare blood group so there was nothing they could do. I touched his burning forehead and he reached for my hand, staring at me with eyes bright with fever.

'Let's go, let's go,' he murmured repeatedly.

Milavić told me that he was one of four HVO soldiers caught in the blast of a grenade and they were all in the hospital. I suggested that he send a message to Bagarić giving him their details. He agreed that it could do no harm and we gave the letter to Tim Clancy. Although determined to stay behind, I'd never been so frightened and was unsure whether I'd survive. Before leaving Britain, I wrote a letter to my parents to be opened if by some chance I didn't make it back; this was the first time I thought it might actually be read.

To my surprise, the very next day a small contingent of UNPROFOR soldiers came to evacuate three of the soldiers who were stable enough to travel. Their arrival was obviously the result of the message Milavić had sent, but when he saw them he flew into a rage, shouting that he'd included a list of the sick and wounded children but that it had been ignored.

'Instead, they come for fighting men!' he cried and ordered them out of the building.

Following the announcement of my presence on Mostar radio, the shelling stopped for a while. I was convinced it was because of the soldiers, but Milavić thought otherwise. This meant that no one was in a rush to see me leave.

When someone left the building, you could never be sure if they'd make it back. Shortly after I arrived a man called Agim came to see me. He was president of the Albanian community, and he asked me to tell his embassy that two hundred Albanians were trapped in east Mostar and most of them wanted to leave. I promised to pass on the message when I reached the other side, but he returned to the hospital several times each day to ensure that I wouldn't forget. Each time he came, he was risking his life unnecessarily, so I was exasperated when the cook mentioned him again.

'You don't understand,' she said. 'He's dead, killed by a sniper. His body has just been brought in.'

Amel Demić was still in a coma. His family kept a constant vigil beside his bed, and Hafid told me that if by some miracle he managed to survive he'd be in urgent need of specialist care.

His brother Emir glanced at me. 'Please help him,' he said.

In Mostar most activities took place at night as this was the safest time. People would use the cover of darkness to visit friends, bury their dead, collect water from the river or search for food. Most people were living in cellars or the lower floors of buildings, sleeping on blankets, mattresses or rugs, completely reliant on aid. There was no black market, as all the roads into town were targeted by the HVO and the Serbs controlled the surrounding hills. The only food available was from a soup kitchen set up in a former department store where they served three thousand bowls of 'soup' each day.

Every evening Hafid set off to deliver half of his food ration to his sister, who slept beneath the local pharmacy. On the way back he'd stop to feed the wounded cat that lived in the ruins of his father's house. I insisted he take my share of the food, wishing there was more I could do to help.

I went over to the War Office every day hoping to secure the departure papers for the children. Sometimes I'd pass a body left there from the previous night, and the stench of rotting corpses mingled with the stink of excrement and garbage that littered the streets. If the shelling was heavy I'd find that it was closed; if they were busy they told me to come back later.

The main street ran parallel with the river and the side streets leading off it were targeted by snipers. I'd wait anxiously at each intersection, trying to gather the nerve to race across. Occasionally a red pinprick of light would flash across my body from the laser beam on a sniper's rifle, which was truly terrifying.

The shelling soon recommenced, and whenever the generator was working we watched the carnage on the news. The staff cheered when the presenter announced that the Muslim counter-offensive had gained ground. Then onto the screen came scenes of a massacre by Bosnian soldiers, including a young boy who'd been butchered. 'They are all as bad as one another really,' said Hafid softly.

The woman doctor showed me the morgue. This was actually just an ordinary room, as it had no refrigeration. Several bodies were piled inside, one upon the other, and she told me that hundreds of bodies had passed through there since the siege began.

On the fifth day I was woken by a familiar French accent and to my delight I saw it was Danielle from UNICEF. She gave me a hug and then to my dismay announced that she was just about to leave. She'd entered east Mostar with Jerry Hulme, head of the UNHCR in Bosnia-Herzegovina, so I quickly told her about the children and the difficulties I was having trying to arrange their evacuation. She suggested I come with her to meet him, so we raced through the narrow streets to where he was parked with an escort of APCs. Jerry was a middle-aged man, wearing a flak jacket and a blue UN helmet. He removed it for a moment to wipe the sweat trickling down from his bald head. His face was suntanned, and he had twinkling blue eyes. After listening to what I had to say, he assured me that the UNHCR would be able to carry out the evacuation on my behalf.

Danielle tried to convince me to go with them, and I hesitated for a moment, tempted to escape from all the death and destruction. Instead I gave them the list of names and urged them to hurry.

Watching them go left me feeling more alone than ever. I was becoming increasingly light-headed from the lack of food and water, combined with the intense heat. After racing across 'snipers alley', I wearily made my way back to the hospital past the blackened shells of burned-out buildings, sharply delineated against the clear blue sky.

Following a night of constant shelling I awoke to find that the ambulance had taken a hit. I knew that no one would dare venture out long enough to try and fix it, and I was unsure what to do next. My head was aching, and I couldn't seem to think straight. When Hafid finished his shift that evening, he found me sitting on the edge of his bed with my head in my hands.

'Sally, you are sick,' he said, feeling my forehead. 'You have a fever, and I think perhaps it is time for you to leave.'

Knowing there was nothing I could do without transportation, I figured he was probably right. In any case I was confident that Jerry and Daniele would soon be back to carry out the evacuation. The UNPROFOR soldiers would be changing shift the following day and Hafid suggested I go with them.

That evening I went to see the woman with the head wound and found her young son still beside her, nursing his damaged arm. I visited the father of a sixteen-year-old girl with a spinal injury and explained the situation, assuring him I would do my best to help her. Following surgery most patients were taken upstairs, where they were lined up on mattresses on the floor. Among the patients was a young girl, her head swathed in bandages. She was obviously in a great deal of pain and I felt wretched knowing there was nothing I could do.

Early the next morning I packed my bag and said goodbye to the staff. Tim had loaned the flak jackets to the stretcher bearers and I decided to leave them behind. They were made from Kevlar and cost £1,000 each, but I figured that no one needed them more than these two men who continuously risked death as they rushed to help the wounded. Hafid was in the middle of an operation, so, not wanting to disturb him, I left a short note on his bed. I thanked him for his generosity and kindness, and I promised to make sure his wife received the things she needed for their baby. I handed the keys of the ambulance to Milavić's wife and ran from the building.

On the main street I waited while a soldier faxed my details to the base in Medjugorje as they'd need permission before I'd be able to travel in their vehicle. I sat down on the dusty pavement and a scrawny young dog limped towards me. He was brown and white with a very large head, and I saw a piece of shrapnel protruding from his paw. As I gently tried to remove it, he licked my face, perhaps sensing that I wanted to help. I was suddenly overwhelmed. Burying my face in his neck, which was thick with dust, I wept for this poor wounded animal and all the other wretched creatures of this once thriving city; for all the men, women and children who were living like rats in dungeons with death on their doorstep.

I left the city in a UN armoured vehicle, and although it was small and very cramped it felt like heaven, for at last I felt safe. The vehicle broke down before we reached the airfield and we had to be shunted along by another APC, so a journey that should have taken about forty minutes actually took seven hours. As we passed through Čitluk I asked to be let out but was surprised that they insisted on taking me to the UN base. When the hatch was opened and I finally climbed out, a man pointed a camera in my face and a microphone was pushed under my nose as I staggered across the compound.

'How does it feel to be rescued by the UN?'

Back at the hotel I was greeted by Ivan, Lynne and Vava, who were obviously relieved to see me. Vava told me that Ivan had hardly slept and had been to church each day, praying for my safe return. We were joined by the other doctors, and they wanted to hear about my experiences in 'enemy' territory. To be fair they did not ask for any military information; they simply wanted to understand why the mission had failed.

I was exhausted, with dark shadows beneath my eyes, and my cheeks were hollow, my clothes dusty and spattered with blood. Collette pushed her way past the doctors insisting that I needed to rest. She took me to her room and insisted I lie down, as I was still running a fever. As I lay between the clean fresh sheets she gave me some aspirin and camomile tea. There were no bursts of gunfire, no explosions and no screams of pain; only the comforting feel of Collette's cool hand upon my forehead as I drifted off to sleep.

11

As soon as I started to feel better I went to see Ivan about blood supplies for the wounded Croat soldier with the rare blood group. He suggested I ask Jerry Hulme to deliver it to the hospital, so I drove to his office and he gave me his assurance that the evacuation would be taking place within days. They were sorting out the paperwork, and in the meantime he'd be going in with a medevac team to assess the patients. This seemed to me to be an unnecessary delay, but he was adamant that it had to be done as part of the process. He seemed very genuine, if a little patronising in his manner, but at this stage I had no say in the matter: it was no longer my operation. Before I left he asked me for a favour. Would I use my influence with Ivan to get permission for him and Danielle to visit west Mostar? They wanted to inspect the orphanages and hospitals there.

It took me a couple of days to persuade Bagarić to allow them to enter west Mostar on an unofficial basis. I pointed out that she'd agreed to arrange an assessment of Nova Bila in return. Ivan agreed, on condition I accompanied them into the city, which was ironic. In spite of my somewhat fraught relationship with the UN, I was now to be cast in the role of chaperone.

While Jerry and Danielle were taken around the hospital, I went to visit Damir and his family. Erna was still trying to get Damir to Britain, but his permit would allow him no farther than Zagreb. He had relatives there who were desperately trying to sort out a visa, but so far it had been refused on the grounds that he'd need to be accompanied by his parents.

Damir's grandfather had at last returned home to his wife. The antibiotics had worked and he was beginning to walk again. Erna told me that the Rozić family had become very popular because they were friends with the 'Angel of Mostar'. I laughed but Damir assured me that it was true, and indeed when we passed through the checkpoint outside their apartment the soldiers vied with each other to talk to me. It was the same in Čitluk, where we were constantly turning down invitations to visit people's homes. Even the hotel receptionists, who'd always seemed indifferent if not downright cold, now treated us with a grudging respect. It was either due to my stint on the 'other side' or because I was drawing attention to Mostar. Either way, I was pleased because it made Lynne feel much safer.

Three days later, Collette and Sean went with the boys into west Mostar to take some photographs of the damage. Before they left, Collette told me that she planned to join me on my next mission. She had decided she'd rather use her nursing skills in east Mostar, where she felt the people would benefit more from her help. Sean was against the idea, but knowing how determined she was he realised that he had little choice in the matter.

Collette was in a room at the top of an abandoned apartment block in an area known as the Rondo, where the boys were observing an area captured the previous day. A grenade fired from an RPG-7 came through the window and exploded behind the couch where she was sitting. Collette was blown to the far side of the room, conscious but horribly wounded.

Sean was hurled backwards by the blast as he came through the doorway. Making his way through the smoke and the dust he saw that Collette was on the floor. The shrapnel had ripped through her abdomen and damaged vital organs. He shouted for help as she clutched her stomach in an effort to prevent her intestines spilling out.

The boys found an abandoned stretcher in the corridor and carried her down the seven flights of stairs. They immediately commandeered a vehicle, and with the stretcher supported across the top of the seats they drove her towards the hospital on the hill. All the while Sean held her hand and told her that he loved her.

As soon as they arrived at the hospital Collette was rushed into surgery. Sean waited outside the operating room while the doctors battled to save her and finally, after four hours, Vladlena appeared.

'Her injuries are very bad,' she said, looking exhausted. 'She's in a very serious condition. Go back to your hotel – there's nothing you can do here.'

Sean did not want to leave her but Vladlena insisted. 'You must get some rest and come back in the morning.'

That evening Sean appeared in the doorway of our room and told us what happened. When he finished, he sat there in silence, his face pale and drawn. Thierry arrived a short while later, and as he sat down he slowly shook his head.

'She won't make it,' he said softly. 'She's in a very bad way. Even if she survives the operation, she'd be on tubes and machines for the rest of her life. Collette is too lively, too vital. She wouldn't want to live like that.' We lapsed into silence once again, shocked by his words.

Sean decided to go and pack some of her things to take to the hospital. He'd only been gone a few minutes when he reappeared at the door and announced that she was dead.

I could hardly begin to imagine his pain. In the few months since they got together they'd rarely been apart, and I recalled how he'd gazed at her photograph on the bus and how we'd teased him. I remembered the poems he wrote about her and the hundreds of photographs he'd taken: Collette in her surgical greens or wearing his uniform and swimming in the lake at Ljubuški with the boys. Those photographs were now all that remained of this vibrant, beautiful and caring young woman.

After a few minutes Sean announced that he was going to his room. When he left I wandered onto the landing, needing some time to think. I felt terribly guilty, knowing how often I'd tempted fate and feeling that it should have been me instead of her. When I eventually turned around to go back to my room, I saw one of the doctors who worked with Collette. Normally quite tough, with a confident, jaunty manner, he looked drawn, punctured by grief.

'She was so pretty,' he said as tears streamed down his cheeks. Until then I was too numb to cry but seeing him in such torment I too wept openly. Tim and Thierry joined us and we talked long into the night about Collette, remembering how happy she was and the funny things she said.

That morning Sean returned to the hospital with Thierry, after spending the night in the bed he had shared with Collette. Later Thierry told us what had happened.

'It was terrible. The morgue was full so they'd placed her body in another room. I begged Sean not to look at her, to remember her just as she was, young and beautiful. I have seen many corpses and, in this heat, with the flies ... I knew it would be bad, but he wouldn't listen. This isn't Collette, I told him. This is just a body.'

We offered to call Collette's family as they still did not know what had happened, but Sean insisted he'd make the call himself. I asked him if he wanted a drink, but he just sat staring into space. Thinking he'd prefer to be alone I started to leave, but he suddenly reached out his hand. There was nothing I could say to ease his pain, so I just held him close until his tears eventually subsided.

The Croat health authorities arranged for her body to be driven to Split and then flown to Zagreb for cremation. Sean and Tim accompanied the coffin and at the morgue in Split twenty nurses stood in attendance, each holding a white rose in one hand and a candle in the other. A gold plaque was fixed on the wall at

Bijeli Brijeg hospital in remembrance of Collette, who'd died in the very place where she'd worked so hard to save the lives of others.

Another week passed with still no sign of the evacuation of the trapped children. Rod insisted that it would only happen if we carried out the mission ourselves, but Ivan was adamant that he'd not get permission for me to cross the front line alone. He wasn't willing to let me risk my life again – but there was another factor. I'd not yet managed to organise a similar mission to Nova Bila, and Ivan's reputation was on the line. Why, his superiors wanted to know, had he allowed me to help the Bosnians Muslims when I'd not helped one single Croat? I knew that it was imperative I try to reach Nova Bila.

Things went from bad to worse, and Jerry told me that it would be at least two weeks before the evacuation of Mostar would take place. The whole operation had been passed on to the International Office of Migration (IOM), which meant that before the children could be brought out, they had to be allocated hospital beds in other countries. Only then would they be issued with visas. This didn't make sense to me because I knew that Danielle had already arranged for beds to be made available at the US field hospital in Zagreb.

'Why can't the children be taken to Zagreb?' I asked, completely bewildered by the bureaucracy. 'Surely the visas can be allocated once they're safe.'

'The IOM doesn't work like that,' said Jerry patiently. 'They prefer to do all the paperwork first.'

'And what if somebody dies in the meantime?'

'That's the way the mandate works I'm afraid,' he said, seeming a little uncomfortable. 'It's their policy.'

'Then it's a load of crap! Children are dying because of these so called "policies". It's appalling! For goodness' sake, forget the IOM. Instead of going in to assess them tomorrow, just bring them out.'

'Sally, we can't evacuate the children ourselves, not now that the mission has been given to the IOM.'

I couldn't believe what I was hearing. 'Why?' I asked him, softly this time. 'Why was the mission passed to them?'

He started shuffling some papers on his desk and replied to my question without looking up. 'It was a political decision. Perhaps the IOM want the kudos for themselves.'

Politics! It was always politics; politics and publicity, even if it meant risking the lives of the children. And I knew that behind the caring faces of aid workers like Danielle, behind all those brave UN soldiers on the ground, were the faceless puppeteers who pulled the strings for their own political ends. I was consumed with anger and frustration.

The Croats had recently opened an embassy near Medjugorje, where I was invited to meet the new ambassador. We had lunch and talked a little about the situation, but I felt uncomfortable when he proudly announced that the area under their control was now called Herzeg-Bosnia, and Mostar would soon be the capital. Later Vava drove me to meet Mate Boban, the president of 'Herzeg-Bosnia', who congratulated me for what I'd achieved in Mostar – and berated me for what I'd failed to do in central Bosnia.

This was the opportunity I'd been waiting for, and I decided to take a chance. Would he, I asked, give me permission for a convoy to east Mostar, providing I did the same for Nova Bila?

'I don't care where else you go,' said the president. 'You can take aid to all sides, evacuate the injured, so long as you include the areas of Vitez, Novi Travnik, Bugojno and Nova Bila.'

At last, I could realise my dream to help all sides – I had his word. I also knew that I was looking at something on a much greater scale than anything I'd tackled so far. I'd need supplies, transport, volunteers and an enormous amount of money. And of course I didn't have much time, for the situation was growing ever more desperate as winter approached. I'd have to go home.

Ivan and Vava drove Lynne and me to the airport, and I asked them what they thought of Boban.

'He doesn't like me,' said Ivan. 'I was once in his office discussing the political situation and he asked me where I wished to be, so I pointed to his chair!'

We laughed, but in fact I too wished that Ivan had been sitting in the presidential chair; the war might have ended long ago.

'It isn't over,' I told Lynne as we walked through the airport. 'This is my chance to help the children of Nova Bila.'

'You know I won't be here to help you?' said Lynne.

'Do you mean that?' I asked, unable to imagine Bosnia without her.

She looked at me sadly. 'Everything changed when Collette died. And now the boys have gone ...'

I suggested she might be exhausted. 'Perhaps you just need a good rest.'

Lynne laughed. 'And what about you? Don't *you* need a rest?'

'Well, I'll get one while I'm in Britain,' I said.

'A rest?' she said, as they called our flight over the tannoy. 'You'll be lucky. You'll need volunteers and aid, funding and vehicles ...'

'Sounds a bit too much like hard work to me,' I said, as we hurried towards the plane. 'I might have to reconsider!'

I found a letter from Hafid waiting for me when I got home. He said that I'd brought light into their lives and he prayed for my swift return. He thanked me for all I'd done for his people and hoped that God would bless me always. He had some tragic news as well, which made me cry.

I am so sorry to have to inform you that despite their promise, the UN have not yet carried out the evacuation of the children. Medina, a child who was wounded by shrapnel in her brain, has died from septicaemia; there was nothing we could do. She was only eleven years old. This war is a travesty. It is destroying us and killing our children.

Naturally I blamed myself for what had happened. I shouldn't have relied on the UN. I should have been more insistent; I should have tried to go back in and bring them out myself.

I wrote a strongly worded fax to the UN headquarters in Zagreb, demanding they carry out the evacuation immediately. A reply came back within an hour: the evacuation would proceed within days.

A short while later I was watching a television documentary about Mostar. Jeremy Bowen was speaking to Medina's mother.

'I thought that Sally Becker would help us,' she sobbed. 'But she didn't come and my little girl died.'

They are words I can never forget.

12

I scribbled the sums on a piece of paper. We'd need, I calculated, about £60,000 to get the convoy to Bosnia, and I'd arrived back in Britain with nothing. And yet on 10 December 1993, World Human Rights Day, Operation Angel assembled at Brighton Pier with over two hundred volunteers and fifty-six trucks, ambulances and even a coach. It was the largest convoy to leave these shores; and it had all been done in three weeks. The story of how it came together is a remarkable testimony to the resourcefulness and generosity of the people of Britain.

It had begun extremely badly. In fact, before we were able to get underway I wasted five precious weeks trying to do things 'through the proper channels'. I had lunch with a man from the Overseas Development Administration, I sent faxes to John Major, the British prime minister, telling him about the children, and I tried every avenue I could think of. But each in turn was a dead end.

I also had fun, as I was presented with awards from the Variety Club, the Celebrity Guild of Great Britain and the Ross McWhirter Foundation, and I was invited to meet Princess Margaret at a luncheon for Women of the Year. When I received notification of the McWhirter award, I was invited to attend a dinner being held at the Inner Temple in London. I needed an escort for this event, so I asked Duncan Stewart, a local GP, to accompany me. It seemed appropriate as I'd known him a long time and he was the first person to donate supplies for me to take to Bosnia. He was the perfect escort, tall, handsome and very charming.

Having lived in a war zone for some time, it felt strange to find myself sitting amid members of the aristocracy, judges and other notables at a magnificent banquet. As they congratulated me, I wondered how I came to be there. My parents and my brother joined us, together with my oldest friend Heather James. As liqueurs were served, I asked Duncan if he'd consider becoming the medical officer for Operation Angel; Dr Mark Porter from BBC *Good Morning* was supposed to come but he had peritonitis and was forced to cancel.

Duncan shook his head and laughed. 'I'd love to but I'm afraid I'm far too busy.'

'Believe me, Duncan,' said my father, 'before the night is out she'll change your mind.' And he was right.

I was presented with the Unsung Heroes award by the actor Richard Wilson, and when it was time to make a speech I was astounded by all the famous faces in front of me. I couldn't quite bring myself to wear an evening gown and high heels (I'd spent too long in jeans, T-shirt and trainers, and knew I wouldn't feel comfortable in a dress), so I settled for a pair of smart black trousers and a white silk blouse. Various interviews were arranged through Mike Mendoza and I used the opportunity to highlight the mission. The *Daily Mirror* had started an appeal, but things were still moving very slowly.

I was asked to speak at an event organised by the JACS (Jewish Adult Cultural Society) that raised almost £2,000. This enabled us to buy our first ambulance, a Bedford, similar to the one I used in Bosnia, but this time fully equipped. From that point on, things really began to happen as I was able to set up a headquarters with telephones and a fax machine – until that point I'd been using my mother's kitchen. Then an old school friend called Stewart Weir offered his assistance. He took charge of recruitment and immediately enlisted two women from the local business school to help me. Justine and Val were to prove indispensable, using their skills to type all the reams of necessary documents, letters and faxes, taking endless phone calls, interviewing prospective volunteers and keeping track of my appointments.

Duncan was president of the Sir Halley Stewart Trust, set up by his grandfather to provide funds for worthy causes, and they donated £1,000. Gloria Macari, who had a beautiful voice and a heart to match, wrote a song together with her colleagues Roger Ferris and Yolanda Beeny called 'Hear the Children', and I found it so moving that I called Neil Morris, producer of BBC TV's *Good Morning*, and played a recording of the song over the phone. He was very interested, and the next day I was invited onto the show to talk about our mission. The BBC decided to get behind us, and Anne Diamond and her co-presenter Nick Owen started an appeal.

A friend of Duncan's designed a leaflet that he printed by the thousand. The leaflet read: 'An angel rushes in where most of us fear to tread' and included a photograph of Elmir, taken by the award-winning photographer Simon Dack, just after we came out of Mostar.

The leaflet was endorsed by several celebrities, including Harold Pinter, Lady Antonia Fraser, Chris Eubank, Christopher Timothy, Andrew Bowden MP, Bob Marshall Andrews QC and Dr Mark Porter. At the bottom of the page were the details of UKJAID, a registered charity that had agreed to handle funds on our behalf – we didn't have time to apply for charitable status.

Stewart Weir appointed half a dozen co-coordinators based around the country, and they began to distribute the literature and start appeals within their own areas. The police in Humberside loaned us a mobile kitchen, and as my cousin Ashley was studying to be a chef, he was put in charge of the catering. His elder brother David had managed to convince the company he worked for to donate a truck filled with aid, which he would drive to Bosnia himself.

The response to the appeal was incredible. People right across the country began raising funds and collecting supplies. Elderly ladies knitted sweaters and children handed their pennies over in school.

Sadly, there wasn't time to release 'Hear the Children' so *Good Morning* chose another song – 'Remembering Christmas', performed by the Bramdean Boys Choir – that was already available on CD. The BBC compiled a very moving video to accompany the song, which raised over £8,000. An appeal in the *Sunday Mirror* raised a further £11,000 and Sally Line Ferries offered us free passage to France; Nissan loaned me a brand-new 4×4, Vodaphone loaned us some mobiles to use while we were setting things up, and Trailblazers provided loudspeakers and CB radios for each of the vehicles.

An extraordinary man called Mansukh Patel, who ran an organisation dedicated to world peace, invited me and Duncan to visit his multi-faith centre in Birmingham. He then marshalled all his followers to prepare hundreds of nutritious food parcels for the journey. A motto was printed on each of the parcels: 'Every little thing we do, no matter how small, can change the world.'

We were offered hand-knitted teddy bears, which we decided to include in the family boxes, by an organisation called Teddies for Tragedies, run by Evelyn and Peter Reese. It started in 1985 and since then hundreds of thousands of teddies have been knitted, bringing smiles to the faces of children all over the world.

Having somehow managed to capture the country's imagination, we were inundated with aid. Perhaps it was due to the fact that people were used to putting a few coins in a box never actually knowing where the money would go or how it would be used; whereas those who supported us knew where the aid was going and who we aimed to help – and they could even follow the whole thing on TV.

There were, of course, the occasional blunders. We appealed for family parcels destined for the refugee camps and a man who worked for the ambulance service offered to help. He made an announcement on television that the parcels could be dropped in to any ambulance station, but he forgot to inform his bosses. As a result, ambulance stations right across the country were inundated with parcels and no one was available to receive them. The phone rang continuously for days until we finally managed to sort out the misunderstanding and arrange for the aid to be collected.

We appealed for volunteers, preferably ex-servicemen or emergency service workers. We needed people who were used to discipline and not easily frightened, and we tried to discourage those with young children by stressing that the areas we hoped to reach were very dangerous. Unfortunately, there wasn't time to vet each volunteer personally, but we did insist on good references and a clean bill of health. Each person was asked to raise sponsorship of £100 towards the costs. I contacted the AA and the RAC, who kindly offered to provide breakdown teams for the convoy. They'd remain alongside us throughout the mission, there to provide back-up.

With donations of medical equipment from hospitals that were closing or refurbishing and medical supplies from various companies, we had over £1 million worth of medical aid, but we were still short of funds for the journey itself. The ship that would carry the convoy from Italy to Croatia was going to cost a further £30,000, and we hadn't yet reached our original target. It was then that Duncan kindly stepped in to offer the use of the building that housed his surgery as surety for a loan. By the time we were due to leave we'd raised enough money and the loan was not needed after all, but I was touched and honoured by his faith in me.

During this time, I was busy trying to clarify the overall plan. It would be no use having the means if we had not sorted out the end. My aim was to help all sides in the conflict, so I approached the respective embassies to request permission to cross their territories. The Croats and the Bosnians confirmed their agreement, but the Serbs failed to respond to any of my requests. We therefore headed to east Mostar, where the Muslims were besieged by Croats, and to Nova Bila, where the Croats were besieged by Muslims.

I contacted the UN in Zagreb to request protection for the convoy and to my surprise I received an immediate response. Karen AbuZayd was chief of mission in Bosnia-Herzegovina, and she sounded very enthusiastic about the mission, even asking whether I'd consider including other enclaves such as Tuzla and Zenica. Her only stipulation was that the selection of the patients would be done by the UNHCR medevac team. I agreed, and the UN issued a press release announcing a joint mission that they called 'Operation Angel'.

I soon found myself caught up in a bizarre Catch-22 situation. I kept receiving messages from the UNHCR informing me that Britain had refused to allocate beds. When I contacted the ODA, the government department responsible for such things, they told me that no beds had been requested. With the planned evacuation of several hundred sick and wounded children and their families, this allocation was essential, so I wrote to them both and suggested they sort it out.

I was contacted by a representative of Veterans for Peace, an NGO based in the States that apparently had access to numerous hospital beds. They put me in touch with Bianca Jagger, who was staying at the Savoy Hotel in London, and Duncan and I went to meet her. She assured us that she'd do her best to help but she'd need details of the patients, so I sent a message to the UNHCR. The Veterans were already caring for some of the children I evacuated from east Mostar, including Maja Kazazić, and to my great delight, they forwarded her letter. It was a wonderful note telling me about her life now and how thankful she and her family were. If ever I found myself wavering through exhaustion or frustration, Maja's letter strengthened my resolve.

A few days before departure, my family was invited to accompany me to the Variety Club Ball. I found myself sitting at the top table beside Dame Vera Lynn. When we were introduced, I told her how honoured I was to meet her. She took my hand and said, 'You are a brave and courageous young woman, and it is I who am honoured to meet you.' Hearing this from one of the best-loved and respected women in Britain, I can honestly say my heart nearly burst with pride.

Towards the last few days we were working day and night in order to meet the deadline, but somehow we did it. On 9 December, 230 volunteers dressed in white sweatshirts and base-ball caps with 'Operation Angel' emblazoned in blue assembled at the Thistle and the Metropole hotels in Brighton, where they'd be staying overnight, free of charge.

The volunteers were a wonderfully varied group of people, both in age and background. There were nurses of all ages, ambulance drivers, medics, firemen, policemen, two female doctors and a psychologist. There was also a team of five doctors from Veterans for Peace who'd flown in from the States, though unfortunately their offer of beds had not yet been confirmed.

As a result of the UN announcement, members of the press had arranged to meet us in Croatia but others, including a crew from the BBC and another from ITV Meridian, would be travelling with us. Meridian were making a documentary about my work and they'd been filming some of the lead-up to the actual mission.

We'd arranged a final briefing prior to departure, and when I stepped onto the platform in the conference hall the place was humming with energy. There was a heart-warming ovation from our 270 volunteers, and when they eventually quietened down I thanked them for coming. I then proceeded to explain as clearly as possible the current situation in Bosnia-Herzegovina. I made it clear how gruelling the journey across Europe would be and explained that the drivers would work in shifts, stopping only for fuel and the occasional meal. Using video footage from a hard-hitting BBC documentary called *Unfinished Business*, I showed them the area where they'd be going and stressed the dangers. I made it clear that they might become irritable and bad-tempered from lack of sleep, that they'd probably argue with one another, but it was important to keep sight of our aim – to save lives.

Next on the podium was Lawrence Le Carré, an energetic man in his fifties with a mop of bright red hair and a very loud voice. Lawrence had run convoys to Bosnia before, and he explained the driving rules and emergency procedures. When he'd finished, Duncan stood up and briefed the volunteers on the medical aspects of our mission.

The briefing lasted from 10 a.m. until three o'clock in the afternoon, after which the volunteers were free to spend the rest of the day as they pleased. The mood among them was a mixture of exhilaration and trepidation. Many had said goodbye to their families, not sure whether they'd make it home for Christmas and perhaps even wondering whether they'd return at all.

Later that night a fax arrived from the UNHCR, a document I should have received much earlier containing a detailed list of the evacuees. There were more than eighty in Mostar alone, including Amel Demić, who was still in a coma. The list also included names from Zenica, Tuzla and Sarajevo, all predominantly Muslim enclaves. It was then that I saw there was only one patient coming from Nova Bila, and my heart sank. According to Ivan, there were still many seriously injured children at the monastery who were in desperate need of specialised medical treatment. The fax stated that heavy snow was blocking the roads into central Bosnia and it would therefore be impossible to take the convoy in with us. Instead, they'd arranged to fly me and Duncan to Sarajevo and bring the evacuees out by air.

I was filled with dismay, knowing that the Croats would be enraged. Not only would it now be impossible to take aid into

Nova Bila, only one person would be evacuated. I was sure that the Croats would feel that I had reneged on our agreement, but there was nothing we could do so soon before departure. Nevertheless, I was determined to get the list amended as soon as we arrived.

Early the next morning when all the supplies had been loaded onto the vehicles, the press began to film the convoy leaving the car park beneath the Metropole hotel. As we prepared to pull out onto the main road, a traffic warden appeared and began working her way along the line issuing parking tickets, seemingly oblivious to the whirring of cameras and gales of laughter.

A crowd of well-wishers had gathered at the Palace Pier to see us off. The convoy comprised seventy-two ambulances and trucks, most of them white and emblazoned with the Operation Angel logo and stickers from Sally Line Ferries, and one by one they began to line up along the promenade.

'Don't worry, I'll take good care of her,' said Duncan, hoping to reassure my father.

'More likely she'll take care of you,' he replied, to the amusement of those within earshot.

I started my engine, a signal to the rest of the convoy that we were leaving, and as we pulled away from the kerb I could see my mother was crying. Standing beside her was her sister Jenny, whose sons Ashley and David had volunteered. Through a loudspeaker secured to my vehicle, Gloria Macari's voice filled the air.

Can you hear them?
Do you care?
Listen to the children, crying out there.
All their pain and suffering, they never asked to play our
    games.

This was followed by the chorus sung by the children.

We are the children,
Listen to our voices,
We are the future but all our dreams are dying.
We have the gift of life;
We have the right to survive.
Oh mankind, please don't take away our world.

One by one each of the vehicles pulled up behind me, the blue lights of the ambulances flashing in unison. Glancing in the rearview mirror my heart swelled – Operation Angel was at last underway.

13

The convoy seemed jinxed from the start. The canteen trailer loaned by Humberside police jack-knifed on the road leaving Brighton and although no one was hurt, we lost our mobile kitchen. Ashley and his friend Nick, who were supposed to do the catering, would now have to travel in the bus.

We made it to the ferry port just in time and found the coach waiting for us. The driver had removed most of the seats and spread mattresses on the floor, as we'd done on previous convoys to enable people to take a proper rest. Somehow Stewart Weir had enlisted too many volunteers, but I hadn't the heart to force anyone to leave. Instead, I borrowed a minibus from Sally Line Ferries to accommodate the extra people.

Once we boarded the ferry, I went to call our representative in France. He was trying to trace the documents that would enable us to pass through the motorway tolls without paying. This was standard for all humanitarian aid convoys, but there was a lot of paperwork involved. When I returned from the office, I over-heard a man making an announcement in a broad Scottish accent.

'We shouldn't follow their route,' he was saying, slurring slightly from an excess of alcohol. 'I know a better way. Anyway, it's all being done wrong and I don't think we should continue with this woman.'

I tugged at his sleeve, for he obviously hadn't noticed me come in. 'This woman would prefer you didn't continue at all,' I said, to the sound of cheering. 'First of all, you're drunk, and drinking is strictly forbidden while driving in convoy. Second, I made it very clear that anyone attempting to stir up trouble would be asked to leave. We are travelling to a war zone, for goodness' sake.'

There was silence as everyone waited for his reaction. I knew that this incident could make or break my authority with the volunteers. The man lurched towards me and started to shout in my face.

'Well, I have to tell you,' he slurred, 'that first I'm not drunk and that second I plan to bring out a couple of soldiers who are stuck in central Bosnia, so I really have to go there.'

I could hardly believe what I was hearing. If this man was being serious, he was actually prepared to jeopardise the whole mission by attempting to smuggle soldiers through a war zone.

'You're no longer part of this convoy,' I said coldly. 'Please remove the logo from your vehicle and travel separately. I'm sorry, but I will not risk you being connected with us. This is an official evacuation, and we are working within UN regulations. I've signed a paper that states I'll not make any unauthorised evacuations, and as leader of this convoy I'm responsible for the actions of all the volunteers.'

On arrival at Dunkirk I still had to sort out the authorisation for the tolls, so while the volunteers were left to catch some sleep, I remained in the office while a persistent Frenchwoman attempted to clear our path. It took until dawn, but at last we set off and Duncan took the wheel of the Nissan Patrol so I could get some rest. When we stopped to fuel up, John Morrison, a university lecturer from Humberside, suggested that we go on ahead to the next toll in order to make sure the convoy wouldn't be delayed. It seemed a sensible idea at the time but I was to regret it bitterly later.

The BBC crew had followed us to the next toll and to my surprise I saw Stewart was with them. He was supposed to be our personnel officer, in charge of the volunteers, so I was disappointed to learn that he was being paid as the BBC's driver instead.

Everything was now in place for the convoy to pass through the tolls and we waited for them to catch up. Hours went by but still no one came, so we drove to the nearest service station to find out where they were, mobile phones not yet being ubiquitous. After a night of frantic phone calls to Meridian TV, we finally had an answer. The convoy had stopped to unload some excess weight from some of the vehicles. The Red Cross later picked up the discarded boxes, which contained clothes and blankets that were sent on to Bosnia. Unfortunately, the scene had already been filmed by Meridian, who gave the impression that the aid had just been dumped. This would do our reputation immense harm before we were able to set the record straight.

Morrison and his wife had arranged a meeting to sort things out, sidelining Lawrence and appointing the firemen as convoy leaders instead. They'd sensibly split the vehicles up into separate groups that were easier to manage and able to make quicker progress, but they'd failed to inform Lawrence. The vital medical supplies and equipment had been transferred to the three largest trucks, which left more space in the ambulances for the drivers.

As each group arrived, Duncan and I spent hours sorting out their grievances and giving encouragement to those who'd begun to lose heart. I was disappointed that even at this early stage, some of the volunteers had already seemed to have lost sight of our aim. One man was complaining that he'd not had a hot meal in hours, and I reminded him that there were poor souls in Mostar who hadn't had a hot meal in months.

Duncan observed that we were taking along a few volunteers with a package holiday mentality. It was our own fault, though, because we hadn't had the time to interview each person in order to weed out those with neither the stomach nor the stamina for such an exercise.

Ashley and Nick had rigged up the Primus stoves in the car park, and while the volunteers ate a hot meal, I received a phone call that was patched through the BBC crew saying that the Italian police wanted a word with me. Feeling exhausted, I set off with Duncan, Lawrence and Mick Fegan, a former policeman who'd been driving one of the large trucks. To my dismay, I saw that the man at the border post was the loud-mouthed drunk I'd dismissed from the convoy. He was held up at the border and I noticed that he hadn't removed the Operation Angel logo from his Land Rover. It soon became apparent that he was demanding free access through the tolls under our name.

Lawrence became angry, his outrage further fuelled because a volunteer had reported that the Scotsman had been boasting about smuggling weapons into Bosnia. A scuffle broke out, and Lawrence landed a punch on the man's nose. As I watched him run off, I shook my head in disbelief. My dream was rapidly turning into a nightmare, and we hadn't even reached our destination.

My next concern was an elderly man being cared for by one of the paramedics. His vehicle had broken down and he'd slept in the open, waiting for a lift. The paramedic told me that the man was suffering from a mild form of hypothermia and was not fit to continue the arduous journey, so we arranged to fly him back to the UK.

We drove on ahead to sort out the tolls and arrived in Ancona ahead of the others. Planning to have a well-earned rest for a few hours while we waited for the groups to arrive, we checked into the Hotel Jolly. The hotel could not have had a more inappropriate name. As soon as I entered my room, I received a call from Mike Mendoza; the news was filled with reports that our coach had crashed and there were apparently several casualties.

I knocked on Duncan's door and told him what had happened, and we frantically tried to call the hospital where the injured had been taken. The coach had been struck in the rear by a speeding truck but fortunately the reports of serious injuries were unfounded; the coach driver had whiplash and some of the passengers were lightly bruised. A few of them were traumatised by the accident and felt unable to face the ordeal ahead so we authorised the funds to fly them home and Mike arranged for them to be picked up at Gatwick Airport. We then spent the rest of the night making sure their families had been informed.

The remaining coach passengers insisted they wanted to continue the journey and they joined us on the quayside a few hours later. Among them were Ashley and Nick, who'd been sitting in the rear seats of the coach until ten minutes before the crash, when they happened to transfer to David's truck. Had they not done so they'd have been seriously injured, perhaps even killed.

There were showers and hot food on board the ship, and cabins were allocated to those most in need. I was invited to dine with the ship's captain to discuss the forthcoming mission and he asked me which route I preferred to take and what time I'd like to dock in Croatia; having never been 'in charge' of a ship before, I found it quite exhilarating. As we crossed the swelling waves of the Adriatic, however, I began to feel seasick and was relieved when we finally sailed into port.

As we docked in the pouring rain, we were met by UN officials who appeared very friendly and polite. They explained that Duncan and I would be taken to Sarajevo while the convoy was escorted to Makarska to wait for our return. We'd booked a hotel on the beach, so that while we were in Sarajevo the volunteers would be able to rest from their journey.

Following a series of interviews with the press who were hanging around the port, I overheard a briefing being given to the volunteers by one of the very same officials. He was informing them that they'd be travelling to Mostar the following day. I marched through the crowd and climbed some scaffolding so that all the volunteers would hear me.

'Please ignore what you've just been told,' I said. 'You will not be going to Mostar tomorrow at all. I have given my word to the Croatian authorities that the mission will not take place until we have carried out the evacuation of Nova Bila. They've made it very clear that this is the way it will happen, and I'm not prepared to jeopardise that. We can't pass through territory held by the Croats without their permission; it would be foolish as well as dangerous, and the operation could fail.'

Some of the volunteers nodded, while others just stood there looking confused.

'As soon as we return from Sarajevo, then and only then will we have permission to enter Mostar. In the meantime you'll be staying in a comfortable hotel where you can eat and drink whatever you wish and take a well-earned rest.'

'Suppose something happens to you and you don't make it back?' called out one of the doctors bluntly.

'Then the situation would be out of my hands,' I replied.

The UN official apologised, saying there had been a misunderstanding. I accepted his apology but remained a little sceptical as we said our goodbyes. The volunteers gathered around to wish us good luck and afterwards I took Lawrence aside.

'Regardless of what happened en route,' I told him, 'you're still in charge of the vehicles and the aid.'

At the UN headquarters in Split we were joined by Mark Dowdney, the foreign correspondent for the *Daily Mirror*, and a cameraman called Roy who worked for Meridian. Each of us was issued with a UNHCR identification card that would enable us to use UN transport and placed us under their official protection. Beneath my photograph was the word 'Consultant', which caused me to chuckle. I'd been given a flak jacket but it lacked the vital Kevlar plates that were supposed to be placed inside. Duncan had a bulletproof vest loaned to him by one of our volunteers, but he was told by an officer to leave it behind as he'd be issued with a better one in Sarajevo.

As we crossed the airport tarmac, a soldier suddenly appeared. 'You're not allowed to travel without a flak jacket,' he shouted at Duncan. 'It's forbidden under UN rules.'

'He has to come,' I replied, raising my voice to be heard over the roar of the engines. 'As our medical officer he'll be needed to assess the patients not yet included on the list.'

The soldier shrugged. 'Well, he ain't going nowhere without a flak jacket, so I suggest you either travel without him or stay behind yourself.'

He seemed unnecessarily aggressive, and I stepped in front of him so that we were virtually nose to nose.

'First, there's no need to be so rude! And second, your boss has caused this problem by insisting that our medical officer leave his flak jacket behind. Something smells a little odd around here, and I'm telling you now that I'll not be going anywhere without him.'

At that moment a BBC cameraman came over. He'd forgotten to bring his passport, thinking that the UN pass would be sufficient, and now he too was unable to travel. He offered his flak jacket to Duncan, and at last we were able to board. After stowing our boxes of food and medical supplies destined for Nova Bila, we sat down beside the medevac representative, a French woman called Geneviève who was in charge of this part of the mission.

The flight was very short, and once we landed in Sarajevo we raced to unload the boxes from the hold. The surrounding area was controlled by the Serbs so the airfield was exposed to snipers, and there was the continuous sound of shelling and gunfire. The sounds, so familiar to me, were completely new to Duncan, but he seemed quite calm as he struggled back and forth beneath the heavy loads.

Beneath the tarmac lay a tunnel that bypassed both UN controls and the siege lines. Protected from Serb shelling and sniper fire, thousands of people, and tonnes of food, arms and other supplies were smuggled through the tunnel every day; eight hundred metres long, it had taken six months to build. The UN denied its existence, but it provided a lifeline for the city throughout the siege.

We took shelter within a darkened room while we waited for transport to our hotel. Mark Dowdney, who resembled a bank manager with his grey hair and glasses, looked incongruous in the stark surroundings. He was chatting to Duncan, who despite his exhaustion was smiling, his fair hair curled by the drizzling rain and his eyes a cornflower blue. He caught my gaze and I felt my pulse quicken as he smiled. Seemingly unconcerned by the darkness and the danger, his courage gave me an unfamiliar sense of security. For the first time in months I didn't feel afraid, and at that moment he seemed like a knight from a fairy tale, wearing a flak jacket instead of shining armour.

A UN soldier appeared and informed us that our transport had been delayed; the vehicle had been detained inside Serb lines and wouldn't now make it before curfew. We were eventually taken into the city in an APC to the Holiday Inn Hotel. The surrounding buildings were pockmarked with shrapnel and bullet holes, and blackened by fire. The city had been under siege for over a year and very few people dared venture out onto the streets. Those who did were desperately trying to avoid the snipers as they raced from one side of the road to the other.

Built to house the athletes during the 1984 Winter Olympic Games, the Holiday Inn was now the only functioning hotel in town, a battered yellow building that had become a familiar backdrop to news reports around the world. Several floors were missing, struck by a shell earlier in the conflict.

Walking through the darkened atrium strung with fairy lights, we were told that the power only ran long enough for the chefs to prepare a meal. We followed Geneviève through the reception area to an alcove where a woman sat behind a glass partition. She noted down our details by the light of a candle and we paid for the rooms by credit card, increasing the feeling that we were in the midst of some strange dream. Geneviève announced that she'd see us in the morning, so we made our way up several flights of stairs by torchlight to our rooms. The bathroom had no running water but to my delight the power suddenly came on. There was a knock at the door and a maid came in to turn down my bed. Duncan handed her a large bar of hazelnut chocolate in lieu of a tip and she gave him a beaming smile.

'She can probably sell it on the black market and buy some food,' I told him.

'She can probably buy a house with it,' he replied, making me laugh.

'We should have got a discount for the rooms,' I pointed out. 'Eighty dollars per night seems a trifle expensive for a view of the Serbian guns.'

He turned on the television and a Western came on. After watching for a moment he turned off the sound.

'Why did you do that?' I asked.

'Because we've got the real thing outside.'

The room was very cold. It was snowing outside and there was no heating. I was tired and wanted to climb into bed but first we needed to eat. Duncan said he'd scout around for food and left me alone in the room. After about ten minutes had passed, the lights went out again and I realised he hadn't taken the torch. I sat there worrying as I pictured him wandering around in the dark, but after what seemed like ages I heard a noise in the corridor. He'd managed to find his way back by feeling for the numbers on the doors.

'Madam,' he said, offering his arm, 'would you care to join me for dinner?'

I took his arm and we carefully made our way down the stairs using the torch. As we entered the dining room I gasped at the extraordinary scene before us. Tables were laid with white linen cloths and cutlery gleamed beneath subdued lighting. Waiters dressed in peach-coloured jackets with starched white shirts and black bow ties bustled between the tables carrying trays laden with food. There was a low buzz of conversation and nearly all of the tables were full. Fortunately, Mark Dowdney had saved us a place, and as we sat down I felt as though we'd been transported from war-torn Sarajevo to a high-class restaurant in Mayfair.

The meal, however, was a stark reminder that we were far away from London. The rolls were freshly baked but the meat had a strange flavour, and I almost choked when Duncan suggested it might be horse flesh. A bottle of house wine cost $40 and the coffee was $10 per cup; we were dining in a city where people were known to strip bark from the trees to fill their empty bellies. Most of our fellow diners were journalists and UN personnel, and Mark informed us that the management paid protection money to the Serbs in order to stay in business.

When the meal was over, we returned to my room to discuss arrangements for the morning. It was still very cold in spite of the fact that we were wearing our coats, and we huddled together for warmth. We chatted about mundane things and for the first time in days I began to relax.

The following morning we were driven to Kiseljak, a former ski resort with panoramic views. We were taken into the UN compound and given our itinerary for the day, which included visits to a hospital and an orphanage from where children would be evacuated as part of the mission. Nova Bila had now been removed from the list; according to Geneviève, the only patient to pass the medevac assessment didn't now wish to leave. I insisted that we go there anyway, if only to deliver the medical aid and to see the situation for ourselves.

The Church of the Holy Ghost in Nova Bila was still being used as a hospital for the sick and the wounded, and we were greeted at the entrance by Fra Franjo Grebenar, a Franciscan monk who said that he'd been expecting me for a very long time. All the beds were full, so many of the patients were lying on wooden pews in the chapel.

There was a sudden commotion and a man with a bullet lodged in his head was rushed into a room where operations were performed. A television crew appeared, and as the doctors prepared to try and help the wounded man, cameras began to whirr. No one attempted to stop them filming, much to our surprise. In fact, one of the doctors, with blood still dripping from his hands, twisted the poor man's face towards the camera to emphasise the horror of their situation.

We were taken around the makeshift hospital and listened to the patients' histories: soldiers wounded in the fighting, missing limbs or eyes and sometimes both; women, young and old, maimed by shrapnel; children, one with no legs and another with no arms, one seriously ill and another horribly burned. Someone placed a baby in my arms. He was eight months old and almost blind, but no one knew why. They didn't have the facilities to run any tests and as I held his small, limp body his mother broke down and cried.

'My husband has been killed and I am alone with my children. Please help us. Take us out of here so that my son can get treatment,' she pleaded.

I tried to comfort her, but the child struck at me with her tiny fists, thinking that I had made her mother cry. Rage welled up inside me. 'Why were these children not included on the list?' I demanded to know.

'You promised beds,' Geneviève began shouting angrily. 'But your government knows nothing about it. In any case this child isn't dying – there are others more in need.'

'She's going blind,' I said calmly. 'Doesn't that count as serious? Surely we ought to try and help her?'

'We don't have enough beds available. Your government insists that you didn't request any, and those we have are needed for more serious cases.'

I was outraged, thinking of all the meetings and phone calls with the ODA, the letters I'd written to John Major, the IOM and the Home Office. I'd tried every tactic I could think of to get this sorted and so had the various people I'd approached. Yet the answer had always been the same: the beds must be requested by medevac and approved by the UNHCR and the International Office of Migration.

On impulse I spun around to face the cameras with the child still lying in my arms.

'Please don't leave the children here to die. John Major, I'm begging you to help them. Let us have the beds so they can be saved.'

We were taken to the staff room where I explained that we desperately wanted to help their children but were being prevented from doing so. The doctors told me that Geneviève had not been near the hospital in weeks and that the only patient to be included on the list was a man who decided he'd rather a child was left in his place. We told them that we'd continue to push for the evacuation – and if it didn't happen, I'd find a way to do it myself.

To our surprise we heard that a convoy was due to arrive later that day. Dr Slobodan Lang, a Jewish Croat from Zagreb, had negotiated with the Bosnian Muslims, and each side was bringing a convoy of humanitarian aid to the area. One was destined for the area of Nova Bila, the other for Zenica. So much for the roads being impassable.

Duncan and I were invited to the maternity ward and watched enchanted as a jolly midwife placed a new-born in the arms of its young mother. There was only one obstetrics bed for the hundreds of women living in the area and this was the 110th child to be born there. We felt immensely cheered by the mother's joy and the midwife's obvious pride in her work. Despite the horrors of the war raging beyond the doors, despite all the confusion and fear, there was still new life to be cherished.

As we prepared to leave, however, our frustrations soon resurfaced. I found Geneviève in the midst of a television interview lambasting me for misleading the UN. I felt suddenly weary at the thought of defending myself yet again, so I just turned away. Fra Grebenar requested an Operation Angel sweatshirt and gave us gifts in return: a black and white print inscribed with the words 'with thanks to the Angel of Nova Bila' and a watercolour for Duncan. We were touched yet saddened, for in spite of our efforts we'd been unable to help them.

When we left Nova Bila, our vehicle was caught in cross-fire and as the bullets ricocheted off the armour plating, we were grateful for the skill of the British soldier who was driving. We stopped in Vitez and were greeted by an officer from the Coldstream Guards who briefed us on the local situation. All sides were encouraged to pass on information knowing that it would remain confidential, with the result that not a soldier nor a weapon moved without UNPROFOR knowing about it. Major Tohler was informative and amusing, and despite the setbacks of the day we found ourselves still able to laugh. He told us about an arms factory, coveted by all sides, which was situated beside a jam factory, and pointed out that if the factory were blown up it could create a very 'sticky' situation.

That evening we ate in the officers' quarters and spent a pleasant couple of hours watching them rehearse their Christmas show. Duncan and Mark were then led away to the barracks together with the other journalists, while I was told I'd be spending the night at the home of the commander of the British battalion, Colonel Peter Williams.

The gallant colonel led the way, stamping a path through the thick, slimy mud – the bane of every soldier's life – so that I could literally follow in his footsteps. As we made our way across the base, I told him about the children who'd been excluded from the evacuation list, and he assured me that if I came back for them his men would be ready to assist with the evacuation.

Despite all the conflicting information whirling around in my brain, I slept very well that night and awoke feeling refreshed. I had a hot shower, a change of clothes and was served with coffee by a young soldier who insisted on calling me 'Ma'am'. I was filled with admiration for these soldiers. For some it was their first deployment, and their job was made even more difficult by the increasing desperation of the local people. So bad had it become that some of the adults encouraged their children to run in front of the aid trucks, forcing them to stop. Other youngsters would then board the vehicle and throw as many packages as they could out of the truck. The soldiers also lived beneath the constant threat of the heavy guns in the surrounding hills.

Geneviève rejoined us as we waited for transport, and we clashed almost immediately. I suggested that she was wrong for criticising me to the press, but she called me a liar, almost spitting the words out, her mouth twisted with fury. She then accused me of 'exploiting a child'.

This made me incensed. 'I held the baby in front of the camera,' I said angrily, 'to convince the prime minister to change his mind.'

On the way back, we heard that Britain had offered sixteen beds as a result of my plea. We cheered and Duncan squeezed my hand, but unfortunately Geneviève was travelling in another vehicle so I couldn't see her face. Silvana Foa was later quoted as saying, 'Sally Becker turns up in Bosnia with a TV crew, and sixteen sick children get promises of admission to the UK in three days, including visas for relatives. It usually takes at least three weeks, and usually the health secretary doesn't get involved personally.'

Upon our arrival at the UN base in Kiseljak, we were informed that we couldn't return to Croatia as there were no more flights that day; the rest of the mission would therefore have to proceed without us. I was shocked and at the same time concerned, for the permission that would enable our convoy to cross the front line into east Mostar rested with me.

'How will my volunteers pass through the checkpoints?' I inquired.

The officer replied that they wouldn't be going. Instead, the evacuation would be carried out by the UN. I knew this made sense on one level – the patients would be safer inside the armoured vehicles – but I didn't see how they could carry eighty patients unless they'd suddenly acquired a huge amount of transport. I voiced my concerns to Duncan, and he reminded me that the new arrangements also meant that our aid wouldn't be delivered to the hospital.

The more I thought about it, the less I believed in the likelihood of the evacuation taking place. East Mostar was the quid pro quo for Nova Bila, and nothing had happened there yet. The officer was called to the phone and returned a few minutes later looking worried.

'The Croats have called off the mission,' he said despondently.

I urged him to help us, saying that if he could get us back to Croatia, I'd try to sort things out.

He was obviously not convinced that I could overturn a decision by the Croatian Ministry of Defence; but then neither was I.

14

It was no real surprise when the officer informed us that he might be able to arrange a flight after all, and twenty minutes later we were on our way to the airport. Inside the small terminal a make-shift sign read 'Maybe Airlines', a satirical reference to the number of planes that never left the ground, and listed among the choice of destinations was Heaven.

It was a great relief when the plane eventually left the tarmac, as we were desperate to get back and continue with the mission. Lawrence and Mick were waiting to meet us when we landed in Split. They both looked worn out and with very good reason. The UN had taken command of the convoy and ordered the volunteers to transport the aid to a warehouse in Metković. I was so furious I could hardly speak as we headed along the coast to Makarska.

The hotel was impressive, nestled among some pine trees within a few yards of the sea. We were greeted by Major Need, the liaison officer acting on behalf of the UN, and I immediately demanded to know why the trucks had been emptied.

'The aid's in a compound at Metković,' he replied. 'Some of the volunteers are there too.'

'Why? What are they doing there? They were all supposed to wait here until we got back.'

I followed him through a door sporting a sign saying 'Operation Angel', and sitting inside was John Morrison and his wife.

'We thought that you weren't coming back,' said John, 'so we decided to proceed without you.'

'Why wasn't I contacted? And who authorised the aid to be removed from our trucks?'

Morrison sighed. 'I don't know why you're so perturbed,' he said in a patronising tone. 'The bulk of the aid is safely inside the UN warehouse and the volunteers have been distributing the family boxes to local refugee camps. Oh, and yesterday the UN took a couple of the firemen into Mostar to deliver some of the medical supplies.'

I stared at the major in disbelief. 'When Boban agreed that I could carry out these missions,' I said, 'it was on the understanding that Nova Bila would be first. The evacuation of Mostar is now in serious jeopardy.'

I marched out of the office, with the major following behind. He was attempting to explain, but I was beyond listening. When I reached the reception area I turned to face him. 'Hopefully I'll be able to arrange a meeting with Dr Bagarić, but I just hope to God that you guys haven't screwed up the whole operation.'

He told me that he'd ensure the volunteers returned before nightfall. 'And by the way,' he said as I began to walk away, 'don't say, "you guys". I'm a Royal Marine who has been appointed to liaise between you and the United Nations, and that is all. I don't make the decisions.'

I knew that he was in a difficult position, caught in the uncomfortable position of go-between, and despite my anger I liked him.

A short while later the other drivers returned. One of them, older with a grey beard, stood right in front of me and started shouting right in my face. 'You must never organise anything like this ever again. You've put people's lives at risk.'

My cousin David prepared to move between us, obviously concerned that he might become violent.

'We believed in you,' he continued, 'and we followed you, but you've let us all down. I have been saying this behind your back, so I feel it's only fair to say it to your face. People could have died in that coach crash.'

As I looked around, I noticed that the ever-present cameras were filming his outburst.

'You're not just saying it to me, you're saying it to the whole of Britain,' I said, pointing to the cameras.

Mick moved towards the television crew.

'No,' I cried, 'leave it. He's had his say, and now I'll have mine.' I turned to face the camera.

'The crash was an act of God. I could hardly have prevented an Italian lorry from hitting the back of our coach. When I started out on this mission, I made my aims clear and invited others to join me. I know that the journey was hard and there were setbacks, but we made it clear from the start that it wouldn't be easy.'

I was worried. Nothing was as it seemed, and it looked as though the mission might fail. In addition to this, I was losing the support of my own volunteers. I was feeling despondent and very weary.

A short while later Major Need informed me that a briefing was underway in the conference room. I entered the room to find Morrison and his wife sitting side by side in front of the volunteers.

When Morrison saw me, he grinned and somewhat facetiously made an announcement. 'Ladies and gentlemen, your leader has returned.'

The volunteers responded with a slow handclap and I could feel the hurt rising inside me. I clutched the edge of the table to prevent my hands from trembling as I started to speak. 'I'm sorry that we haven't been around but Duncan and I have been in central Bosnia trying to arrange the first part our mission.'

One of the drivers stood up. 'The journey from Britain was exhausting,' he said, 'and we were assured that we'd get to rest when we arrived. Instead, we were taken to Metković and told to wait in our trucks. We've spent two days sleeping in a UN compound.'

'I'm really sorry,' I said earnestly. 'I know you must have been exhausted when you arrived, but that's exactly why we'd arranged for you all to spend a couple of days here in this hotel. Any alternative instructions you've been given were certainly not mine.'

I glanced meaningfully at Morrison before continuing. 'As I told you during the briefing back in Brighton, people in east Mostar are dying for want of the most basic medical supplies. The area has been under siege for several months, so they only get one meal a day. They live in basements and cellars because it's too dangerous to go outside.'

I paused for a moment, looking into the sea of faces, some of them openly hostile.

'This mission was my dream, and the day we left Brighton, the day it all finally came together, well, that was one of the happiest days of my life. We came here to help the innocent victims of a war not of their making and beyond their understanding – so let's focus on that and do whatever we can now to help make a difference.'

As I prepared to leave the room, some of the nurses came over. 'Sally, we joined this mission because we believe in what you are doing,' said one. 'Be assured that you have our undivided loyalty, no matter what.'

I thanked her, then turned away, not wanting them to see my tears.

When I finally got through to Ivan's office, I was told that he was unavailable. They put me through to his secretary, who informed me that the UN had requested the mission be delayed until Tuesday.

'But that's impossible,' I said, urging her to let me speak to Ivan.

The volunteers were supposed to be leaving on Sunday, and our budget wouldn't stretch to the costs of further accommodation and food for two hundred people. Apart from the costs, those who worked for the emergency services would be expected back at work, especially over the Christmas period. I asked her to explain all this to Ivan, and she promised to call me back. After pacing the floor for a while I finally got a call to say that Ivan would discuss the situation with his colleagues and get back to me later. I repeated the conversation to Major Need but he insisted that it was the Croats who requested the delay, not the UN. The situation was becoming more confusing by the minute. We went upstairs to wait for Ivan's call to be put through, and when the phone rang it was Vava on the line.

'Vava, I don't understand what's going on,' I said, relieved to hear his voice. 'According to the UN, the Croats have requested a delay.'

Vava assured me that this wasn't the case. He said that he'd try to persuade Ivan to come to the hotel. I repeated the conversation to Duncan and suggested that we were being misled. Duncan looked a little embarrassed and nodded towards the major, who was standing in the doorway.

'How dare you insinuate that we've been lying,' said the major, his face red. 'I've had enough of this whole business,' and before I could reply he turned on his heels and left the room.

Now it was Duncan's turn to lose his temper; cool, calm Duncan from whom I'd hardly heard a word uttered in anger. 'For goodness' sake, Sally, you've blown the whole operation now. Why on earth can't you be more diplomatic?'

I was surprised and disappointed by his outburst, as he was the one person I thought would understand.

'Diplomatic? Diplomatic?! It wasn't diplomacy that enabled me to cross the front line or diplomacy that stopped me getting killed by snipers. In fact, the last time I depended on the diplomacy of the United Nations, a little girl died.'

'You should apologise immediately,' he said, heading to the door. 'I'm going to try to prevent him from leaving. I just hope that it's not too late.'

'He won't be going anywhere, Duncan,' I called after him, but he ignored me and strode off down the corridor, leaving me dismayed that he had so little faith.

He was on his way to the elevator, and I followed him. 'They've been using me,' I said. 'Don't you see? This is all about publicity, it must be. Why do you think they were so keen to include the press on this mission?'

He seemed to hesitate.

'Think about it, Duncan. They've commandeered our aid and convinced the volunteers that we wouldn't be coming back.'

The doors of the elevator closed quietly behind him, and I returned to my room feeling emotionally drained. It was all so stressful and twisted. Nothing was as it appeared to be. There was obviously something going on behind the scenes, but I didn't know what. Alone in the room I decided to take a shower to cool down. Ivan would be here soon, and I felt I should at least try to look presentable. The success of our mission now rested on him.

A short while later Duncan reappeared and told me that the major was still around. 'You were right,' he said grudgingly, 'he isn't leaving after all. But he said that he came very close. Apparently, he's never lost his temper before.'

I decided that Duncan was probably right – perhaps it *was* time for some diplomacy after all. The major was sitting at the bar, though he was only drinking coffee.

'May I join you?' I asked, and he immediately gestured to a chair. 'I just wanted to say that I'm sorry. I know that you're not to blame for all this.'

After ordering another coffee he told me that the UN had arranged to carry out the evacuation of east Mostar without me. 'They'd have collected the patients in their APCs and transferred them into your ambulances at Metković. But now that the Croats have cancelled the mission, what happens next is anyone's guess.'

That evening Vava arrived with Ivan, and when they entered the room I could see the bitter disappointment in his eyes. We spent over an hour trying to clarify the position, and he remained adamant that the UN had requested the delay. I pointed out that it was irrelevant now and asked him to arrange for us to proceed with the evacuation as soon as possible, preferably the following day.

He shook his head emphatically. 'It would be impossible to get a ceasefire agreed at such short notice. And besides,' he reminded me, 'you still haven't helped the children who are trapped in Nova Bila.'

Dr Lang was planning to create a route through Bosnia-Herzegovina that would provide safe access to all the hospitals, enabling aid and medical staff to be taken in and patients to be brought out. This was the White Roads project that Ivan had started several months earlier, in which I'd played a very small part. Dr Lang's convoy would enable the project to finally be fulfilled, but Ivan explained that the vehicles were currently being held up by the Bosnian Army; one man had already been killed and the drivers had been taken hostage.

'If you wish to go ahead with your mission, you must try to get the other convoy released,' he said, causing my head to spin. It was all becoming more and more confused. I wondered how on earth I'd manage to salvage anything out of this mess.

Leaning forward, I looked into Ivan's eyes. 'If you allow me to carry out the evacuation of Mostar, I give you my word that I'll travel to Nova Bila the very next day and remain there until the convoy is released.'

I could see him giving serious thought to my proposal. Ivan knew that the press were following me and this would put pressure on those who were preventing Lang's convoy from reaching its destination. He stood up, gathering his papers together and putting them into his briefcase.

'I cannot promise anything,' he said. 'But I am Ivan Bagarić, and I too want to save lives. Therefore I'll do whatever is in my power to help Sally Becker, Angel of Mostar and Nova Bila.'

15

Later that night we were invited to attend another briefing in the hotel basement. Major Need explained that the UN had decided to proceed with the mission into east Mostar without official permission.

'Surely you don't intend to defy the Croats?' I asked. 'That would put the patients' lives at risk. In any case you'd be stopped at the very first checkpoint.'

'That's where you come in,' he replied. 'You'll travel at the head of the convoy and as usual the press will follow you. If the Croats hold us up, you'll use the media to embarrass them into letting us pass.'

I had a sense of déjà vu, as it seemed that the UN were prepared to try and use me once again.

'Well, I'm telling you now that you can forget it,' I told the major bluntly. 'I'll endeavour to carry out this mission without resorting to blackmail.'

The next day the volunteers were invited to the airport at Split to see the first fifty patients arrive under the auspices of Operation Angel. I was escorted across the tarmac to where the Sea King helicopters had landed with their precious cargo, and my anger and frustration disappeared. The patients came from Tuzla, Zenica and Sarajevo, and among them was a ten-year-old boy called Senad Zukić. He had been playing in the garden with his friend when a grenade exploded, causing serious injuries to his stomach and legs. On his head he wore a baseball cap bearing our logo and as he was carried across the tarmac there was a broad smile on his face. I wasn't the only one profoundly moved by the moment. The volunteers were watching from the terrace above and many of them were crying.

Upon our return to the hotel I was given a message from Ivan. He stated that I'd need to send a fax to Mate Boban's office confirming my intention. I knew this was a sign that it could all be OK, and within a few hours we were told to prepare for the mission.

At the final briefing we were informed that Duncan and I would be entering Mostar with the three British doctors and the doctors from Veterans for Peace. When I asked about the supplies I'd brought for the hospital, they said it would be impossible to take them as we'd be travelling in an APC.

'And what about all the paediatric medicines and the antibiotics? These are things they really need.'

The officer thought about it for a few moments and then made a suggestion. 'The only way you can take those in would be in your own vehicle,' he said, rubbing his chin thoughtfully. 'Though of course that would be dangerous and might in fact be considered reckless.'

'We went to a great deal of trouble to get those supplies,' I said, 'and we've brought them all the way from Britain. I certainly don't plan to leave them in a UN warehouse.'

He sighed irritably. 'OK. We'll sandwich your vehicle between the APCs to give you some protection.'

Duncan offered to travel with me, but as much as I wanted him beside me, there seemed no point in us both taking a risk.

That night we went to bed early as we'd be leaving in a few hours. Most of the volunteers would be waiting in Metković, just a couple of kilometres from the front line, so it was important they remained alert.

As I was about to get undressed, Mick knocked on my door. 'Sally, please take care of yourself,' he said, giving me a hug.

I couldn't sleep, my mind reeling with the forthcoming mission. I was truly terrified at the thought of crossing the front line once again, even with protection. Having made the journey three times under fire, I couldn't help feeling that my luck might be running out.

We left Makarska at 3.30 a.m. and arrived in Metković two hours later. I was finally issued with plates for my flak jacket and headed towards the rendezvous point on the outskirts of Mostar. As we reached the last HVO checkpoint, we could see the UN convoy parked up ahead. There were several armoured vehicles driven by the Spanish UNPROFOR, along with Jerry Hulme's bulletproof Land Rover. He seemed slightly bemused as he came over to my vehicle to collect Duncan. As we waited for permission to continue, I tried to hide my fear, gripping the steering wheel to prevent my hands from shaking. Duncan wished me luck and I watched him walk away, a tall, slim figure silhouetted against the light of dawn.

The officer from the briefing appeared at my window and demanded that I hand back the identity pass issued by the UNHCR, as I'd no longer be under UN protection. 'You've chosen to travel in an un-armoured vehicle,' he said, 'therefore we're no longer responsible for your safety and you'll have to travel at the rear of the convoy.'

That isn't what he'd told me at the briefing but there wasn't time to argue; the convoy was already moving. The back of the Nissan was loaded with boxes of antibiotics, liquid paracetamol for children, dressings, antiseptics and a sterilisation unit. I also carried some personal things for Hafid, such as a powerful torch he could use for operations and a whole load of surgical equipment. There were also plenty of cans, dried food and coffee.

As we approached the now familiar front line, I remembered the faces of all the children, those I'd managed to help and those I'd been forced to leave behind. When I reached the main street, a Bosnian soldier stood in the middle of the road and refused to let me pass. Instead he directed me to the War Office, where I was ordered to park the vehicle and get out. He led me up the stairs to the first-floor landing, where a man was waiting to speak to me.

'I want to thank you,' he said, smiling warmly. 'You saved my daughter. She had a serious injury to her spine and because of your persistence the UN finally came to get her out. She's had an operation and thanks to you is now safe and well. We'll always be in your debt.'

Before I could respond I was taken into an office where I was told to sit down and wait. Mark Dowdney was already there with another reporter, both of them looking confused. Decorating the wall was a mural of Stari Most, the beautiful old bridge that gave Mostar its name. Having survived five hundred years of war, earthquakes and other disasters, the bridge had finally been destroyed on 9 November after heavy shelling by the HVO. A symbol of civic pride and tradition, its loss had been a terrible blow to the morale of Mostar's citizens, Muslims and Croats alike. EC Monitoring Mission Observer Brendan O'Shea noted the significance of this 'senseless vandalism' in his book *Bosnia's Forgotten Battlefield: Bihac*:

> While it made it obvious to everyone that the values of the past were now well and truly gone, it also triggered a reaction from the politicians who were at least theoretically supposed to be in control of their military ... Mate Boban fired his top general, Slobodan Praljak, replacing him with the more moderate Ante Roso ... Five days later in Geneva all three sides signed a declaration ... purporting to guarantee the free passage and security of all humanitarian convoys operating in Bosnia.

But how would that translate into practice on the ground?

Two men entered the office. One of them, a soldier, was pale and his eyes were red. 'You do not have permission to enter the city,' he said, interpreting for the larger, older man dressed in civilian clothes. He looked feverish and was trembling as he spoke. 'None of you were included on the UNPROFOR list. We have new rules which state that UNPROFOR must provide a list of all names to be included on a convoy and the list must be submitted twenty-four hours in advance of any operation.'

'Surely my name must be on there somewhere,' I said. 'I organised the mission.'

The interpreter repeated my words to the official, who looked puzzled.

'He wants you to explain what you mean,' said the young man, looking as though he was about to pass out. 'This is Operation Angel, an official UN mission.'

'*She* is Operation Angel,' said Mark. 'This whole thing was her idea.'

The two men withdrew, and we waited for almost an hour. I thought of the supplies in the Nissan and wondered how to ensure they reached the hospital. As we sat there discussing what had happened, it slowly dawned on me that the UN might have deliberately withheld our names from the list in order to prevent us from reaching the hospital; that way they could still take the credit for the evacuation. I was becoming used to the way in which they worked, but if only they'd told me. It wouldn't have mattered to me who got the credit, so long as the children got out.

After a while the journalists were told they could leave but I was ordered to remain behind in the office. As I stood alone, looking out of the window, I spotted Duncan standing on the pavement below. I called to him and he looked up in surprise.

'I'm being held here against my will,' I shouted, hoping he could hear me.

A short while later a man came to take me downstairs. 'There's been a misunderstanding,' he said apologetically. 'We know who you are, and if you still wish to visit the hospital then you may.'

As I came out onto the street, I found Duncan talking to Jerry Hulme.

'This whole thing is utterly pathetic,' I told Jerry, who stood there in silence while I continued to rage. 'You allowed me to drive in without protection on the understanding that this was the only way I could bring in the supplies. You failed to protect my vehicle and then made damn sure I was prevented from reaching the hospital. It's appalling and you ought to be ashamed of yourselves.'

An ITN cameraman began filming the row, and Jerry addressed me as though trying to calm down a hysterical child.

'Now, now, Sally,' he said, 'if you want to reach the hospital so badly, I'll take you myself. Unfortunately a man has just been shot by a sniper, but of course if you'd rather they welcomed you instead of helping him, we'll go now.'

I felt sick to my stomach. 'Of course, I wouldn't expect to go to the hospital while they're recovering the wounded,' I said.

'Then you'll leave with us now,' said Jerry. 'The patients are already in the vehicles, forty-four in all.'

'There were supposed to be eighty-four,' I said.

'Unfortunately, some of those on your list did not reach the hospital this morning,' he replied.

'Well, can't we go and find them?' I asked, aghast at the news.

'No,' he said emphatically. 'There was shelling last night and they're scattered all over the place.' Seeing my despair, Duncan pulled me close.

'We have to go now,' said Jerry, striding towards his vehicle.

Duncan offered to drive the Nissan but I was past caring about the snipers and oblivious to the danger. As I climbed into the vehicle I was thinking of the other names on the list, so near yet so far. My thoughts were interrupted as I heard a familiar voice and looking up I saw a mop of red-gold hair. It was Tim Clancy, the American volunteer I hadn't seen for weeks.

I jumped out and gave him a hug. 'What are you doing in Mostar?' I asked.

'We've got permission to bring a mobile hospital unit across the front line. It should be here any day now.'

I realised that this meant Tim would be staying. 'Please, take these things to the hospital,' I said, opening the rear of the vehicle.

He helped me to unload the heavy boxes onto the pavement and then I reached in to get the packages for Hafid. I pulled out the last of the boxes, which contained all manner of clothing, food, chocolates, vitamins, coffee, beer and cheese. There was even a small Christmas cake. Tim called to his friends to come and help while I scribbled a quick note to Hafid.

'I'd better go now,' I said, seeing the convoy approaching. 'Take care.'

My flak jacket still lay beside me on the passenger seat and I handed it to Tim. As I drove along the muddy track that wound its way along the side of the hill, the vehicle started to slide and I panicked. I couldn't remember how to use the four-wheel drive. Fearing that the vehicle was about to go over the edge, I shut my eyes hard. To my surprise, somehow the wheels began to grip and I managed to regain control. Looking back in my mirror I saw that I'd just missed a series of stick mines protruding from the ground.

Once we were out of the war zone, I passed through the Croat checkpoint and stopped to wait, in case the HVO soldiers tried to hold up the convoy. I was carrying my original documents signed by General Praljak and the minister of health, and I hoped these might prove useful if a problem arose. Jerry was waiting up ahead and when he saw me he put his vehicle into reverse. Both he and Duncan got out of the Land Rover and strode towards to my vehicle.

'Come on,' said Duncan sharply, 'move over, I'll drive.'

He thought that I was having some kind of breakdown but I explained that I was fine.

'I'm waiting for our patients,' I said. 'But you're welcome to join me.'

He shrugged and slid into the passenger seat as Jerry wrenched open my door.

'You can't stay here,' he said abruptly. 'We're going on to Metković.'

'You go,' I said. 'We'll follow on behind with the others.'

Jerry hesitated for a moment and then looked at me. 'Stay if you must, but I wish you'd stop being paranoid. Operation Angel was a UN thing. Oh, you helped us, of course, because without your ambulances we wouldn't be able to carry the patients to Split, but the rest of it had nothing to do with you.'

When all the armoured vehicles had passed safely through the checkpoint, we followed on behind, and forty minutes later we pulled into the UN compound at Metković and were greeted by a wondrous sight. Our ambulances were arranged in a large circle like a wagon-train camp in a Western. Beside each of the vehicles were our medical teams, waiting to escort those who could walk while others were borne in on stretchers. When it was time to leave I went over to Major Need. He was overseeing the transfer, and to my surprise he put his arms around me and gave me a hug.

'Well done,' he said, smiling.

As I returned to my vehicle, I saw one of our paramedics from West Sussex talking to the Meridian presenter. 'Yes,' she was saying in reply to a question, 'seeing this today has made it all seem worthwhile.'

'Would you do it again?' asked the presenter.

'Yes,' she replied, tears streaming down her face. 'But without Sally Becker. The woman was never around.'

I didn't care, for at that moment a stretcher went past me carrying Amel. It looked as though Hafid would have his miracle after all.

As the convoy headed back along the stunning coastal road, the sun was setting and the sky was a myriad of colours. In the mirror I caught a glimpse of the flashing blue lights of the ambulances following behind us and I caught my breath: inside each of those vehicles were the children – safe at last.

Once we reached the airport in Split, we drove onto the tarmac and watched as the patients were transferred to the waiting aircraft. Someone came with a message from Ivan. Dr Lang's convoy had reached Nova Bila, so I wouldn't need to stay behind after all. Duncan and I were invited to escort the patients to Italy, so we said goodbye to our volunteers who were preparing to catch the ferry.

When we arrived in Ancona there was only one more job to do; transfer some of the patients and their families onto a medevac flight to Britain. The plane had been chartered by a team of paediatric specialists from the trauma centre at the Staffordshire Children's Hospital in Stoke-on-Trent. Veterans of Operation Irma, they'd be involved in the ongoing care of our patients. During the flight I talked to Suad, Senad's elder brother, who told me that he hoped their mother would be able to join them one day. Those patients on the plane who were well enough to eat were given a hot meal, and some of them were taken to visit the flight deck.

We landed at Birmingham Airport to a media scrum, and at the press conference a journalist called out, 'Sally, the United Nations say they could have done this without you.'

'So why the bloody hell didn't they?' I replied.

16

The press was cruel: 'Angel Has Wings Clipped' read one of the headlines, 'A Tarnished Halo' read another. One minute I was hailed as a heroine and the next I was a 'loose cannon', a 'maverick' or a 'publicity seeker'. I was terribly hurt by the things that were said, for despite all the setbacks, the quarrels and confusion, we'd come through – ninety-eight people were safe at last, and for them at least, the war was over.

I was planning one more operation, this time by air, taking supplies into central Bosnia and bringing out the wounded. I called the UN headquarters in Zagreb and wrote to the chief of missions with a request for assistance with the evacuation of Nova Bila. At the end of January I received a reply: the UN had no plans to evacuate the children, and it was clear they were not willing to assist me.

When I tried other avenues, Paddy Ashdown MP, leader of the Liberal Democrats, was the only politician who bothered to reply. He wrote to Malcolm Rifkin, secretary of state for defence, and to General Sir Michael Rose, the newly appointed chief of the UN in Bosnia, asking them to support my next mission. He couldn't be involved any further than that, but I was immensely encouraged by his support.

I also made contact with Dr Lang. He was planning another convoy, this time with the extraordinary combination of Muslim and Croat drivers, and was planning to reach Zenica, Sarajevo and Nova Bila. I immediately offered to help.

I'd heard nothing from Bagarić since my return, despite sending a stream of faxes and making endless calls. It was obvious that he hadn't yet forgiven me for letting him down.

Dr Lang invited me to join the convoy, and within five days I was ready to go. On the evening of Sunday, 4 February 1994, Duncan drove me to Heathrow Airport for my flight to Split, and as I prepared to go through passport control he took me in his arms.

'I love you, Miss Becker.'

'I love you too, Doc,' I said, and tears pricked my eyes as I waved him goodbye.

We'd just spent our first weekend together and leaving wasn't so easy for I realised that I'd fallen in love. The tension in the conflict had become heightened by the threat of air strikes against the Serbs. They'd been given one last chance to lift the siege of Sarajevo, and the countdown was about to begin.

The flight was almost full. British soldiers, UN personnel and aid workers filled the seats, and when we landed the airport was teeming. I took a taxi to the Hotel Split in the centre of town, where I'd have to wait while arrangements were made. The hotel had few guests apart from some EC monitors, but it was packed with refugees. I spent the first couple of days in my room trying to make contact with the Bosnian-Croat Ministry of Defence and waiting to hear from Dr Lang. To while away the time I watched the news on CNN.

Being quite impatient, I found the waiting almost intolerable. I'd already wasted several weeks and was impatient to get on with the job. I was also increasingly concerned about the impending air strikes and their effect upon the people of Bosnia-Herzegovina. Having lived through the Gulf War, I knew just how imprecise so-called surgical air strikes could be.

Eventually I received the long-awaited call from Dr Lang. He told me that the convoy was delayed due to the atrocious weather in central Bosnia, where thick snow had again made the roads impassable. He told me that the only way to get there would be to fly, and he suggested that I travel with him to a conference the following day. There would be important people there who might be able to help me. I'd already tried the aid organisations but they'd either halted operations due to the threat of air strikes or were grounded because of the snow. There was one organisation that might try going in, but they were unwilling to take an outsider with them.

Dr Lang arrived at the hotel and as I joined him in the chauffeur-driven car, I saw that we had a police escort. Lang had become a heroic figure since the success of his White Roads mission in December, and on hearing of my own experiences he urged me to press my case with the Croat authorities. I knew, however, that the person I really had to convince was my first and best ally.

I saw him as soon as we arrived, Brigadier Doctor Ivan Bagarić, a head taller those at his side. He gave me a bear-like hug, but I still sensed some distance between us. After a few moments he excused himself and I was left alone to watch the proceedings.

The conference was vital – chosen by Mate Boban to announce his resignation as president – but it was all in Serbo-Croat and I could hardly understand a word. It was freezing cold in the auditorium, and I couldn't stop shivering, despite my fleece-lined jacket. I eventually managed to corner Ivan during lunch and tried hard to convince him of my sincerity.

I was here, I said, to keep my promise to the people of Nova Bila, but I'd need a helicopter to reach the area. His first reaction was to laugh, until he realised I was serious. I pressed him throughout the day, and towards the end of the conference he finally agreed to make some inquiries.

I had to wait a further ten days in my hotel room in Split waiting for his decision, and my only solace was Vava, who kept in touch with me by phone. At last the news came: a helicopter was standing by in Posušje to take me to Nova Bila; we'd take off as soon as the weather permitted. I immediately packed my bags and drove down to Čitluk, where I'd been told to await final instructions.

As soon as I set foot in the Čitluk hotel the memories came flooding back. I received a very warm welcome from the staff and was given a key to one of the rooms. It was similar to the one I'd shared with Lynne for so many weeks, and I could almost hear her voice and those of Thierry, Domi, Paul, Paddy, Sean ... and, of course, Collette.

The weather was the only thing that had changed. Instead of the oppressive heat of the previous summer, snow now lay several inches deep and the temperature was well below freezing. I called Stipe and Erna as the phone lines were working, and they came over with a couple of their friends – a police inspector and his Muslim wife. They arrived in the Renault 4 and we drove to a restaurant that had been their favourite before the war robbed them of an income. I saw that Erna had at last put on a little weight and looked lovely. They both missed Damir, but he wrote often and occasionally they managed to call him on the phone. He was staying with Erna's sister in London and with support from the '35s' he was able to continue his studies. We ordered a platter of seafood, Erna's favourite, and shared a bottle of wine. Over dinner we talked politics, and I caught up on the news.

Ivan had arranged for Zoran to deliver mail and parcels to the people living in east Mostar. Those who'd been separated from their friends and families during the war could now keep in touch. Hafid's wife had given birth to a healthy baby girl and was now living abroad. Erna told me excitedly that Bella, her little dog, had a litter of puppies.

'The father,' she said, with a serious expression on her face, 'has been killed, so she's now a war widow.'

As they prepared to drive back to Mostar, they all wished me luck with the forthcoming mission.

'We have constant electricity now,' said Stipe, 'so we'll be able to follow your work on television.'

Ivan's driver came to collect me a couple of days later, and we drove to Siroki Brijeg to pick up Vava. I'd been feeling nervous about my mission, but his warmth and humour immediately lifted my spirits. I'd bought him a bottle of Jack Daniel's, which he opened on the way to the Ministry of Defence in Posušje.

'Do you think the NATO ultimatum will affect our mission?' I asked as we drove across the snow-covered landscape.

He laughed out loud. 'Are you crazy? It's just talk, as usual. We lost our faith in them a long time ago. Their threats are empty.'

I spent the night with some friends of his in Posušje. Dr Jurić and his family made me very welcome, but it was even colder than Čitluk. I found it impossible to sleep because my teeth wouldn't stop chattering. In the morning I was taken to an office where I was able to make some phone calls. I rang the helicopter pilots; I rang my mother, who was torn between wanting me to succeed yet wanting me out of danger; and finally, I called Duncan. This would be the last time we'd talk for a while, and I wondered whether I'd ever hear his voice again.

I also called Karen AbuZayd, Chief of Mission at the UN headquarters in Zagreb, and asked whether there were any plans to evacuate the children from Nova Bila. She was adamant that there was nothing on record; when I requested permission to enter the no-fly zone in central Bosnia, she assured me that Croatian military helicopters used the route often.

The days dragged by and I thought I'd go crazy. Every time I prepared to set off, a message would come through: fog has come down, we can't fly. I passed the time sending messages to Nova Bila and the Bosnian Army, and fretting over the weather reports. I'd never before taken such a keen interest in meteorology.

On 20 February the fog finally lifted and we were told that it was safe to fly. Vava was coming with me, which was immensely reassuring. He'd been trapped in Sarajevo for several months during the siege, and after hiding in the airport for several days in fear of his life, he'd managed to escape. He always swore he'd never go back, and when I asked him what had changed his mind, he shrugged.

'We'll fly in, wait for the children to be carried on board and we'll fly back out. I won't even have to leave the aircraft.'

'If that's the case, why don't they carry out the evacuation themselves?' I asked. 'Why would they need me?'

'In wartime there are things that take priority over wounded civilians – even children. Don't ask me why. I'm not a soldier or a politician. Also, it's considered too dangerous to evacuate civilians, as the helicopter could be shot at. Your presence here and the fact that you've informed the Bosnian Army have enabled Ivan to convince the military authorities to make an exception. They've allocated one slot.'

The helicopter was a Russian Mi-8MTV, which was missing some essential equipment. Peter Churdo, the pilot, had never flown this type of helicopter before, but he'd volunteered because he wanted to help the children. He managed to convince his commander to let him go, and he found a co-pilot and a flight technician willing to join him. The helicopter was loaded with medical supplies and we had to sit astride the boxes. Vava winked at me from his position behind a huge pack of dressings as the rotors whirred into action.

We flew without lights, unseen but not of course unheard, and I tensed as I pictured the big anti-aircraft guns below and the damage they could do. The flight took around thirty minutes, and after circling the area three or four times we finally landed in a quarry thick with snow. The supplies were quickly off-loaded and the patients were then lifted in on stretchers. I saw they were all wounded soldiers – where were the children? I searched around for Vava but couldn't see him.

The helicopter blades were already rotating faster and faster as the heavy machine prepared to lift off from the ground. However much these people needed help, I'd not waited so long nor travelled so far to abandon the children. But what could I do? I knew I only had a few seconds to make a decision.

I cursed under my breath as I picked up my bag and jumped to the ground, the powerful blades whipping the snow into a blizzard. I was wearing a soft white scarf that I wrapped around my face, but icy particles blew into my eyes, half blinding me. It was much too dark to see anything in any case, and I had no idea in what direction the hospital lay.

Suddenly a figure appeared in front of me. To my relief I saw it was Vava.

'Hi, man,' he said, as the helicopter rose into the air. He grasped my hand and helped me to my feet. 'I saw you leave so I jumped out too.'

'Why didn't you go with them?' I asked, surprised he hadn't left while he had the chance. He glanced at me as we trudged along side by side, knee deep in snow.

'How could I leave you alone here? First, you don't speak the language, and second … Ivan would never forgive me!'

17

We scrambled up the side of the quarry and found an ambulance parked at the top. It was the vehicle that had been used to transport the injured soldiers and was just preparing to leave. Vava asked the driver to take us to the hospital, assuming that our messages had not got through. We were met in the entrance by Fra Grebenar.

'You came back,' he said, and pulled down the neck of his robe to show me that he was wearing his Operation Angel Sweatshirt. He then led us to a warm room and an even warmer welcome from the staff.

To my astonishment their phones were working, so Vava started to make some calls while I was taken to the ward.

'The children were told that you were on your way back,' said a woman doctor. 'It will give them great pleasure to see you have arrived.'

I was surprised to see that Robin White, a reporter for ITN, was there. Having been accused of being a publicity seeker by the UN, we hadn't informed the press about this mission. Without the media it would have been impossible to highlight the plight of victims of war, and without them we'd never have managed to raise funds and aid for Operation Angel. However, I was funding this mission myself and I was working alone, so there was no need for the press to be involved this time.

Ironically, Robin had heard about the mission during a briefing by the UN, with the British Army based in Vitez being told to refuse entry should I turn up with the children. 'It would be a shame for Becker to grab the limelight!' read the UN staff order. That was not part of my plan, but I was disappointed to think that British soldiers would have been forced to turn away injured children. In fact, I'm sure that Colonel Williams would not have approved.

The room was filled with young patients and their relatives, and I visited each child in turn, explaining that I'd come to take them to safety. A fourteen-year-old girl called Maria had lost both her legs.

'Thank you for coming,' she said quietly and Fra Grebenar told me she'd been on a UN waiting list for months.

One of the doctors handed me a sheet of paper with fifty-five names on it, and when Vava had finished making his calls I asked him if we'd be able to fit them all in.

'We'll just have to try,' he said.

Vava was told there would be no more flights that night, but they'd send the helicopter back the following evening, 'providing there isn't any fog'. I resigned myself to another long wait and was offered a bed in the staff room. It was three in the morning and I was pretty worn out.

The next day I spotted Elvis, the fixer from ABC News I'd last seen in Mostar. He was now working for another news crew and he told me that his shrapnel wounds had healed well. A few hours later a British soldier arrived from the battalion at Vitez and informed the doctors that an evacuation would take place the very next day.

One of the doctors confronted him. 'We have been asking you to evacuate our wounded for several months, so why would you decide to do it now? Could it have something to do with Miss Becker's arrival?'

The soldier looked extremely embarrassed. He was obviously only following orders.

'I have my own thoughts on that,' he replied, 'but I'm not allowed to express them.' He turned to me. 'Please can I see the names of the children you plan to take out? I think three of them might be on our own list and we don't want a mix-up.'

Fra Grebenar stepped between us and insisted that I wasn't to give him the list.

'We'd prefer you to take them out yourself,' he said. 'The UN have let us down too many times and we're not willing to trust them again.'

That evening the children and their relatives were gathered at the entrance to the church. A small boy was clinging to a nurse and crying. He had an ugly leg wound that was pinned together by an external fixator. The nurse explained that he'd been orphaned by the war, and she and the other nurses had become his family. His cries broke my heart, but she assured me that he had an aunt in Croatia who was waiting to take care of him.

We planned to fly all the children and their mothers to Split because many of them had relatives in the city. The hospital had the facilities to treat all the patients and of course they could speak the same language. One by one the patients were carried into the ambulances that waited outside.

When they were ready to leave, I climbed inside and sat opposite a woman with a baby on her knee. He had a dummy clamped firmly in his mouth and was staring at me with wide-eyed curiosity. Beside me was Maria, who was lying on a stretcher. She was shivering from the cold, so I took off my scarf and placed it around her neck. We soon began the treacherous descent down the side of the quarry and she screamed as each jolt of the vehicle sent an agonising pain through her mutilated body.

The vehicles finally stopped outside a hut built into the hillside and completely covered in snow. First the stretchers were carried inside, followed by the walking wounded and the relatives. The cold bit into my face and hands, and I could feel my toes going numb inside my boots.

With the patients safely huddled inside around a warm stove, I stood outside with Vava and scanned the night sky, straining to see any sign of the helicopter. It was pitch dark, but we could just make out the silhouettes of trees surrounding the quarry. A group of soldiers were standing guard a few feet away, their cigarettes glowing like fireflies. The cold wind whipped against me, slowly freezing each part of my body.

'Will they come?' I whispered anxiously.

Vava shrugged and bent over to light a cigarette, shielding the flame with his hand. 'They said so,' he replied, though his voice betrayed his uncertainty.

In the distance I heard the crack of rifle fire and I hoped to God that the doctors were right when they said that the quarry was hidden from view.

All of a sudden from out of the darkness, a young couple appeared with two small children. I could see one of the doctors ushering them away, so we went over to see what was happening. One of the children, a five-year-old boy, was in need of an operation and he'd been on an evacuation list for over six months. Hearing of our arrival, his father had decided to try and get him out, and they'd walked for miles through the snow. The doctor was adamant that we couldn't take them; they hadn't been included on our list and there was no space.

The man told me that he didn't care about himself, but he begged us to take his wife and children. The doctor became angry and started shouting, insisting that they go back. My heart ached as I watched them turn to leave, the young man's shoulders slumped in defeat. I pleaded with the doctor and offered to give up my place, but he ignored me. Vava offered to do the same, and finally the doctor looked at us both and sighed. The small family were trudging back up the hill huddled together for warmth when we caught up with them and explained that they might get to leave after all.

'Thank you,' said the man, tugging the boys' woolly hats down over their ears.

Suddenly one of the soldiers looked up and pointed, and we could hear the murmur of anticipation among them. Straining our eyes, we peered into the sky and saw a small dark shape passing in front of a cloud. I held my breath as the shape grew larger, until at last I could see the outline of a helicopter. There were no lights on the ground but the soldiers darted forward with torches and helped to guide it into the quarry. When it was almost overhead, the pilots switched on the landing lights and the helicopter settled clumsily on to the snow like a giant blue-bottle.

The women came rushing outside, overjoyed at the sight of the machine, and as the blades whipped up the snow I quickly removed my coat to cover the two little boys. Snowflakes melted into icy rivulets and ran inside my sweater, but I barely noticed in the joy of the moment.

We had to wait for an hour while they unloaded the supplies, stamping our feet and rubbing our arms in an effort to keep warm. Finally, the stretchers were carried on board while those who could walk followed behind them. The doctor ticked off each of their names. At last they were all inside, but there seemed to be no space left for the new arrivals.

The doctor looked at me helplessly. 'I'm sorry,' he said.

I turned to Vava, desperation on my face. 'We have to get them out. Please, try to convince him.'

'I really don't think there's any more room,' he said despondently.

The doctor suddenly pushed us towards the doors, but I gestured to the family waiting patiently at my side.

'Please, let them go instead of us.'

He looked at me for a moment and then shrugged. 'OK,' he said, and told them to climb on board.

While the woman was saying goodbye to her husband, I felt a small, icy hand slip into mine. It was the youngest boy and I choked back the tears as I lifted him gently inside.

I turned to Vava. 'Sorry,' I said, feeling wretched that he was stuck there because of me.

He shrugged. 'Life's a bitch!'

As they prepared to close the doors, the doctor suddenly insisted that we get inside. I didn't see how we could possibly fit, but before I could say anything Vava grabbed my arm and we carefully edged our way through the crush of bodies. It was dark and absurdly cramped; arms, legs, feet and elbows dug into my back as I squeezed in behind the cockpit. Sitting with my knees against my chest, I tried hard not to crush the medical records given to me by the doctors, with the soldiers heaving and pushing against the mass of bodies as they struggled to close the door.

During those first few tense moments nobody made a sound, and then suddenly everyone's faces were bathed in a glow of light as Maria's mother lit a candle in prayer.

As she spoke, her face pale in the flickering light, Vava translated her words: 'Thanks be to God and all good people; for we are saved.'

Her careworn face was transfused with a look of utter peace, such as I'd never seen.

The pilots soon strapped themselves in and the rotors started turning overhead. Vava gripped my hand, and I hoped with all my heart that Maria's mother was right. The great machine lifted from the ground, swaying from side to side as it rose into the air. I could just make out the faces of those around me, some anxious, others filled with anticipation. Only the babies were oblivious to the danger.

The helicopter climbed higher and time seemed to stand still as we flew over the Bosnian countryside, where the war still raged below. I kept up a silent entreaty, 'Please let us make it, please, please …'

And then the lights of Split appeared below us, like a carpet of jewels spread out in the night. Vava passed the news around, and suddenly everyone was laughing and cheering, trying to hug one another in that cramped space. Tears streamed down my face as we came in to land, and I made no attempt to wipe them away. I had kept my promise.

18

I returned to a media storm. Lyndall Sachs, spokesperson for the UN, was quoted as saying that my mission had caused 'the entire aid operation in the area to grind to a halt'. Ray Wilkinson, spokesman for the UNHCR, issued a statement to the press announcing that I'd hijacked a UN operation and had put patients in danger by using a helicopter in a no-fly zone. Both of them also stated that we'd been shot at, which of course wasn't true.

Wilkinson was busy making the rounds of all the national television and radio stations, and although I was invited onto the programmes, I declined. Mike Mendoza convinced me that I ought to defend myself against the allegations, and in the end I agreed to do an interview by telephone. When I was asked to respond to the accusation that I'd hijacked a UN mission, I pointed out that Karen AbuZayd had assured me that there were no plans to evacuate Nova Bila. I tried to say that some of the children had been on a list for months, but Wilkinson kept interrupting me and my words were lost. When I asked him to account for what happened to our aid, my question was ignored.

With help from a wonderful man called Michael Harris, Operation Angel became a registered charity, and while the ceasefire in Mostar seemed to be holding, Nick Jacobs, an ophthalmic surgeon, offered to do some surgery. Although snipers were still occasionally taking pot-shots across the front line, the shelling had ceased. The fortifications and checkpoints that divided the city had been dismantled, and in west Mostar – for the first time in two years – the sidewalk cafés were full. Even on the eastern side of the city, people were beginning to venture out from their underground shelters, taking advantage of the uneasy peace. Based in the mobile hospital that Tim Clancy helped bring into the city, Nick performed thirty-five successful operations.

When I next returned to Mostar I was accompanied by Mark Norman, who was reporting for the BBC. We were staying with Erna, who told me about a project that she thought might interest me. Edina Kajtaz and a vibrant redhead called Azra Hasanbegović had set up a centre for Muslim and Croat women called Žena BiH. The association, which started with thirty-two women, enabled them to work and earn an income. Apart from providing support for one another, the women made clothes and toys for local refugees, and as more women began to attend they needed more space and materials. We applied for a grant from the Sir Halley Stewart Trust, and Zoran, who'd known Azra for some time, set about finding more appropriate accommodation. With the money from the trust we were able to pay for a lease and supply them with sewing machines and the materials they needed, and within three months the membership increased by several hundred.

Damir was keen to return home, and now that the ceasefire seemed to be holding, his parents relented. The European Union had sent a police force to Mostar to help keep the peace, so Damir applied for a job and was soon working as an interpreter for them, earning more in one month than his father Stipe received in a year.

During my next visit, Erna and I went to meet Damir at the Hotel Ero during his break. Since the ceasefire, the restaurant had become popular with staff from the international organisations and I saw Jerry Hulme sitting in the bar. His skin looked yellow and he'd lost a great deal of weight. He invited me to join him, and to my surprise he apologised for what had happened during the Operation Angel mission in December 1993.

'It seems that I was grossly misled.'

I was about to ask him what had made him change his mind but someone came over with an urgent message. 'We'll meet again and have a talk,' he said, as he hurried away.

Sadly that wasn't to be, as he died a short while later from a serious liver disease. He was a remarkably brave man who helped a great many people. Jerry shouldered a heavy burden and his problems had been our problems, but multiplied and complicated by official responsibility.

I visited Senad Zukić in Birmingham, where he was living in a small apartment with his mother, who was eventually able to join her sons. He'd undergone countless operations at Heartlands Hospital, and although he could only move around on crutches, the prognosis was good. He'd got taller, but otherwise hadn't really changed much and still had the same beaming smile. He was doing very well at school and spoke English with a broad Brummie accent.

Žena BiH continued to grow, and very soon there were two thousand members, most of them refugees. Among the women were 250 former prisoners of war, many of whom were severely traumatised, and I was taken to meet one of them, a woman named Mira. She lived alone in a darkened basement, barely eating and afraid to go out. During my visit she sat with her arms wrapped around her body and trembled as she told me her story.

Mira was driven from her home in north-west Bosnia and had taken shelter in the UN compound at Potočari in the municipality of Srebrenica when it fell to the Serbs. Srebrenica was a UN-mandated and NATO-protected 'safe haven', but when Ratko Mladić, the Serbian commander, ordered his forces to surround the area, the UN were unable to protect the refugees.

While his bodyguards handed out chocolates to the children, Mladić, who was responsible for the siege of Sarajevo in which 10,000 people died, assured their mothers they wouldn't be harmed.

The men were separated from the women and taken to collection centres around Srebrenica. Everyone was terrified, and Mira remembered two girls being dragged outside and returning later with their clothes in shreds. Following negotiations between the UN and the Serbs, the women and children were eventually herded onto buses to be deported, but as she prepared to leave with her young son, he was taken from her arms and she never saw him again.

Mira was now clearly severely traumatised and in need of counselling, but as she didn't feel able to go to the Žena BiH centre, we arranged for a psychologist to visit her at home. Azra and her colleagues took statements from these women and prepared a series of reports, which were later submitted to the United Nations Human Rights Commission.

In August 1995 NATO ordered air strikes against the Bosnian Serb Army, code-named Operation Deliberate Force, following the Srebrenica massacre. Four months later the Dayton Peace Accords were signed, bringing an end to a conflict that had claimed at least 100,000 lives and driven around two million people from their homes.

PART II
The Accursed Mountains

19

When the Dayton Peace Accords were signed, there was little attention paid to Kosovo, which continued to remain under Serbian control, nor any mention of the fact that 300,000 Serbs were still living as refugees, having been ethnically cleansed from the short-lived Republic of Serbian Krajina in Croatia. As Brendan O'Shea so presciently pointed out in his book *Bosnia's Forgotten Battlefield: Bihac*, before the tragedy of Kosovo had begun truly to unfold, 'Milosevic may well live to regret that no provision was made for this region when the Dayton deal was cobbled together.'

Since 1989, when Milošević revoked their autonomous status, the ethnic Albanians who made up 90 per cent of the population of Kosovo had suffered oppression under the Serbs. Ibrahim Rugova, who became president of the Republic of Kosovo in 1992, led a civil resistance movement, insisting on a path of non-violence. Despite ten years of peaceful demonstrations and appeals to the international community, the situation continued to worsen. Those who were not of Serbian origin were subjected to random assaults and mass arrests, and 185,000 people were dismissed from their jobs in the state-controlled economy and forced to travel abroad for work in order to support their families.

Hashim Thaçi, a young Albanian known as 'the Serpent', went underground to join the hitherto unknown UÇK (Ushtria

Çlirimtare e Kosovës), also known as the Kosovo Liberation Army (KLA), and Rugova's pacifist tactics were abandoned in favour of the KLA's campaign of armed struggle. The KLA began attacking Serb forces, wearing masks to prevent identification and subsequent action against their families. The Serbs called them terrorists but the members of the KLA saw themselves as freedom fighters, determined to release their people from the tyranny of the Serb regime, and they were prepared to die for the cause.

In December 1997 I began a campaign on behalf of the people of Kosovo. Having experienced the horrors of the war in Bosnia, I wanted to try to prevent something similar from happening again. The majority of the international organisations based in Kosovo came under the authority of the Yugoslav Red Cross, meaning they had problems trying to retain their impartiality, and the ethnic Albanians suffered from lack of aid, especially in outlying areas.

With help from my old friend Karen Turner, we began to raise funds for aid and medical supplies while appealing for vehicles and volunteers to drive them. Mitsubishi Motors loaned me a white Shogun with a long wheel base, which was customised with our logo. Most of our volunteers were from the emergency services or veterans of the mission to Bosnia in 1993.

Sean Vatcher offered to be convoy master. He'd formed a close relationship with a young British woman and although he was obviously still grieving for Collette, his new girlfriend accepted the fact and was very supportive.

Following a night at the Metropole Hotel, we left Brighton seafront with a convoy of thirty vehicles carrying several tonnes of aid.

After an uneventful drive across Europe and through Montenegro, we arrived in Pristina, where we were introduced to Jak Mita, director of the Mother Teresa Charity, the only organisation still able to assist the ethnic Albanians. During a briefing he told us that the Kosovo Albanian population constantly risked being harassed or arrested at one of the numerous police checkpoints. This risk was all the greater since many ethnic Albanians lacked the requisite papers.

We were taken to a school in Pristina, the Kosovan capital, that was in serious need of help. Since taking control of the region, the Serbs insisted upon Cyrillic being used in educational facilities, and Albanian textbooks were banned from the classroom. The Albanians rebelled and chose to fund their children's education from their own pockets, but as the majority were now unemployed, this wasn't easy.

Unable to tolerate this rebellion, the headmaster ordered a wall to be built through the centre of the school, dividing the children by their ethnic origins. On one side of the wall there were 2,500 Albanian students, who shared two toilets. Broken glass littered the playground and the children studied cross-legged on the stone floor. The walls were bare and the books were old and tattered. On the Serbian side, where five hundred students gathered to study, the classrooms were well stocked with books and educational materials and the furniture was new.

The state hospital in Pristina provided free treatment for Serbs but the unemployed Albanians, unable to afford health insurance, were forced to pay. They were also forbidden to speak in their own language, which caused difficulties when trying to explain a medical problem to a Serbian doctor, creating an environment of fear and mistrust. As a result, Marta, a vibrant woman in her forties, had set up a number of clinics that were funded by the Mother Teresa Society. Most Albanians preferred to use these clinics rather than the state-run hospital, but the staff could only provide the minimum of care as there was a lack of equipment.

Although we'd brought supplies for both the state hospital and the clinics, we were told on our arrival that it wouldn't be possible to give any of the medical aid to the Albanians as they were classed as separatists. We were also refused permission to take food and other supplies to Drenica, one of the areas most in need.

I complained about these restrictions during a meeting with the Yugoslav Red Cross, then signalled to our camerawoman to start filming. The presence of the camera seemed to sway the decision and permission to distribute aid to Albanians was duly granted, albeit with obvious reluctance.

With help from Jak Mita and Marta, we negotiated our way through Serb paramilitary check points, and apart from some worrying moments when our male volunteers were ordered out of their vehicles, we were able to reach our destination. As we arrived in one of the small villages, we were greeted by women and children who were poorly dressed and looked malnourished. Heavy grey clouds hung over the landscape and I caught a glimpse of some men watching from the hills. They were armed with Kalashnikovs, their faces hidden behind masks, and I guessed they must be the soldiers of the KLA. A gust of wind whipped across the hillside and I reached down to my bag for my jacket. By the time I looked up again they were gone.

Upon our return to the UK I received an invitation from the Queen and Prince Philip to attend a 'Reception for the Arts' at Windsor Castle. On approaching Windsor Great Park I got caught up in traffic and began to worry that I'd be late. Fortunately, the Shogun still sported the Operation Angel logo, and a policeman on horseback who spotted it immediately stopped all the traffic and escorted me into the Long Walk that leads to the castle.

Once out of the vehicle I smoothed down my skirt and, trying not to trip in my high heels, followed the other guests through St George's Hall. The walls were lined with paintings by Rubens, Van Dyke and other old masters, and we passed fine tapestries and suits of armour. I'd been gazing up at the incredible gilded ceiling when I found myself standing beside the actress Joanna Lumley. We chatted about my forthcoming convoy. I told her that we were aiming to recruit female volunteers this time, in the hope that we'd appear less threatening to the Serbs. She said that if she hadn't currently been under contract to the BBC she'd have willingly joined us.

There was a sudden hush as the Queen entered the room, looking far smaller and more beautiful than I'd imagined. She was escorted by Prince Philip and Prince Edward, her youngest son. As she stopped to speak to some of the guests, her equerry informed me that I too could be introduced to Her Majesty if I wished. Feeling understandably nervous and wondering whether I'd be expected to curtsy, I was shocked when a man she was talking to started to shout in her face. The Queen seemed completely unperturbed by his outburst and addressed him calmly but firmly before moving on.

'Her Majesty will see you now,' the equerry informed me, so I inclined my head and placed one foot behind the other in what I hoped was a curtsy but probably looked more like a bowling alley lunge. The Queen shook my hand and I was surprised to see that she was not wearing gloves.

'I know about the wonderful work you have done in Bosnia,' she told me. 'What a tragedy that was. Do you believe the same thing is going to happen in Kosovo?'

When I told her that it was already happening, there was genuine sadness in her eyes. 'Those poor people,' she said, 'it must be so awful for them.'

The room was filled with famous faces and I wandered around feeling completely out of place. Each of us was given a booklet that listed the names of each guest, and I was surprised to find myself described as a 'war artist'.

I was invited to meet the Duchess of Gloucester, wife of Prince Richard, the Queen's first cousin. She seemed genuinely interested in my work, and after we sat and talked for a while, she introduced me to Anne Wood CBE, creator of some of the world's best-loved children's television programmes. Anne told me that her Ragdoll Foundation was considering becoming a sponsor of our charity, and within two or three weeks a large truck arrived at our warehouse with a delivery of aid.

During an interview with Lorraine Kelly on Talk Radio I was invited to make an appeal for volunteers. When the phone lines lit up with women keen to apply, I made it clear that the trip would be dangerous, so we'd prefer to enlist those with relevant experience. Having already learned harsh lessons on previous trips, we were planning to interview all prospective volunteers in advance, although this wasn't always possible as some of them lived too far away.

On 29 May a Serb policeman was killed and another wounded in the Decani region. This was followed by a Serb offensive that left over sixty Albanians dead, some of them children. As a result the fighting intensified, and a week before we were due to depart the Yugoslav embassy informed us that our visas had been refused. I met with Isa Zymberi, head of the Kosovo Information Centre in London, and asked him what he thought we should do. Isa suggested that we take the aid to 15,000 refugees who'd just crossed the border into Albania, as he knew they'd be in desperate need of help, and he offered to speak to some people who'd help to facilitate our mission.

By the end of June we'd enlisted twenty-six volunteers, ranging in age from thirty to sixty-five. I bought an old camper van that would serve as a mobile office as well as somewhere to sleep, and we managed to rent six large vans. We were also taking the ambulance and a coach, and I still had the use of the Shogun. All the vehicles would be loaded at our warehouse in Brighton, and the day before we were due to depart, Karen and I waited to greet them.

Mary Banks, a bus driver from Yorkshire, had offered to pick up the coach, which would carry some aid as well as providing a place for the drivers to rest en route. Karen and I were waiting on the pavement when the vehicle pulled up alongside us. The doors opened to reveal a short woman with a round pale face and bleached blonde hair. Although close to seventy, she posed on the step with her hands on her hips and announced in a broad Yorkshire accent, 'My real name is Mary but my friends call me Doris Day.'

'More like Dockyard Doris!' muttered Karen.

Mary was accompanied by Maud, a retired bus driver who'd agreed to co-drive the coach. She was a tall, slim woman with wavy blonde hair and a broad Irish accent, and although quite outspoken, she was funny and very kind. Pat, a local woman in her sixties with short grey hair and piercing blue eyes, had spent many years in South Africa, where she led a high-profile campaign against apartheid. Pat and Marie, another local woman, came along to the warehouse every day to help sort out the aid.

Liz Dack, a nurse who worked in the intensive care unit at Southlands Hospital in Shoreham-by-Sea, had volunteered as our medical officer. She had short brown hair, with a fringe that flopped across one eye, and a great sense of humour. Another of our volunteers, Brian, wanted us to take his girlfriend Jenny Wheatley, but I wasn't sure if this was such a good idea. She had no relevant experience and no driving licence, but he pointed out how helpful she'd been in the warehouse, so in spite of my reservations, I agreed.

Joycey, a paediatric nurse, was now retired after many years working as a missionary in isolated parts of the world. She was the oldest volunteer but very fit and capable, and I knew we could depend upon her if any difficulties arose. There were also a few former soldiers who'd flown over from Guernsey. Every volunteer except Mary Banks had managed to raise sponsorship money to contribute to the costs of the journey. Susan, a hospital matron, took charge of the funds, and a former police inspector called Brenda was appointed convoy master.

20

The convoy set off at the end of June and two days later we reached Bari where we boarded the ferry to Durrës in Albania.

While the vehicles were being checked by customs. we were approached by a young Kosovar called Riki. He was in his early thirties, with thick black hair and a warm, friendly face. Riki had been living in Switzerland but was hoping to visit his family. He'd been chatting to one of our volunteers, who told me that Riki had offered to be our guide and interpreter, and as none of us spoke Albanian, I readily agreed.

When all the vehicles were finally through, we were met by Ismet Shamolli, a Kosovar who'd been sent by the Albanian government to assist with our mission. Ismet was a member of the LDK – the Democratic League of Kosovo – headed by President Rugova, and had been sending truck-loads of aid into Kosovo since the conflict began.

We set off early the next morning and drove through Tirana, Albania's bustling capital, which still bore the grey patina of communism. The road was clogged with small trucks and ancient buses belching clouds of black smoke, and weaving dangerously between the traffic were primitive carts pulled by horses and mules. Mercedes-Benz limos with darkened windows played dodgems with rusty old bangers, and the air was thick with dust and diesel.

Ismet had arranged an armed police escort for the convoy; the area through which we planned to travel was a haven for bandits. As we left the city and headed north, we passed the rusted carcasses of automobiles and mountains of discarded rubber tyres. The dry, barren landscape was dotted with grey concrete domes that resembled giant mushrooms. The bunkers, installed by Enver Hoxha, Albania's communist leader until 1985, were built with slits in the walls for snipers, ostensibly to protect Albanian citizens from foreign invasion.

Although the escort changed at various points throughout the journey, one police officer remained with us constantly. A big fellow with black hair and a thick moustache, he chose to travel with Janey, a buxom blonde with a sharp wit. In between staving off his advances, she kept us amused with her impressions, and we'd often hear Mary Banks's raucous tones echoing down the CB radios fitted to each of our vehicles, only to find that it was in fact Janey.

As we headed into the mountains the road began to twist and turn, and we were forced to negotiate a particularly narrow pass where the coach got into difficulties. I was in the lead vehicle when the call came through, and above the sound of screaming I could hear Mary Banks shouting and swearing. Hurrying past the long line of vehicles, I was shocked to find that the back end of the coach was jutting over the edge of a ravine.

Mary and Maud were in the midst of a blazing row while six of our volunteers and two armed guards looked on. Jenny Wheatley explained that Mary had insisted on driving while Maud was told to navigate. Somehow they'd taken a bend at the wrong angle and Maud was now being blamed.

I asked the police to help move the coach and under their direction, Mary gamely inched it back and forth until the entire vehicle was back on solid ground. Jenny was telling me how frightened they all were, so I suggested that they travel in the Shogun.

'We won't leave the coach without Mary,' declared Jenny. 'If she stays, we stay.'

I offered to swap places with Mary but her face darkened in anger.

'Nobody drives this coach but me,' she said emphatically, and I saw Maud raise her eyes.

We reached our destination at about 10 p.m., and as we drove down the main street we had to avoid stray dogs that were roaming around in packs. Bajram Curri is a small town in the isolated region of Tropojë, not far from the Kosovo border. The local population, already stricken with unemployment and poverty, had increased by thousands over the past few weeks as refugees fled from the fighting. The police led us to a secure compound where we left the vehicles under guard. We were taken up the road to a hotel, and near the entrance I was surprised to see someone I knew.

Bob Edge was a tall, lean man who was rarely seen without his baseball cap. He'd been part of Operation Angel in 1993 and was now working for Children's Aid Direct. He introduced me to Halil Gjongecaj, the hotel director, a short, slightly built man with shifty eyes. He didn't speak English and looked like Mr Rigsby from the TV show *Rising Damp*.

The Hotel Ermal, a mustard-coloured four-storey building, was originally a government guest house. When members of the OSCE (Organisation for Security and Co-operation in Europe) arrived to take up residence, the building had long been abandoned, having been vandalised by the locals. The rooms had no windows but the OSCE offered one month's rent in advance for four rooms, which meant $6,000 cash (a very large sum of money). Within a day the rooms were habitable, each of which cost $50 per night, although electricity and water were not always available.

This set the price, so when we arrived, Halil demanded a cash payment in advance for the ten days accommodation we required.

There were still only half a dozen rooms available, but fortunately some of them were quite large. I bunked in with Liz Dack and Christine, another nurse. The toilet, situated just down the hall, was a hole in the ground, which also doubled as a shower. It stank and we were disappointed to learn that there was currently no water. We had just unpacked our belongings when the lights went out too – the electricity had just been shut off owing to unpaid bills.

Bob appeared with his torch and invited me to his room, which was stacked high with tins. He explained that he was currently in charge of the distribution of canned meat on behalf of ECHO (European Community Humanitarian Organisation); the people of Bajram Curri were deemed to be undernourished and the cans were from a consignment left over from the so-called 'European meat mountain'. This had earned him the nickname 'Bobby Mish', the Albanian word for meat. He poured me some raki and I began to relax after the long, stressful journey.

Bob was a mine of information and advised me on the best way to distribute our aid, suggesting that we deliver the medical equipment and supplies directly to the local hospital. We were also carrying large quantities of rice, pasta and tinned food, as well as blankets and cooking materials for the refugees in Tropojë. None of us got much sleep that night because a dog started barking, which set off all the others, a common chorus throughout our stay.

Although the town was in an idyllic setting, nestled at the foot of snow-capped mountains, it had witnessed a great deal of violence. After the communists were defeated in the 1992 elections and private enterprise was introduced, Albanian inexperience with capitalism led to the proliferation of pyramid schemes, which were left unchecked by the corrupt new government. These schemes eventually collapsed, resulting in anarchy, and following a nationwide raid on Albania's armouries, law and order for a while became virtually non-existent.

We were invited to a meeting with the local representatives of the UNHCR, where an English field officer called Mark Cutts requested our assistance for refugee families unable to reach the town. The next day our teams set off with boxes of food and medical supplies to be delivered to the addresses provided by the UN. The nurses were able to use their paediatric skills to help sick children in these outlying areas, while the rest of us stayed in the vehicle compound, sorting out aid for further deliveries. It was gruelling in the heat, and I was filled with admiration for the older volunteers who kept going regardless.

Escorted by the OSCE and the local police, we took the bulk of the aid to the UN warehouse in Tropojë, not far from the border with Kosovo. We also delivered individual boxes to families housing refugees and therefore desperate for extra food and clothing.

That evening Dawn, Alison and Jenny decided to go home. Mark Cutts was driving to Tirana the very next day, so he offered to give them a lift. I wasn't aware of their decision until the next morning when Jenny came and told me they were going.

'I suppose you think I'm a coward,' she said, somewhat defensively.

'Not in the slightest,' I assured her. 'Our aim was to get the aid here safely, which you have helped us to do. We're just waiting for Ismet to collect some things for Kosovo and then the convoy will go home. Please don't feel bad. You've done a brilliant job!'

I found Dawn and Alison waiting in the car, but they chose to ignore me.

Mary went to a local shop and bought fresh bread for breakfast every day, and when eggs were available she made omelettes. In the evenings there was electricity and we usually ate in the hotel. The food mainly comprised tough pieces of meat described in the menu as 'steak' and 'kebab' or pasta with cheese. The meat was served with chips and a little salad and was just about edible, but most of us supplemented the food with Imodium, a treatment for diarrhoea. Alcohol was cheap, and some of the volunteers, relaxing after a hard day's work, helped to boost the bar takings.

One evening we were all having dinner on the terrace when a man strode over to our table. He had wavy copper-coloured hair and a moustache, and was wearing a metal hook in place of his left hand.

'Major Bill Foxton, OSCE,' he said. 'It's an honour to meet you, Miss Becker.'

Throughout the mission Bill afforded us every assistance, from briefing the volunteers daily about the local situation to arranging armed escorts for the convoy.

Some of the volunteers complained that their bras and cameras had been stolen, so Bill spoke to the two Albanian women who did the cleaning for the hotel. He'd nicknamed them 'Wagon and Trailer' because they went everywhere together. The bras eventually reappeared but the cameras were never returned. Each week, Bob Edge wrote a satirical news-sheet based on local gossip, which he copied and distributed to all the aid workers. We provided the perfect material, and much to our amusement we saw that he called his latest article 'Hell's Angels'. We delivered some toys and food to the orphanage, and later the women challenged the local schoolchildren to a football match. The children won by twelve goals to three but nobody minded.

Bill introduced us to Phil Figgins, the OSCE field station co-ordinator who'd just arrived in Bajram Curri, and Liz and I were invited to join the two of them for dinner. Bill led us to a small 'restaurant' in the back streets of town where we were seated at the only table. There was no menu but our order was taken by an elderly woman who was both the waitress and chef – I think we were in her front room. We were given four bowls of a rich beef stew called *fërgesë*, and while the three of us shared a bottle of the local red wine, Bill called for a large beer.

This was Phil's first visit to Bajram Curri and over dinner he recalled the events of the day.

'We decided to come via the Lake Koman ferry in order to avoid the dodgy road route through the aptly named villages of Pukë and Rrapë, before potentially getting robbed at Qafë-Mali, a popular place to be stripped of everything. When we arrived at the entrance to the tunnel that leads through the mountain to the ferry terminal, there were vehicles trying to force their way in both directions through what can best be described as a collapsed cave, with room for the width of a couple of donkeys. How we got through was baffling. Forty minutes and four hundred yards later, we reached the far end. I was beginning to think we should have travelled the road route after all.

'Boarding the ferry ahead of us was a camper van with so much weaponry and ammunition aboard it had to be eased onto the ferry by ten men trying to take weight off the inverted springs. I was leaning against one of the upper deck rails eating a burek when a gun went off about ten feet away. Some crazed diaspora Albanian (probably from California) was blatting away into the hillside. The captain of the ferry appeared at the top of the ladder and rushed over to the young gun, and I was expecting him to have a go at the idiot. Instead, he grabbed the pistol and started firing into the same patch of ground fifty-odd yards from a bunch of scuttling villagers. Welcome to north-east Albania, I thought, as me and Bill withdrew to a safer hangout.'

A few days later Ismet arrived with a truck destined for Kosovo, and among the medical equipment we gave him was a mobile X-ray machine. Although he hoped the vehicle would get through, nothing was certain. The situation across the border was becoming desperate; no aid had reached the area for some time as supplies had to be taken in across the mountains on the backs of mules since the aid organisations had pulled out.

Knowing that there were sick and wounded children in need of help, I'd brought a large bag of paediatric medicines that I planned to deliver to Kosovo myself. Thousands of refugees had crossed the border in recent weeks, so I figured it shouldn't be too difficult.

One afternoon I was asked to go to the office of the UNHCR to speak to Daniel Enders, the young Frenchman in charge. He told me that there were many children in need of types of medical treatment that were unavailable in the region, and he asked whether I'd be able to organise some hospital beds in Britain.

'If you can do this,' he said in his charming French accent, 'I can guarantee that the International Red Cross will assist with the evacuation and we'll provide our full support.'

I told him that I'd send a message to Duncan, who in turn would speak to his medical colleagues. A few days later, Daniel was replaced as head of office by an Italian woman called Alessandra Morelli. Having heard about my intentions, she wanted to know how I planned to enter Kosovo now that the borders were closed.

I shrugged. 'To be honest, I've no idea, but it's vital these medicines reach the children.'

I was expecting her to tell me that it was a bad idea, but instead she said that she'd received a report that over a hundred refugees were supposedly trapped in the forest just across the border. Some of them were thought to be children who might be injured, and she suggested I try to locate them.

'As you know, the UNHCR have been pulled out of the region, so there's nothing we can do. If you happen to find them, perhaps you can try to bring them out.'

Later that same evening I was summoned to the OSCE office by John Mattson, an American who worked with Bill Foxton. Bill was waiting to speak to me, and once I sat down, John left the room.

'I know about your plans,' said Bill, 'and although I don't doubt there is a shortage of medicines, it's just as important that you use the mission to highlight what's happening. You can focus on the kids who've been wounded and those who'll be at risk if nothing's done to protect them. You managed to bring a spotlight to Mostar, so I'm sure you can do the same in Kosovo. With your reputation, people will take notice.'

He popped his head around the door as if to ensure that no one was listening.

'We've had reports that Junik is virtually surrounded and will soon be taken by the Serbs, so you'll need to get in and out fairly quickly. Of course, the only way to get there at the moment is across the mountains, but the Serbs have tightened their security to prevent smuggling of arms by the KLA. I suggest that you'd be best to cross the border at night to avoid Serb patrols. Artan, my interpreter, will take you to Tropojë and someone will meet you there. I'll give you a long-range walkie-talkie so that we can keep in touch. Let me know if you come across the refugees, and we'll arrange to meet you at the border.'

I was very surprised to be offered this kind of support from what was in effect a government agency, and I said as much.

'You mustn't mention this to anyone,' he responded, 'and if you get captured do not, under any circumstances, reveal who gave you the radio. It would cause an international incident.'

On the eve of the convoy's departure, we were warned that bandits were operating in the area and that they might target the vehicles. Bill suggested that the volunteers leave after dark; they would then drive straight to Fierzë to await the early ferry.

Gathering in the gloom of the reception area, we said our goodbyes. Mari, an Irish woman who lived not far from me in Brighton, admitted that before leaving Britain she'd begun to have doubts.

'But actually I'm delighted that I came,' she said, giving me a warm hug. 'It's been an amazing experience and I wouldn't have missed it for the world.'

Karen was in tears, worried about leaving me behind and concerned for my safety.

'I'll be fine,' I reassured her. 'I'll deliver the medicines and then come straight home.'

21

The muffled sound of explosions echoed from the rugged mountain range that loomed before me. These 'Accursed Mountains', as the Albanian Alps are sometimes known, run the entire length of the Kosovan border from Montenegro to Macedonia. Spectacular and virtually impenetrable, a few high passes link the small number of farmsteads nestled within them to the valleys below. The landscape is savage and journeys are measured in days rather than hours. As I reached the tent above Padesh, the distant explosions reminded me of Bosnia and I hesitated, almost overwhelmed by the familiar sense of trepidation and doubt.

I entered the tent dragging a bag filled with antibiotics, dressings and liquid paracetamol destined for the besieged hospital across the border. Originally set up by Médecins Sans Frontières as a rest station for the sick and exhausted refugees fleeing from the conflict, the tent was now serving as a refuge for the KLA. Around two dozen soldiers were sprawled across the floor, while an older man in army fatigues was heating some coffee on a camping stove.

'Angel of Mostar!' he declared with a smile.

I was surprised that they were expecting me. This was an isolated region in an isolated country. Avdyl explained that he normally worked in the Ujeze Highland close to Padesh, but since Médecins Sans Frontières pulled out he also took care of the rest station. A few of the soldiers gathered around us, and I noticed they wore sneakers instead of boots and their uniforms were mismatched. The badges on their upper sleeves bore a twin black-headed eagle against a red background with the letters UÇK (Ushtria Çlirimtare e Kosovës) embroidered in yellow, the official emblem of the KLA. Kalashnikov rifles, grenades and ammunition belts were littered across the floor.

'It's an honour to meet you,' said one of the soldiers, speaking in French. 'You've saved many lives.'

I thanked him and gratefully accepted a cup of sweet Turkish coffee. Having no idea when or with whom I'd be continuing my journey, I asked the caretaker to enlighten me, but he simply shrugged.

Stepping outside to find the toilet, I soon realised it was non-existent, so I headed towards some foliage on the brow of the hill. In the distance I could hear the sound of shelling and occasional gunfire, but apart from the soft murmur of voices coming from the tent, the immediate area was quiet. Dusk was approaching and by the time I returned an oil lamp had been lit, casting shadows across the canvas.

My rucksack had been placed on Avdyl's camp bed, where he insisted I should sleep. I was wondering whether to remove my outer clothing when another group of soldiers arrived. Their commander was in his late twenties, with a thin, tanned face, heavy-lidded eyes and shoulder-length brown hair. He was carrying a hefty Goryunov machine gun and a large hunting knife hung from his belt. Unlike his colleagues, he wore green camouflage uniform and tough army boots. With bandoleers of ammunition slung across his chest, he reminded me of a character played by Sylvester Stallone.

'Rambo,' I declared smiling, and to my surprise he nodded and held out his hand. Soldiers of the KLA used pseudonyms in order to protect their families, and this was the name he'd chosen for himself. We shook hands, and following a short discussion with the caretaker, Rambo asked me some questions. Speaking in

German, he wanted to know how and where I intended crossing into Kosovo. I explained that I was supposed to be travelling with an escort from the KLA. After briefing his men, their eyes red from strain and fatigue, Rambo announced that we were leaving.

As we made our way along the mountain ridge, two of the soldiers carried the heavy bag of medicines between them on a stick. I found it hard going, but Rambo reached out to help me whenever the track became too steep. The light was beginning to fade and soon it was difficult to see. We stepped around a dead mule with a bullet wound in its flank and fresh blood staining the stony ground on which it lay, obviously quite a recent victim. After a while we stopped to rest and Rambo offered me a cigarette, but feeling somewhat breathless I declined. As he dragged on his, he cupped the lighted end within his hand to shield the glow from snipers.

When we set off again I caught a glimpse of the soldiers struggling along with my bag. We kept going, then finally stopped to take a rest, with Rambo going on alone to scout the area. I had no idea how, where or when we'd cross the border, and I realised that I'd put my faith in a complete stranger.

I heard the drone of a Mi-8 helicopter, used by the Serbs for reconnaissance of the border and the tension rose. Rambo reappeared, and in hushed tones he explained that the appearance of the helicopter made the crossing far too dangerous. He ordered his men to turn around, and I found myself following him back down the track. I was disappointed and frustrated, impatient to proceed with my mission. When we arrived back at the tent I asked him when he thought it might be safe to try again, but he just shrugged.

While the soldiers climbed into sleeping bags or covered themselves with rough army blankets, I lay on the camp bed wondering how to get a message home. I wanted to let Duncan and my family know that I hadn't yet crossed the border. I had the radio

Bill had given me but I was loath to use it in case the men became suspicious. They trusted very few people and often refused requests from journalists wanting to interview or accompany them, on the grounds that information could be passed to the enemy. I decided to try and sleep as I was exhausted.

I awoke the following morning to find Avdyl heating a small pot of coffee while Rambo paced up and down. The tent was now virtually empty, and I went outside and found a tap where I brushed my teeth and splashed my face with the icy water.

'You have friends close by in the valley,' said Rambo, appearing alongside me.

I looked at him blankly.

'Italian journalists who say they know you.'

I recalled three Italians who'd turned up at the office of the OSCE in Bajram Curri. They'd come to interview Bill Foxton, and when they asked him whether anything interesting was happening in the area, he suggested they talk to me. They were apparently hoping to follow some KLA soldiers into Kosovo, but as this was the intention of most journalists in northern Albania, I hadn't taken much notice.

'I remember meeting them,' I said, 'but they're not part of my mission.'

'We are going to join them in the valley,' he said, dunking his head in the icy-cold water.

I collected my rucksack and thanked Avdyl for his hospitality. It was mid-July and the sun shone brightly as we strode across the alpine landscape. Rambo told me that the paediatric supplies would be taken across the mountains on the back of a mule.

We made our way into the valley where a few soldiers were sitting around. A number of small fires had been lit and the smell of wood smoke scented the air. The journalists were sitting beneath some pine trees on the edge of the forest, slightly apart from the soldiers. Rafaelle Cirielo, a slightly built man with dark hair, invited me to join them. Before sitting down, I removed the heavy blue waistcoat in which I carried the walkie-talkie, my passport, a penknife and two disposable cameras. Around my neck were the dog tags bearing my name and blood group.

He asked me when I intended crossing the border. 'We're really hoping they'll take us with you,' he said. 'We've wasted a lot of time getting here and now we're being told that we just have to wait.'

Gian Micalessin and his colleague Fausto Bilaslavo worked for an Italian television station. They both wore glasses and light grey reporter vests with bulging pockets and baseball caps turned back to front.

Rafaelle produced a tin of tuna and some bread, and using water that had been heated over a fire I made some instant coffee from sachets I carried in my backpack. It was obvious that we'd have a long wait, as there would be no chance of crossing during daylight. A low-hanging mist enveloped the valley, so I pulled on my jacket and, using my rucksack as a pillow, I lay down to sleep. When I awoke a few hours later I found Rambo huddled in conversation with a group of young soldiers.

'We'll be leaving shortly,' he said, and suggested I gather my belongings.

The journalists asked if they could follow me and Rafaelle promised that I'd have access to their film. Rambo agreed to let them tag along on condition they keep their cameras under wraps for the time being. The soldiers wouldn't want to be filmed for fear of Serb reprisals against their families.

Kosovars who'd been working abroad were now returning to fight, and northern Albania had become a launch pad for some of these units. Training camps had been set up in Kukës, Bajram Curri and Tropojë using unoccupied or appropriated commercial properties, including a factory and a hotel. Rambo, whose real name was Abedin Sadrija, had been living and working in Germany until the recent escalation in fighting brought him home.

Following a ragtag band of new recruits, we made our way along a shepherds' trail towards the high mountain meadows. The jagged pinnacles and snow-capped peaks of the mountains rose above us, in some places six thousand feet high. According to local folklore, the area had been fashioned by the devil himself, unleashed from hell for a single day of mischief. It was late afternoon by the time we reached the mountain ridge that separated Albania from Kosovo, and beyond the ridge was a forested valley framed by steep limestone cliffs.

We took cover in the elephant grass, where we'd wait until nightfall before moving on. Rambo went ahead to scout the area, and by the time he returned it was so dark I could barely see. He signalled for us to follow, and keeping our heads and shoulders low to avoid being spotted we ran as fast as possible through the long grass.

As we reached the open meadow there was little cover and I tried not to stumble as we scuttled along in single file. All of a sudden I found myself lying flat on the ground with Rambo's hand across my mouth.

'Serb patrol,' he hissed in my ear.

Small pinpricks of light were moving up ahead and I held my breath, wondering what would happen if we were caught. A couple of young Americans had recently been discovered in Pristina without visas and were subsequently arrested. They were released again after a few days – but they weren't travelling with members of the KLA. I'd been advised to wear dark clothing and had replaced my white T-shirt with a blue one. I knew that in the dark I could easily be mistaken for a soldier and I was terrified, knowing the Serbs might shoot first and ask questions later.

When it was safe to move on I looked around for Rambo, but he'd disappeared. Rafaelle, Gian and Fausto were still with me, but we'd no idea which way to go. Bill had been adamant that the area was not mined, but I couldn't help thinking of Paddy in Bosnia, who'd lost both his legs. While the others were thinking of turning back, I wasn't sure what to do. I really didn't want to give up, but travelling without a guide would be too dangerous.

Suddenly there was a noise, something between a bird call and a whistle, and Rambo appeared. He'd come back to find us, and as he stood in silhouette against the night sky I was reminded once again of his namesake. He took hold of my arm, and with the others following behind we crossed the border into Kosovo.

Rambo was much fitter and faster than me, and it would've been hard to keep up with him if he hadn't kept a tight grip on my hand. Brambles and branches tore at my face and hands as I followed him blindly through the forest. As he pulled me down a slope, I caught my foot on a tree root and hit the ground with a thump, twisting my ankle. Before I had time to complain I was hauled unceremoniously to my feet. Rambo wrapped his bandoleer around my wrist, the bullets digging deep into my flesh, but this left him free to carry his machine gun in both hands.

I felt as though I were in a painful waking dream, stumbling on and on through the darkness but seemingly getting nowhere. I tried to ignore the throbbing pain in my ankle as I was pulled along the banks of unseen rivers and streams, over slippery rocks and through the icy water.

We continued this way for an hour before the signal was given for the column to stop and for us to get some rest. I immediately sank to the ground, not even bothering to remove my rucksack, and I cursed myself for wearing the wrong kind of shoes. They were made of canvas, more suited for the beach, but my boots had been stolen in Bajram Curri.

It was nearly midnight and I was dismayed to learn there was still another four or five hours' travelling before we reached our destination. The years of smoking and lack of proper exercise were taking their toll. I was exhausted and wanted to rest awhile, but when the signal came to leave, Rambo put my rucksack across his shoulders and pulled me along behind him.

As we penetrated deeper into the forest, he used a special torch with a diffused light, and although this improved matters a great deal, even he was beginning to tire. The journalists were still with us, somehow managing to carry their camera equipment as well as their personal kit.

We'd left the valley at seven in the evening and it was 4.30 a.m. when we finally arrived. By this time I was unable to bear any weight on my foot, so I was helped by Rambo and the officer, who half carried me along a dirt track to a farmhouse.

The soldiers went off down the road, leaving us at the door. It was dark inside as there was no electricity, and Rambo explained that Serb forces had cut the local power supply. He led us upstairs where there were two bedrooms. The journalists went into one of the rooms and I took the other but to my surprise Rambo followed me inside.

I pointed out that there was only one bed, but he just shrugged and took off his jacket. Having left my shoes at the front door as was the local way, I removed my heavy waistcoat and stretched out on the bed. The yielding comfort of the soft mattress felt like heaven beneath my aching limbs, and I was already drifting off to sleep when Rambo climbed in beside me.

22

When I awoke I went downstairs and found that my shoes had been washed and were drying in the sun, an old Albanian custom, typical of the warm hospitality shown to guests. Rambo was sitting outside in the garden, talking to an old man in the shade of a tree. The man was wearing the traditional white domed cap of an ethnic Albanian, and Rambo explained that he and his wife were refugees who were staying at the farmhouse.

I sat down beside them, and in a faltering voice the old man told me how Serb paramilitary police had driven him and his wife from their home. The tanks had surrounded their village while soldiers set light to his house and then burned his cattle. They'd walked for miles with what little they could carry, eventually reaching this farm on the outskirts of Junik where they were given refuge. He told me of his relief that his children and grandchildren were living in Switzerland. He had angina and the medication he needed was no longer available, so his health was suffering. His face was brown and wrinkled, and he gazed at me with watery blue eyes.

'I don't expect to live much longer,' he said. 'Kosovo is dying, so I may as well die too. I only wish that I could have kissed our grandchildren, just once.'

'There will soon be intervention,' I said, trying to instil some hope. 'The British prime minister said they will not allow another Bosnia to happen.'

The old man patted my hand. '*In sha' Allah*,' he said. 'Let it be God's will.'

We were called in to breakfast and sat on cushions around a low wooden table. The farmer's wife served flat bread, sheep's yoghurt and a plate of fried green peppers, which we ate with our hands.

'What happens next?' asked Rafaelle, licking the salt crystals from his fingers.

'You will be taken to Junik,' said Rambo. 'What you do then is up to you.'

As the farmer's wife handed me a glass of sweet black tea, I asked Rambo whether he'd be coming with us.

'Of course,' he replied, seeming surprised by my question. 'My orders are to help you accomplish your mission. I'll be with you the whole time.'

'We'd like to film Sally in Junik if possible,' said Gian.

Rambo shrugged. 'You're not my responsibility. I'll take you to meet the commander and he'll decide.'

A car pulled up on the track alongside the house and we thanked our hosts for their hospitality. I climbed in to the front of the rusty old vehicle, which had a bullet hole through the windscreen, and Rambo and the journalists squeezed into the back. The driver told us that there were snipers up ahead and that we'd need to travel at top speed. I couldn't help wondering what top speed might be for such an old banger, and inadvertently slid further down into my seat. The car backfired as we pulled away, causing me to duck, and we were careering down the bumpy track towards the town.

Once again I was reminded of Mostar, experiencing the same cold tingling on the back of my neck as I wondered whether a sniper was about to pull the trigger. I was greatly relieved when we finally reached the town and the driver slowed down to light a cigarette.

Junik is a small town in south-west Kosovo between the districts of Deçani and Gjakova. Being so close to Albania, the town was a major staging post for the KLA, and the Serbs had recently begun a major offensive in the area. By the time we arrived they'd almost succeeded in surrounding the remote mountain stronghold, and the only way in or out was across the mountains.

We pulled up outside a large concrete building set back from the road, which seemed to be the command headquarters. The walls were pockmarked with shrapnel and there were bullet holes in the glass. Young men in combat fatigues were hanging around the parking area and in the hallway, watching us closely. After about ten minutes we were taken upstairs to an office on the first floor where a man came forward to greet us. Gani Shehu, a former officer in the JNA (the Yugoslav People's Army) was about thirty, clean-shaven with a rounded face and thick dark hair, and unlike the other soldiers he was dressed in a grey flying suit.

With Rambo interpreting, the journalists requested permission to visit the local hospital and talk to the doctors, and if possible they also wanted to interview some officers from the KLA. We were offered glasses of warm Coke while Gani explained that the only hospital inside the town was a small health centre just along the road. As for meeting with KLA officials, he said that would have to be discussed.

'We will find you somewhere to stay,' said Rambo. 'In the meantime, he wants to talk to Miss Becker.'

When the journalists had gone, we were served Turkish coffee and Gani addressed me directly in English. He was actually an Albanian American from Manhattan, a former lawyer fluent in English, German and French. He'd returned to Kosovo as chairman of the LDK, the Democratic League of Kosovo led by Ibrahim Rugova, and was now commander of the battalion based in Junik. He looked at me and ran a hand through his shock of black hair.

'I know of your work, Miss Becker, and we're glad that you've chosen to help us. There's a shortage of everything so we're very grateful for the medical supplies that came in last night. If we can assist with your mission in any way, please don't hesitate to let me know. In the meantime, you're invited to our military canteen for lunch.'

He stood up and escorted me to the door. 'Welcome to Kosovo,' he said.

As we walked along the street, I noticed that many of the buildings bore the battle scars of war. Some of the roofs were completely destroyed and one house had a hole blown through the side.

The mess hall was lined with long wooden tables and benches, and as soon as I sat down I received a bowl of thick soup and large hunk of bread. A soldier dressed in the green camouflage and black beret of the KLA came and joined us. He had short black hair, a neatly trimmed beard and glasses.

'Miss Becker, it's a pleasure to meet you,' he said, shaking my hand. 'My name is Lum Haxhiu.'

Formerly a political prisoner, Lum, a writer and poet, had spent several years living in Denmark and was now the KLA's 'morale officer'.

A couple of weeks earlier he and Gani Shehu had hosted a meeting in Junik with Richard Holbrooke, the United States envoy who'd come to Kosovo to negotiate a peace agreement between the Serbs and the ethnic Albanians. Upon his departure, Holbrooke admitted that the meeting was unsuccessful. Lum spoke fluent English, which was a relief to me after struggling with Rambo in German.

'How do you hope to help us?' he asked, leaning a worn Kalashnikov against the table.

'I don't know exactly,' I replied. 'I wanted to bring you the medical supplies but I'm also here to highlight what's happening. When atrocities take place, the media flock here and you have the ear of the world, but as soon as the journalists disappear, people forget that the innocent are still suffering.'

'But how do we change that?' He tore off a piece of bread and dipped it in the soup. 'We've requested help from the international community for a very long time but no one cares. As a result we've been forced to take up arms in order to fight for our freedom.'

I nodded, for I knew only too well how hard it was to make people listen.

'But you can't expect to beat the Serb Army with a handful of guns and grenades,' I said. 'I know that your soldiers are prepared to lay down their lives for Kosovo, but that won't save your people. In Bosnia it was the media that eventually made people sit up and take notice. In order to get help, you need to highlight the effects of the war on the women and children.'

He looked thoughtful. 'That wouldn't be easy,' he said finally. 'Most of the children are living in cellars and basements on the outskirts of town.'

'What about those in need of medical treatment?' I asked.

'We can't get them to the hospital because snipers watch the roads, so it's extremely dangerous,' said Lum.

'That's exactly the kind of thing I want to highlight.'

'But you'd need to travel through Serb territory in order to reach them.'

I told him I was willing to take the risk.

'And suppose you get hurt, or even killed?' he asked, looking straight into my eyes.

I shrugged. 'Well, that would certainly get their attention.'

He nodded slowly and stood up. Lifting the rifle onto his shoulder, he shook my hand and told me we'd meet again. When he'd gone, Rambo took my hand.

'I'm honoured to have been chosen to accompany you, Sally,' he said. 'I understood some of what was said and I'll do my best to protect you.'

I smiled and thanked him as we walked out onto the street.

Around the corner we came to a house built in the style of a Swiss chalet. It was two storeys high and backed onto a large garden where chickens were roaming. A cow pulled lazily at the grass and in a shaded corner of the garden five old people sat around a large wooden table while a cooking pot rattled on a wood-burning stove.

Alberta, a tall, slim woman about my age, explained that she was looking after the place for her neighbours, who'd gone abroad. She lived next door with her husband and sister, but her daughter was living in Britain and she'd been unable to make contact for several months. All the phone lines were down and the post no longer operated. I suggested she give me her daughter's address so I could pass on a message.

She showed us into the house, which was bright and airy with modern furnishings, and I smiled with delight when I saw the shower room. Then they told me there was no water supply to the building. Instead she fetched me a bucket of hot water heated on the stove. Apart from clean clothes and underwear, I was carrying a toothbrush, toothpaste and shower gel. Stripping off my clothes, I rinsed the dirt and dust from my body and washed my hair. I dressed in a clean pair of jeans and a white T-shirt but decided not to wear shoes as my ankle was swollen. Alberta looked horrified when she saw I was barefoot and she rushed to fetch me a pair of slippers, kept on the doorstep for guests.

Sitting in the sunshine beneath an azure sky, it was hard to believe that the town was the target of an offensive. They told me that the shelling usually went on day and night, and this was the first peaceful day in weeks. She invited us to join them for some chicken soup, and I guiltily eyed the hens pecking in the grass, wondering if they were related to the contents of my bowl. Of course they were.

When we finished eating, Rambo took me to meet his family, where the Italian journalists were staying. I was shown around the house by three giggling teenage girls and was served the inevitable sweet Turkish coffee. I noticed that Rambo turned his small cup upside down on the saucer when he'd finished, and when I asked him about it he told me that his uncle could read the coffee grains left in the cup. He suggested I turn my own cup over so his uncle could read mine too. After a few minutes an old man joined us and Rambo spoke to him in Albanian. The old man nodded and began peering into my cup, although it seemed a long time before he finally spoke.

'You have a long and arduous journey before you and there will be children involved,' he said. 'Success will be the eventual outcome, but in the months to come you will suffer and the suffering will take its toll.'

When he looked into Rambo's cup he spoke in Albanian, so I couldn't understand.

Later that day we were driven to a hospital on the outskirts of Junik. The journalists didn't accompany us, and Rambo explained that they weren't trusted. In one of the wards there were about twelve men, some of whom had lost a limb, others with stomach or chest wounds. Bekim, who was twenty, had a gunshot wound that had paralysed part of his neck and shoulder. The doctor in charge informed me of the grave lack of medication. He showed me the store cupboard in which there were just a few packets of antibiotics and a small number of dressings.

'We've got no anaesthetics at all and the only medicines we have are what was brought in last night.' His eyes were ringed with dark circles from lack of sleep. 'Serb attacks have reduced the local population from 12,000 to 2,000,' he continued. 'Those who are most vulnerable, like the elderly, the women and the children, have been moved to safer places, and in some areas they're sheltering underground. Apart from the aid that can be smuggled through the lines, nothing has reached this area for a very long time.'

I was approached by a young blind man with black hair and a pale, thin face. Speaking perfect English, he told me that he'd been arrested by Serb paramilitaries and taken to the local police station. During the interrogation his tormentors would silently creep up on him. He'd been detained for two days while his mother continuously begged for his release.

He assured me that there was no reason for his arrest, but they continued to harass him in this way every couple of weeks. Eventually, he, his mother and his sister had left their village and travelled to Junik, where he now worked for the hospital. He wanted me to organise visas for him and his family to go abroad, but I explained that this wasn't possible.

'But you evacuate the sick and wounded children,' he said. 'We've seen you on television and read about you in newspapers. I'm only twenty-one and I'm blind.'

'An official evacuation wouldn't be possible from here,' I said. 'The situation is totally different.'

'But you managed to do it in Bosnia,' he said.

I tried to explain. 'The only way to obtain an exit visa here is through the embassy in Belgrade. I understand how difficult things must be for you but I don't want to give you false hope. The only way out of here is across the mountains into Albania, and for you this would not only be extremely difficult but also foolish.'

He agreed that he wouldn't be able to attempt such a journey, but he gave me his name and a contact address, in case I could think of a way to help him in the future.

Due to the extensive media coverage, people tended to assume that I had some special means of getting people out of besieged areas. Of course that wasn't true; there was no Ivan Bagarić here, and unlike the larger aid agencies, we didn't have unlimited funding and government support.

On our return to Junik, the driver stopped the car on the only stretch of road where I could get a signal and I quickly sent a message to Bill. Using the call sign 'Oscar Alpha' assigned to me, I told him that I'd reached my destination. We arrived back at the chalet to find Lum Haxhiu waiting with three officers. Lum explained that he'd made a call to Smolicë, a small village about thirty miles away.

'The journalists have been refused access,' said Lum, 'but the Angel of Mostar is welcome.'

One of the men, a commander, leaned towards me as Lum spoke, looking hard into my eyes. 'The area is very dangerous,' he said. 'The journey will have to be made across country as it's surrounded by Serb forces and you may have to walk part of the way.'

I thought of my ankle but decided not to mention it.

'We have sick and wounded children living in the area who are seriously in need of medical treatment,' he went on. 'We'll send our own cameraman in with you and afterwards he'll give you the film so that you have a record of what you encounter.'

I nodded, and after a short discussion between Rambo and the men, they left us alone. That night I lay in bed listening to the sound of explosions. I was awake for some time, wondering what the next day would bring.

We ate breakfast outside in the sun with Alberta and her family. She'd heard about our forthcoming journey and was very concerned, insisting that I eat plenty, afraid that I might not get another chance. After a meal of yoghurt, fried peppers and flat bread, we went to see the Italians, but Rambo insisted that I keep quiet about the meeting the previous night.

When we arrived, they were in the process of interviewing a general who was reported to have been killed in the fighting. He told them that the KLA was being restructured and he didn't yet know what rank or position he'd hold. I was surprised that he'd agreed to talk to the journalists, especially as he was supposed to be dead. Perhaps there was propaganda value in that very fact.

23

The following evening Lum Haxhiu pulled up outside our house in an old Yugo and I climbed in beside him. Rambo sat behind us with a soldier carrying a small video camera. As he drove, Lum talked about his son who'd fallen ill when he was just a few months old. He'd taken the boy to see a Serb doctor who prescribed some medication, but a short while later the baby died.

'An Albanian specialist told me that my son had been diagnosed incorrectly and that the medicine had killed him,' said Lum, his eyes fixed on the road ahead.

After a few minutes we came to one of the many checkpoints set up by the KLA. Two soldiers waved us through with the victory salute. These checkpoints were placed every few kilometres along the route, and after some discussion with a soldier at the third checkpoint, Lum informed us that we wouldn't need to cover any ground on foot after all as the soldiers had secured a route by road. Instead we drove at top speed along country lanes, often without lights as we passed through Serb-controlled territory.

We eventually reached a small village and Lum parked the car outside a house damaged by shelling. I followed Rambo down some dark concrete steps into a large cellar, and in the candlelight I could make out about a hundred faces staring up at me, most of them children. Rambo explained that they were forced to shelter there beneath the rubble, afraid to go above ground for fear of shelling and snipers. The room was freezing cold and smelt of damp, and upon sitting down we found that even the mattresses were wet. A baby was planted in my lap, gazing up at me placidly, a dummy protruding from his mouth. I wondered if he'd ever known anything other than this dank cellar.

When I asked how they managed to eat, Rambo explained that whenever there was a lull in the fighting, the women would race upstairs to try to bake some bread in the stone oven outside. They were often forced back underground by gunfire or RPGs, and the bread would be ruined. As a result they were all thin and malnourished, their faces pale from lack of sunlight, their lips cracked and sore from the cold and damp.

Tears stung my eyes, and I saw that Rambo was also crying; despite his macho appearance he was highly emotional, especially where his people were concerned. I felt so helpless sitting there in my clean clothes, surrounded by the desperate faces. I looked up to find the soldier filming me, and although I was aware of them all watching, I knew I had to speak.

'I'm here in a cellar beneath what used to be someone's home, surrounded by women and children living in the most appalling conditions. They're afraid to go out into the sunlight …'

As if on cue, a mortar exploded overhead, followed by rapid machine-gun fire. One or two of the children and even some of the adults began to cry, although the baby continued to stare at me unconcerned.

'These people are being ignored by the outside world while they sit here, day after day, night after night, waiting and praying for NATO to save them.'

As we prepared to leave, the women gave me a hug and thanked me for coming. An old man took my face in his hands and kissed my forehead, causing the tears to stream down my face as I climbed the stairs. I knew that those frightened faces, their paleness emphasised in the candlelight, would continue to haunt me for a very long time.

We drove on to other villages, where each trapdoor led to another cellar filled with old men, women and children, and as we entered I'd hear the whispered Albanian words 'Engjëlli i Mostarit'.

Finally, when it was completely dark, we arrived in Smolicë. The village originally consisted of seventy homes, all but two of which had been destroyed. We went to one of these undamaged houses and were introduced to a family who welcomed us inside. Rambo offered to take a photo of Lum and me sitting together on the couch, and I passed him one of my cameras. There was a knock on the door and some soldiers entered, dressed in black. They were members of an elite commando unit who were using the house as their headquarters. I guessed they were members of AFRK (Armed Forces of the Republic of Kosovo) who were loyal to Ibrahim Rugova. Rugova, who'd been president of Kosovo since 1991, had followed a policy of peaceful resistance to the Serbs until the massacres in Drenica that began earlier that year. Unlike the KLA, these men were professionals, moving in smaller groups and usually avoiding contact with outsiders.

There were a couple of regular soldiers staying at the house, and one of them sat down beside me and asked if I could help his family. Uli's parents were in Switzerland but the Serbs had refused permission for his sister and two brothers to join them. Their house had recently been shelled while the three children were inside and they'd all been wounded, the boys quite seriously.

'Khalil, the eldest, has infected wounds where his arms were torn by shrapnel and Musa was badly burned. My sister wasn't really hurt but she can't stay here alone because I have to fight and cannot take care of her.'

I glanced at Lum, who shrugged and said, 'If you think you can help them, if you believe you can get them reunited with their parents in Switzerland, that would be fine.'

'There are others who need help too,' said Uli. 'I have a friend, an officer called Nik Hiseni whose child is in need of an operation.'

I looked at Rambo, who immediately nodded. 'We can take them out the way we came in,' he said.

We stayed up talking with the soldiers for a while, and they told us that earlier that day a fifteen-year-old boy had been shot by a sniper. I wondered what kind of monster could pull the trigger knowing he was killing a child. There were loud explosions and the rattle of machine-gun fire; we were only about a mile from the front line. Fortunately, the immediate area was screened by trees, making it relatively safe.

Early the next morning I was taken to Uli's house to view the damage. We had to run as fast as possible to reach the house as the area was targeted by snipers. The commandos ran alongside me, shielding me from the bullets that ricocheted through the empty streets.

A shell had entered through the roof and shrapnel had exploded in all directions, ripping through wooden beams and becoming embedded in the walls. Once again I was shown the basement of a ruined house where people huddled together in fear. As we left, I saw a missile lying on the ground. It was about five feet long and from the writing on the side I could see it had been manufactured in Russia. The Geneva Convention banned this kind of munition, so I photographed it, intending to show the type of weapons being used against civilians.

When we returned to the command post, Lum arrived in a jeep and drove us to a village called Nec, where I was introduced to Nik Hiseni, the officer Uli had mentioned. Aged around thirty, he was about the same height as me and was wearing army fatigues and a camouflage cap. Nik's youngest daughter Doruntina was sixteen months old. She was suffering from a hernia and when I first saw her she was screaming in pain. She was a lovely baby with rosy cheeks and a mass of blonde curls.

As I stopped to consider what I should do, another man joined us. His name was Hili Krasniqi and he was a good-looking man in his late twenties. Speaking English with a soft accent, he introduced me to his three-year-old daughter Marigona, who had short dark hair and a small, bow-shaped mouth. Her eyes were dark and serious, but she was smiling. She had cataracts. Perched on my lap, she peered intently at my face and I could see the milky white patches over her pupils. Whenever the sun appeared from behind a cloud, she'd squint.

'I took her to Russia in January for an operation,' said Hili, 'but she had a temperature and couldn't undergo the surgery. I was supposed to take her back in March, but war broke out and it became impossible to travel. They tell me that unless she has the operation soon she will go blind. Please, can you help us?'

I told him of the risks, explaining that I had no ceasefire arranged, and no guarantees for their safety. I figured that I could probably arrange an operation once we reached the other side, but as for the journey, I was dependent upon the KLA.

'We're desperate,' said Hili. 'My wife and children are in danger here all the time, so we're willing to take the risk.'

I suggested he discuss it with his wife, as it was vital that she be made aware of the danger. He went off to speak with a young, attractive woman called Valbona, who had long dark hair and dark eyes. She was breastfeeding her baby, Arbresha. Their oldest daughter Miranda, who was five, came and held my hand but Marigona tried to push her away.

Hili soon rejoined us. He said that his wife insisted she'd rather take a risk on the mountain than continue living in danger and watching her child go blind. He'd also spoken to Nik and his wife Hane who felt the same. Nik had gone to call his parents in Switzerland on an army satellite phone, and Lum indicated that we should leave. The families would join us in Junik later.

Valbona's mother, an elderly woman with wisps of grey hair protruding from a headscarf, came to kiss me and thank me for helping her grandchildren. She was crying and I felt wretched for I was being thanked for something I'd not yet done.

The children waved as we drove off in the jeep, stopping only once at what seemed to be a farm building used as a mess hall for soldiers. I was offered some suspect meat, which I politely declined. It was 40°C outside, so I just drank some water instead. To my surprise, the journalists appeared, but before they could ask any questions I was whisked back to the jeep. On the return trip to Junik, my mind whirled with doubts about the mission that I'd just agreed to undertake.

We arrived in Junik to find a family waiting for us at the chalet. Hamez Shala was an engineer and his wife an architect, but neither had worked for several years. Hamez began to cry as he told me how they'd struggled to survive in recent years, both forbidden to work. When war broke out in March they desperately wanted to leave the area but it hadn't been possible. To make matters worse, their two-year-old daughter Besa was deaf; she couldn't hear shelling or gunfire and had to be watched all the time.

'I'd prefer to jump into the nearest river with my family than to stay here under these circumstances,' he said. 'Please, will you help us?'

I told him that I had no guarantees for their safety but got the now familiar answer.

'We'd rather take that chance than to continue living in fear,' he said.

I tried to explain that the evacuation had not been planned and we'd be dependent on others, but he insisted that he and his family would die if I refused to help them. Despite my reservations I agreed to take them, and they quickly left to gather some belongings from their home on the outskirts of town.

I was told to be ready by 5 p.m., so I dressed in a pair of jeans, a T-shirt and my waistcoat, which still held some of my kit, and

I carried my other clothes, water and toiletries in my rucksack. Rambo arrived and we went to meet the others, who were waiting on the edge of the town with some mules.

Uli was there with a group of soldiers and three children. Khalil, who looked about thirteen, was tall and rangy and his arms were swathed in bandages. Musa, his eleven-year-old brother, was grinning broadly, despite the severe burns to his face. Lira, the youngest, was eight years old. She was wearing a grey spotted tracksuit and across her forehead was an angry-looking scar. The three of them giggled as I attempted to greet them in Albanian. When Uli was leaving he took my hand and I saw he was wearing a gold ring with a large red stone.

'I entrust you with their lives,' he said solemnly. 'When you reach the other side, please contact our parents in Switzerland so they can be reunited.'

He handed me a piece of paper with his parent's details and I put it inside my waistcoat. He hugged the three youngsters, and as he walked away Lira slipped her hand in mine, reminding me of the great responsibility I'd accidentally assumed.

Hili was saying goodbye to his family and Valbona was crying as he kissed the sleeping baby in her arms. Miranda, the eldest, was oblivious to the seriousness of the moment, gazing fondly at the mules being loaded with the meagre supplies the families had brought with them. Marigona just stood there peering up at me with a solemn expression on her face.

At that moment Nik arrived with Hane and their three children. Dede, the eldest, was twelve, with a thick mop of blond hair. He stood quietly to one side while his sister Drita, a beautiful ten-year-old with long dark hair, hugged her father, tears rolling down her cheeks. Doruntina was crying, so Hane placed a dummy in her mouth to soothe her.

'Time to go,' called Rambo, starting up the hill. The Shala family walked alongside him, and I noticed they weren't carrying any bags. Hamez told me that a sniper was now operating in the area where they lived, so it had been too dangerous to collect any of their belongings.

Bekim was seated on one of the mules, a jacket draped across his wounded shoulder. He was escorted by his younger brother, dressed in jeans and a T-shirt and carrying a rifle. We were also joined by a large middle-aged woman dressed in black, accompanied by Dino, her sixteen-year-old nephew.

As we prepared to move, the Italian journalists appeared. Gian demanded to know what was happening, and when I explained, he asked if they could join us. I suggested he talk to Rambo, who clearly wasn't happy.

'You have to let us come with you,' said Gian. 'There's no other way out of here.'

I took Rambo aside and eventually convinced him to let them tag along. They wanted a couple of mules to carry their equipment but they were told that they'd have to wait until we reached the next village.

The soldier had been filming the group, and when we passed he gave me the cassette, which I zipped inside my waistcoat together with the disposable cameras. The sun was shining and it was still quite hot as we set off up the hill. Apart from the soldiers, there were twenty-six of us in all, and as we strode along the dusty road I was reminded of a book I once read called *Pied Piper* by Nevil Shute. The main character is an elderly man who travels to the Jura mountains on a fishing trip. Germany has invaded France, and a couple at his hotel ask him to take their children to England. Their harrowing journey proceeds first by train, then on foot, and they're joined by other children in need of help along the way.

24

About an hour into the journey we stopped at a small village, but there were no mules available for the journalists to hire. We sat down to rest, and the mothers gave the children biscuits and water that they carried with them. Gian came over to tell me that mines had been dropped on the border by helicopters the previous night, so we wouldn't be able to continue.

The information had come from two men who appeared to be very drunk, so I was sceptical and asked to see the head of the village. I repeated what Gian had said about the mines but he was sure it was just a rumour; in Kosovo information was currency and people thrived on rumours. Gian had begun filming the group and suddenly Rambo shouted for him to put away the camera.

'It's still daylight and the Serbs can see us. Are you crazy? You're deliberately drawing attention to us!'

He was shaking with anger, his face bright red and his fists tightly clenched.

'OK, OK,' said Gian as he lowered his camera. 'But I think you're overreacting.'

Rambo looked as if he might punch him, so I stepped in and tried to calm him down. Eventually he backed off, but it was clear the two men had become enemies.

Rambo sent a messenger back to Junik with a note for Gani Shehu, and while we waited I was approached by an elderly soldier called Chamed, who was tall and skinny with a weathered face. Chamed insisted that he knew for a fact that the rumour about the mines was simply not true; several of his colleagues had crossed the border the previous night. Half an hour passed before Gani himself appeared in a white jeep. I asked him what he thought we should do, and taking me to one side, he lowered his voice.

'I don't think it's likely that mines have been dropped at the border but I can't be sure,' he said.

'Where is our escort?' I asked, noticing that the soldiers were no longer with us.

His discomfort was obvious. 'They'll meet you en route,' he said. 'They've gone on ahead to assess the situation.'

I nodded, fully aware that the decision was being left to me. I returned to the group and told them what I knew.

'I can't guarantee there aren't any mines. All I can do is cross the area ahead of you, and if I make it across, you can follow in my footsteps. Those of you who'd rather not take the risk must make your decision quickly. We've got to get moving.'

'You're being totally irresponsible,' said Gian.

I spun around to face him. 'Junik will soon be overrun by Serb forces. Surely these people have more chance of crossing the border than surviving a Serb offensive. They've got to make their own decision. No one invited you to come. In fact, you were the one who insisted there was no other way out. If it's safer to stay, then why haven't you turned back?'

Rambo announced that the women wanted to continue, and Valbona, who was just buttoning up her blouse after breastfeeding the baby, spoke confidently. 'We trust you and we'll follow wherever you go.'

The other women nodded in agreement, but Hamez Shala was obviously not sure what to do. He wanted guarantees, which I couldn't give. I told him that if he had doubts then he should take his family home. He said that he'd prefer to do that but his wife wanted to go on. We were losing time and it would be getting dark before we reached the border. I hadn't forgotten how difficult the inward journey had been, and I didn't relish the thought of trying to find our way through the forest in the dark. I was hoping to reach the border by nightfall, where we could wait until it was safe enough to cross.

'It's time to go,' I said.

Among the group was a man in his thirties called Sadedin, who was helping to lift the children onto the mules and making sure that the cumbersome wooden saddles were secure. The sun was rapidly disappearing behind the mountains and it was already getting a little cooler. The road soon narrowed to a track that led into the forest. Dusk was falling and the trees looked menacing as they towered above us, casting long shadows. I noticed that Khalil flinched every time we heard the sound of an explosion, so I put my arm around his thin shoulders to try to reassure him. He was leading the mule that was carrying his brother and sister, and my heart went out to him. He was so young yet he'd already experienced so much. He was now forced to depend upon a stranger, a foreign woman he didn't even know.

Rambo and I set off with the mule carrying Bekim, and behind us rode Marigona, Miranda and Drita. Valbona and Hane walked alongside them, carrying the babies. They were followed by Hamez and his family, together with the widow, who was leaning on her nephew for support. I could just make out the figures of the journalists and Sadedin bringing up the rear.

Large drops of rain began to fall, spattering the leaves, slowly at first, then faster and heavier. Digging out my jacket from the rucksack, I handed it to Valbona, who pulled it on over her shirt. The other women quickly attempted to cover the children but within minutes we were soaked. It was now completely dark and we could hardly see ahead of us. The rain turned torrential and the ground became thick, slippery mud. Rambo stopped and shouted that we'd have to turn back, but we were a third of the way to the top and the thought of giving up now filled me with dismay.

'Can't we take shelter under the trees?' I asked. 'It might not last for long.'

He shook his mane of wet hair. 'The children could die out here.'

I felt he was exaggerating. It was wet, but it certainly wasn't cold and I knew we'd be safer in this weather as the border patrols would be holed up and the noise of the heavy rain would mask the sound of the mules. I pointed all this out, then to my shock and dismay, Rambo broke down.

'I can't do this anymore,' he said, 'because I don't know what's best. I can't make decisions right now because I'm so tired. Please, let's go back.'

Without Rambo to guide us it would be impossible to carry on, so I reluctantly agreed. The whole procession turned around on the narrow path and with the mules slipping and sliding in a mixture of wet mud and clay, we retraced our steps. To my amazement I saw that the journalists were wearing large waterproof capes that covered them from head to toe, while the children were all getting soaked.

For what seemed like an eternity we slipped and stumbled down the mountainside. It was dark and the rain was so heavy that we could barely see, so we each held on to the person in front or grasped the tail of a mule. It was nearly midnight when we finally reached Gjoçaj, the small village we'd passed through earlier. We knocked on the door of an old farmhouse but nobody answered, and we huddled together, soaking wet and frustrated, desperate to get the children out of the rain. Finally, an old woman pulled back the heavy wooden doors and ushered us inside.

We must have presented quite a sight but she didn't seem surprised by our impromptu arrival. The women and children were taken inside and the men were led upstairs. Mattresses were placed side by side across the floor and once we'd stripped the children of their wet clothes, the youngest were tucked beneath blankets on the makeshift beds. It wasn't long before they were all sleeping soundly, exhausted by their adventure.

I helped Khalil to remove his shirt and saw that the dressings on his arms were damp. The wounds were already infected and this would make things worse, so I gently peeled away the wet bandages. He stood there bravely while I cleaned and covered his arms with sterile dressings that I carried in my bag. Musa was watching, and when I'd finished he reached into a pocket of his jacket and gave me a KLA badge. I realised that I was being given what was probably his prize possession, so I thanked him with a kiss, bringing a sheepish smile to his anxious little face.

One of the women asked me what was going to happen. She said that they were all desperate to continue, afraid that if they gave up and returned to their homes, they might never get another chance to leave. As I prepared to answer her, the rest of the women and the older children gathered round to hear what I had to say.

'Well, tonight we had to travel through the forest in the dark,' I said, crouching down low and blindly feeling my way around the room, 'but tomorrow we'll travel in the sunshine.' I stood upright. 'We'll climb the mountain like sunflowers with our heads held high.'

The children began to copy me, marching around the room with their arms swinging, and the women responded by laughing and clapping their hands. For months their children had been forced to shelter in the dark, damp cellars away from the snipers and the RPGs.

I realised that my clothes were soaked, so I quickly changed into some dry jeans and a T-shirt. My shoes were also wet and I left them beside the door in the hope they might dry off a little by morning. I went upstairs and found the men were already lying down. Some were sleeping, but Rambo gestured for me to come to his bedside. He apologised for having lost control, and I patted his hand and assured him that it didn't matter.

'You were probably right anyway,' I conceded. 'At least the children are dry now and they'll get some rest. We'll leave early in the morning and try again.'

Rambo nodded, and as I quietly headed for the door I was aware of Gian watching me from his bed across the room.

Downstairs the children were all asleep, and in the adjoining room I found their mothers were also in bed. There was a spare place for me, so I swallowed a couple of painkillers before wearily lying down and closing my eyes. Everything was spinning around in my head and it wasn't until dawn broke that I was finally able to sleep.

We awoke to find the rain had stopped but heavy grey clouds cast their shadows across the landscape. A group of soldiers were lounging around outside, their mood jubilant as they told us how they'd made a successful attack near the border the previous night. I immediately inquired about the mines, and one of them assured me that the rumour was untrue. I asked whether any of them had been sent to accompany us but all I received in reply were shrugs. There seemed to be very little order or discipline within the group. As an army, the KLA were lacking co-ordination. We ate breakfast in the courtyard of the house, tearing freshly baked bread from a large flat loaf and dipping it into homemade yoghurt.

Hamez Shala came to tell me that although his wife would prefer to continue, he'd decided that she and the children would return with him to Junik. He explained that because of the sniper in Junik they had no spare clothing and what they were wearing was still wet. He made me promise that once I reached the other side I'd do what I could to arrange treatment for his daughter Besa.

'The doctors say that there's an operation that will enable her to hear,' he said. 'If you can promise to help us, I'll find a way for us to get to Albania. But I must be sure. I wouldn't want us to become refugees in Bajram Curri.'

I assured him that if they reached the other side, I'd do whatever I could to help. When the mules were loaded, we watched them begin the journey back down the hill. As we prepared to set off, I was surprised to see that one of the mules was unable to carry more than one child because Gian's rucksack was tied to the saddle. Rambo was already confronting him about it, so I didn't interfere.

We set off into the forest once again, the path becoming steeper as we climbed. Everyone seemed in good spirits and dappled sunlight was shining through the trees. The ground was wet and occasionally a mule would slip, frightening the children on its back. When one of the mules suddenly took off in the wrong direction, Rambo grabbed the reins, hitting the unfortunate animal on the nose. It reared away from him, nearly throwing the children off its back, and I begged him not to hurt it again.

We'd been travelling for a couple of hours and it was nearly noon, so having reached a clearing we settled down to rest. The children ate biscuits and drank some water while I wandered off to find a suitable place to send a radio message. Within minutes I made contact with Tony, one of the border monitors on the other side, and I quickly told him to inform Oscar Charlie Bravo (Bill Foxton) that we'd reach our destination in about six hours. As I waited for an answer, the radio began beeping and I realised that the battery was flat. I had no spare batteries, but it didn't matter as I hadn't intended to use it again until we reached the other side.

Rafaelle joined me on a small plateau, from where we could see the group resting beneath the trees. Some of the children were stooping to gather handfuls of wild strawberries, tiny explosions of sweetness. I tried to see if there were any signs of the refugees who were reported to be hiding in the forest, but I was sure they'd have seen or heard us by now.

Rafaelle asked me if he could interview me, to go with the photos he'd taken. When the interview was over, I asked him why the other journalists tended to stay at the rear of the group; why it was that every time I turned around, they disappeared behind the trees as though they were playing hide and seek.

'They are professionals,' he explained, 'they are always prepared for an ambush.'

'Is that why they never help with the children?' I asked. 'Everyone else, including you, takes a turn in carrying a child.'

He shrugged, obviously not wanting to criticise his colleagues.

It was time to move on, so we lifted the children onto the mules and set off once again. We clambered over jagged rocks and waded through rivers and streams. One of the mules was slipping and sliding as it tried to negotiate a steep bank and the children looked as though they might fall off, so Rambo suggested that I sit behind them. He lifted me onto the large wooden saddle and I put my arms tightly around the two youngsters. The mule swayed and seemed about to lose its footing, and as soon as we made it up the steep incline I immediately got down, not wanting to add to its burden any longer than necessary.

The journey was arduous, especially where there were rocky inclines that were almost too steep to climb. My calves were aching and my ankle was starting to cause severe pain. I looked around and found a perfect stick, thick, strong and just the right size.

After a while it became apparent that Rambo appeared to be lost. Valbona told me he wasn't the experienced soldier I'd assumed him to be; in fact, she said that this was his first visit to Kosovo in seventeen years. Gani had assured me that the soldiers would rejoin us for part of the way, but there was no sign of them. Rambo was convinced they'd soon arrive and insisted we wait. An hour passed by and still nobody came. No one seemed to know the way. Sadedin suggested that he and

Rambo should scout up ahead to see if they could locate the right path.

Shortly after they left, Chamed, the old soldier from the village, appeared through the trees. He was carrying food for the children, and as they gathered round him to eat, he assured me that he knew the way to the border and would take us across – unimaginable relief. I was touched by the fact that he'd decided to follow us.

As we waited for the two men to return, I played with Marigona while her mother sat breastfeeding the baby beneath a tree. I was hot and thirsty, having given away my water bottle, so I went to find a stream. Lying on the bank, I sipped the ice-cold water from my hand and it was the most marvellous thing I'd ever tasted. I splashed my hair and face, then bathed my sore and swollen ankle in the soothing water. The mules grazed, taking advantage of the welcome break.

It was four o'clock by the time the two men returned. Rambo thought that we should wait until dusk before going on, but Chamed and I disagreed. We both felt that it made more sense to travel this last section in daylight as the going was already difficult enough. We included all the adults in the discussion, and the majority chose to move on immediately, not wanting to continue through the forest after dark.

This part of the mountain was the most difficult and the children were tired. Doruntina was in pain and she cried constantly as Hane carried her along the narrow path. I gave her my dog tags to play with and they kept her distracted for a while. We were hot and our limbs ached from the relentless steep climb. When we finally reached the edge of the forest, I suggested that Rambo and the other two should keep their weapons hidden in case they were spotted.

Finally, at 6 p.m. we came in sight of the ridge that marked the border. We settled down beneath the trees to wait for nightfall, and Gian began asked me to explain what was happening for the benefit of the camera. Speaking softly into the microphone I said that we were waiting for darkness before attempting to cross the border into Albania.

'Don't you think that this mission is dangerous?' he asked, pointing the camera at my face. I watched Marigona as she carefully spread a small white cloth on the ground before sitting herself down.

'Yes, of course it's dangerous,' I replied, 'but if these children remain in Kosovo they could die.'

Through the trees I spotted Rambo and was surprised to see that he was out in the open, brandishing his gun. He'd obviously seen something. Then there was the sudden, gut-churning rattle of machine-gun fire. I caught a glimpse of Sadedin ushering the group into the undergrowth, but somewhere behind me a baby was screaming. Hane was crouched beneath a tree with her two daughters, obviously unsure what to do. I was afraid that if I told them to run they might get killed, but I couldn't just leave them behind. As mortars exploded around us and bullets whistled overhead, I scrambled across and pushed them flat on the ground. I managed to shield Drita completely, while Hane covered the baby, who was screaming in terror.

'Mama, Mama!' she called, over and over again and I felt wretched, cursing myself for putting them in danger. I'd often come under fire in Bosnia, but never when children were with me. They'd placed their faith in me, and I knew that I'd failed them. Tears streamed down my face each time the baby screamed, but all I could do was try to protect them and pray they'd somehow be saved.

Whenever I attempted to raise my head, another burst of gunfire erupted close by, so we were forced to stay where we were. Bullets ripped through the branches, splintering the bark above our heads and soon a helicopter gunship was hovering overhead. I'd have to make a decision. The only options were to run or to surrender. Running would almost certainly draw fire, so

I decided to surrender, for at least then the others might have a chance. I had to find the courage to get up, knowing that when I did so, I might be killed. Gesturing for them to stay where they were, I took a deep breath and slowly stood up.

25

I shouted as loud as possible, trying to make myself heard over the sound of the guns – '*Nema pucanja!* Stop shooting!' Amazingly, the guns fell silent. Leaving the cover of the trees, I walked out into the open calling in English: 'Operation Angel, humanitarian, women and children!'

A man's voice replied from somewhere up ahead. 'Put your hands up and come towards us.'

I raised my hands in the air and saw a cluster of green helmets just beyond the ridge. One soldier raised his head slightly and gestured for me to approach. As I climbed the steep hill he became impatient, urging me to hurry up. When I was halfway up, he called for me to remove my waistcoat, which I dropped at my feet before continuing. They must have assumed I was armed, as when I reached them I was grabbed, roughly searched and told to keep my arms raised until they were sure I presented no threat. I explained that I was accompanying a group of women and children, and the first soldier ordered me to call them, assuring me that they would not shoot.

'Hane, it's okay, you can come out,' I called, not sure whether she'd hear me.

The soldier shouted in Serbian and then in Albanian, and at last I saw Hane climbing towards us with the children. Once they reached the top, Hane was searched while I was ordered to retrace my steps back down the hill, followed by three of the soldiers. I slipped and fell a couple of times as I was forced at gunpoint to move quickly down the steep grassy slope.

They insisted I walk on ahead of them while they took cover behind the trees, presumably fearing an ambush. After a few minutes, the one who spoke English jabbed at my back with his rifle and told me to call the rest of the group. I decided to use the opportunity to give the men a chance to escape.

'They say that there will be no danger if you come out. They know there are only women and children,' I called, my voice echoing through the forest.

There was no response, and suddenly the soldier pulled a pistol from his belt and held it to my head.

'Tell them if they don't give themselves up now, I will kill you!'

I was so completely overcome with anger that I was no longer frightened, and I spun around to face him, my hands upon my hips.

'How dare you threaten me,' I said, and cupping my hands to my mouth I shouted as loud as I could,

'Get away; run as fast as you can!'

I expected to feel a bullet slam into my skull, but instead he grabbed my arm and ordered me to collect the mules. One of them had escaped from where it had been tethered, but the other two were standing patiently beneath a tree, still carrying the bags tied to their saddles.

I took their reins and led them back up the hill, with the soldiers following behind. It was getting dark and as we approached the top, I saw that Hane and the children were lying in a small bunker dug into the hillside and that they'd been given blankets, food and some water. Doruntina was sleeping but Drita just sat staring straight ahead, tears streaming down her face. Hane managed to smile at me reassuringly.

'Can I take my bag?' I asked the soldier, gesturing to the small blue rucksack tied to the saddle of one of the mules.

'No, wait,' he replied.

I watched as they unloaded all the bags and emptied them onto the ground, but I grew worried when I realised that one of them belonged to the journalists. Inside was a box of slides and some camera film.

'That isn't mine,' I said quickly, moving towards the contents of my own bag. 'This one is mine.'

He glanced at me briefly and then collected the items together.

'They aren't mine,' I insisted, worried what the photographs might contain, but he ordered me to move away.

I sat on the grass beside the bunker, suddenly feeling very cold. Whether it was the change in temperature, shock or the after-effects of adrenaline in my system I don't know, but my teeth were chattering and I couldn't stop shivering. A blanket was thrown towards me, which I gratefully wrapped around my shoulders.

'What'll happen now?' I asked the soldier nearest to me.

He shrugged. 'We're waiting to speak to our headquarters.'

'Couldn't you just let us continue across the border?' I asked. 'We haven't done anything wrong.'

'Do you have permission to cross?' he asked.

'No, but 15,000 refugees have crossed here recently. What difference would it make if we joined them?'

He just looked at me blankly.

'At least let them go,' I said, gesturing towards Hane and the children.

'We'll wait to speak to headquarters,' he said.

'Have you heard of Operation Angel? We delivered aid to Kosovo a couple of months ago and it was broadcast on Serbian television.'

'We've been here a long time and we don't have access to television.' He then started speaking into a hand-held radio.

As I watched the landscape slowly being swallowed up by nightfall, I wondered if the others had managed to escape or whether they were still hiding in the forest. Somehow Hane had become separated from her son Dede when the attack began, and

I hoped to God that he was with the others and not alone on the mountain. Now that I had time to think, I was again overwhelmed with guilt, asking myself questions to which I had no answers. Should I have refused to attempt the evacuation? Should I have left them to their fate? I was completely exhausted and sat for a while with my head bowed. Eventually one of the soldiers sitting nearby offered me a cigarette, which I accepted gratefully.

'What's happening?' I asked.

'No English,' he said. '*Parlez-vous français?*'

He told me that they were waiting for the military police to come and take us to Djakovica, the town where their headquarters were based.

Djakovica is the Serbian name for Gjakova, a large town mainly inhabited by ethnic Albanians. The area had recently been surrounded by Serb forces, but it was one of the few places that still had electricity and water. I could hear the distant drone of an engine and saw a vehicle climbing the hill. When it reached us, I saw it resembled an APC but with windows made of plastic, which were flapping in the breeze. Hane was ordered into the vehicle with the children and she glanced back at me, afraid we might be separated. Her English was limited, and I spoke no Albanian, but I tried to assure her that I'd do my best to stay with them.

Inside the vehicle were two benches running lengthways on either side. Hane and the children were seated alongside an army officer, while I sat opposite between two military policemen. The engine strained as we bumped and rolled across the hillside, but thankfully Doruntina was asleep. Drita was softly weeping, and even in the dark I could see the fear on Hane's face following ten years of oppression and violence. To make matters worse, both mother and daughter were doubtless thinking of Dede and wondering whether he was still alive.

I was cold and exhausted, but most of all I was consumed with worry. A tear rolled down my face, which Drita must have noticed, for all of a sudden she began to sob. Hane tried to comfort her daughter but she pushed her away.

Seeing this, the officer shouted to me above the roar of the engine. 'You must be strong. Don't let them see you cry.'

I realised that of course he was right, and I quickly tried to regain control. Holding back the tears, I wiped my face and tried to smile, which must have helped a little, as Drita's tears soon subsided. We drove on across the rough terrain for about an hour before stopping in the middle of the countryside. The officer explained that our vehicle had broken down and we were waiting for a relief vehicle to arrive. He opened the rear door and lit a cigarette, cupping it in his hand to hide the flame.

'This area is controlled by the terrorists,' he said, referring to the KLA. 'Any moment now we could be targeted by snipers.'

I responded with a shrug, hoping the others wouldn't hear.

One of the men offered me some roast chicken from his ration pack. First, I offered some to the others. Hane refused, as did Drita, and it was only when they agreed to accept sealed packs of Amita, a cherry-flavoured drink, that I realised they were suspicious of the food being poisoned. Not having been raised in a country filled with murderous hatred between communities, I didn't have the same paranoid concerns and gratefully accepted a piece of chicken.

After a while, another vehicle came along and we were transferred inside. This one was even noisier than the last, and only two men accompanied us this time, including the English-speaking officer. The temperature had dropped considerably, causing me to shiver, and to my amazement the officer draped his jacket around my shoulders. Hane had brought a blanket with her from the dugout, and she and the children snuggled beneath it along the bench. As we travelled through the darkness, I tried to sleep but the interminable grinding of the engine and the bumpy terrain made it impossible, and I stared into the darkness, wondering whether the rest of the group was safe.

It was around 2 a.m. when we arrived at our destination; a large military base on the outskirts of Gjakova, where rows of tanks and trucks stood in silhouette against the moonlit sky. Doruntina was still sleeping as Hane carried her into the building, where a cell awaited us. There were two sets of bunk beds at the side, and in the centre were a table and some chairs.

Two men entered, both dressed in civilian clothes, one of them carrying a small video camera. I was ordered to join them at the table while Hane and the children were taken outside. One of the men sat opposite me, his hard eyes focused on mine as the other man began to film.

'What were you doing on the mountain?' he asked. I explained briefly I'd come to deliver medicines to Kosovo and that, having found children in need of medical help, I'd agreed to evacuate them to Albania.

'We have hospitals here. Why would they need to go to Albania for treatment?'

I shrugged in reply, loath to commit myself to an answer he would not appreciate.

'We killed two terrorists who were with you,' he said. 'They were firing at us.'

I was horrified, believing that he meant Rambo and Bekim's brother, but I tried hard not to show it.

'There are no terrorists with us,' I stated calmly, aware that it might be a ruse to obtain information. It was difficult trying to maintain that outward calm whilst thinking of the two young men and what might have happened.

'How many terrorists did you see in Junik?' he demanded.

'None,' I replied truthfully, not considering the KLA to be terrorists. For more than an hour he questioned me, often repeating the same thing over and over.

'Why were you there? Are you working with the terrorists? Was it a planned operation? Are you a spy?' Throughout the whole interview the camera whirred away.

212

I was tired, and in the end I wasn't even sure if my answers were the same as when he first began the interrogation. He must have realised that we were just going round in circles because he eventually signalled to the cameraman that the interview was over.

As he prepared to leave the cell he told me that the soldiers would be searching the mountainside for the people who'd escaped – 'There are helicopters in the air and dogs on the ground. We will find them, of that you can be sure.'

A few minutes later I was taken into another room where all the contents of the baggage from the mules were laid out on a table. There were a few dollars and some Deutschmarks, clothing, nappies, papers and passports, some film canisters left by the journalists, as well as my two plastic cameras, the video cassette tape given to me by the KLA soldier and my hand-held radio.

'Please indicate which of these items belong to you,' said a soldier standing behind the table.

I pointed to my belongings and asked if I could have them back, but I was told I could only have the toiletries and clothes. I asked to use a bathroom and was taken past a number of guards to a washroom down the hall.

I was concerned for Hane. The interrogator was now talking to her, and of course I'd no way of warning her of what had been said. I had not, for example, told him that three journalists accompanied us, hoping he'd believe there had only been one, the photographer whose film they had in their possession. I was afraid that if they thought there were other journalists with the group, they might make a greater effort to track them down.

The washroom was lined with old sinks, and behind a partition was a hole in the floor. The smell of urine was so overpowering that I decided to wait, blessed as I was with a strong bladder. I opened my sponge bag and proceeded to do what I could to wash my face and hair. The water trickled slowly from the tap, but I was able to brush my teeth and scrub away some of the mountain dirt ingrained on my hands and feet. My shoes were still wet from trekking through rivers and streams, so I carried them and walked barefoot back to the cell.

When the interview with Hane had ended, a guard delivered a tray of food and we were left alone. To my astonishment it contained four chocolate pancakes, four glasses of milk, some yoghurt, biscuits and several small cartons of Amita. It was hardly typical prison fare, especially at this hour of the morning. Once again Hane was suspicious of eating anything prepared by Serbs, but when she saw me tucking in with no immediate ill effects she too began to pick at the food.

Drita refused to join us, remaining curled up on the bunk with her face to the wall. In hushed voices we swapped information, although I couldn't be sure that we really understood each other. Speaking in broken English she told me that she'd admitted there were three journalists with us. When asked about her husband, she told them that he lived in Switzerland. Keeping an eye on the door, I removed Uli's piece of paper and a pen and asked her to list the names of all the people who'd been with us on the mountain. I knew that I might not remember all their names and I was determined to trace them later if possible.

We were exhausted and dawn was breaking, but I didn't sleep. My mind was filled with images from the mountain: Marigona with her dark eyes and cheeky grin, and Rambo's tears mingling with the rain. I relived the interminable climb through the forest, the sound of mortars exploding and Doruntina screaming.

26

It wasn't long before the sun rose and a guard entered the cell to tell us we should prepare to leave. Hane had fed and changed Doruntina, who was starting to cry. I suggested we ask for a doctor, but Hane was adamant that she wouldn't have her baby treated by a Serb. Picking up our few belongings, we followed the guard down the corridor and went outside, where tanks and military trucks were parked in neat rows. Soldiers were milling around preparing for departure and as a vehicle pulled up alongside us, I saw that the English-speaking officer was sitting inside.

As we drove out of the base, I was able to study him in the light of day. He was a tall, handsome man dressed in a green army uniform and steel helmet. We drove for some time with the sun beating down on the roof of the vehicle, making it hot and stuffy inside. The officer removed his flak jacket and offered it to me. His manner was gentle, and it was hard to imagine him condoning the atrocities and ethnic cleansing perpetrated by the paramilitaries.

'There are snipers in the area,' he said. 'These windows are plastic so I suggest you place this behind your head.'

When Hane saw him pass it across, she must have known we were once again in danger, as she promptly crossed herself.

I handed him the flak jacket and said I'd rather it was used to protect the children. He looked at me askance but nodded and passed it across to Hane. I suggested she and the children lie down between the seats with the jacket placed over them.

'She's a Christian,' he said. 'We're passing through a Christian area now and as you can see, none of the buildings have been damaged because they don't support the terrorists. They don't bother us and we don't bother them.'

I said nothing. Most of the children I'd recently met wore plastic rosaries around their necks, yet some of their homes had been razed to the ground.

We arrived in a small village and were transferred to another armoured vehicle for the onward journey. It was very claustrophobic and the noise was almost unbearable, so I was relieved when the vehicle finally stopped. As we got out there was the sound of a bugle call, so I guessed we were in an army barracks.

We were taken into a large square surrounded by long, low buildings. The officer gestured for Hane and the children to follow him, and this made her look worried. I begged him to keep us together but he said it wasn't possible. He did, however, assure me that we'd be reunited later. I asked him to explain this to Hane and although she looked sceptical, she agreed to go with him.

I was taken across the square and shown into a long, narrow room furnished with a boardroom-type table and a number of chairs. The soldier told me to sit down and wait, and I was left alone for a while. When he returned he handed me a strong Turkish coffee, and as soon as I drank it he brought another. After a while, another man came in and sat down opposite me. He explained that he had to take a statement, and once again I'd have to relive the events of the last few days. He asked some questions, mainly to make sure that he had the facts in order. I was offered yet another coffee but declined, for I could feel my pulse racing, even though caffeine doesn't usually affect me at all.

I was then taken into a small prefab where I was told to sit down. To my relief it was air conditioned, as it was now

The Baby Brigadier in Bosnia

On a mission

Lead vehicle in the Operation Angel convoy, Brighton

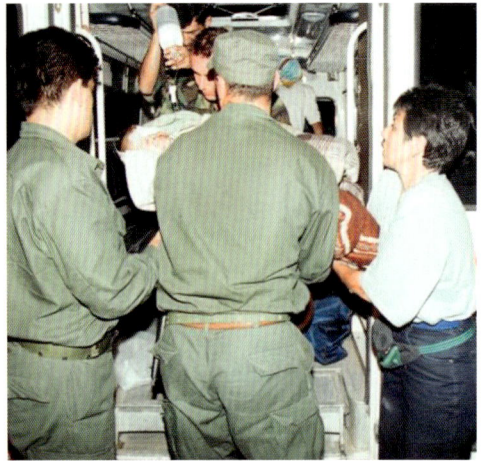

Evacuating Elmir and Lela

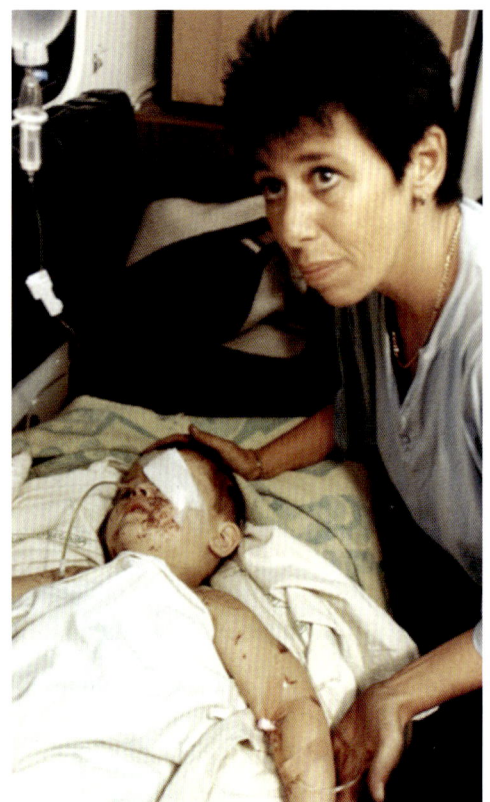

Tending to Elmir in
the ambulance

Arriving back in the UK from Kosovo

Major Bill Foxton

UNHCR, OSCE and ECMM waiting for Sally and the children at the border

Selma, the beautiful bride

With newborn baby Billie

With Billie and Maja in Florida

The field clinic
in Mosul

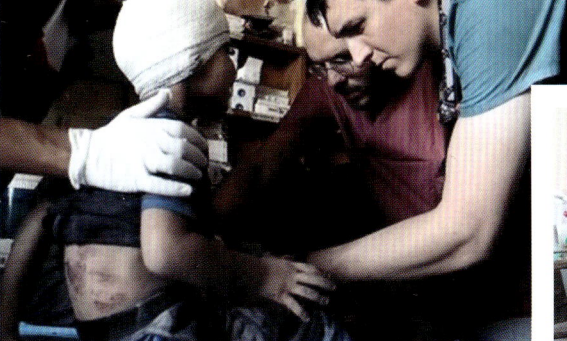

Ryan treating an injured child

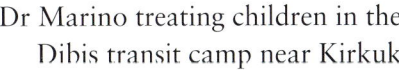

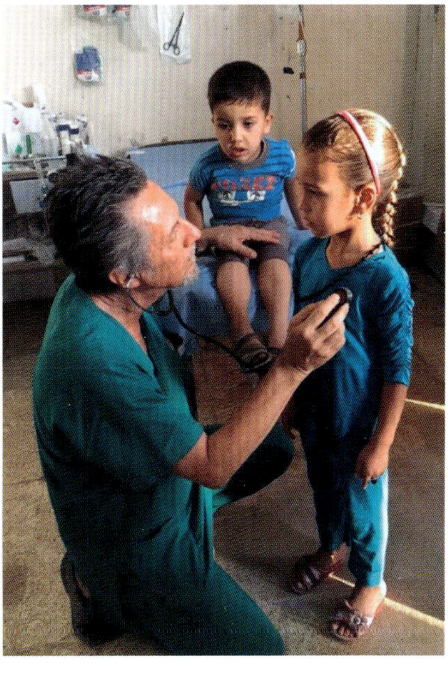

Dr Marino treating children in the
Dibis transit camp near Kirkuk

Dr Marino treating children in the Dibis
transit camp near Kirkuk

With Billie

Carrying the Flag for Peace and Justice at the opening
ceremony of the London Olympic games in 2012

Waiting to board the plane to Italy from a military airbase in Cairo

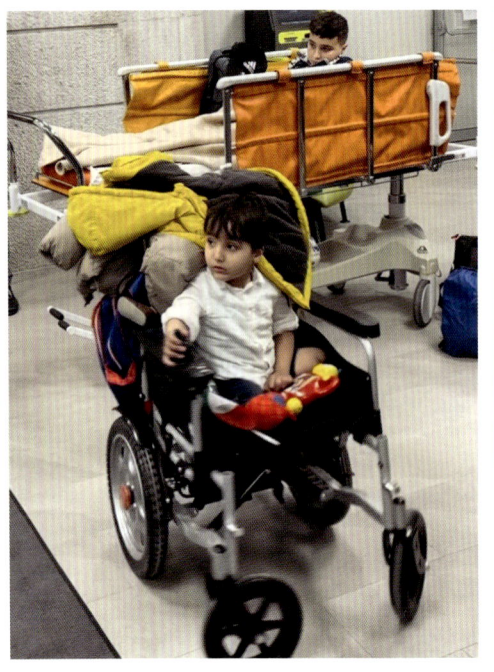

Ahmad   Zeina's father says goodbye

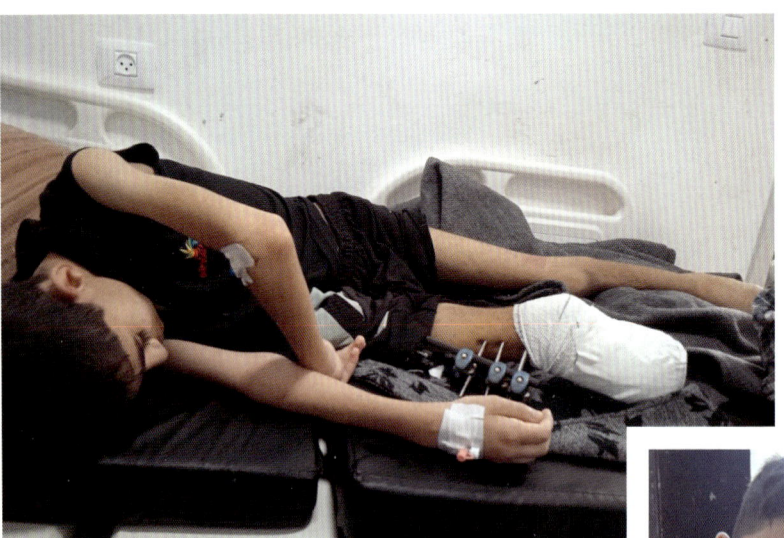

Kareem after his amputation

Kareem on his way to Abu Dhabi

unbearably hot outside. There was a desk in front of me and sitting behind it was a middle-aged man with slicked back hair. He reminded me of a man my father once described as a 'crook in a suit'. Peering at me from over the top of a pair of reading glasses he asked where I was from.

'England,' I replied.

He then said something that I couldn't understand. Sitting beside him was the soldier who'd taken my statement, but when I looked to him for an explanation he just kept quiet, shifting uncomfortably in his chair.

'I'm sorry,' I said, 'my Serbian is limited and I don't understand what you're saying.'

His face reddened with anger and suddenly he began to shout.

'Tell him,' I said to the soldier, 'that I only know a few words of your language.'

The soldier tried to explain but the man banged his fist hard on the table, startling us both.

'He says that you're lying. That you speak the language fluently and he thinks you're a spy.'

I had a severe headache and was beginning to wonder whether this was going to develop into a full-scale interrogation. Looking him straight in the eyes, I sighed and spoke slowly and clearly: 'My knowledge of Serbian is restricted to words such as *dobar dan* [good day], *hvala* [thanks] and *molim* [please]. Oh, and *nema pucanja* [stop shooting].'

His mean, beady eyes bored into mine, making my skin crawl. I was feeling nauseous, which might have been fear, but having been in more difficult circumstances than this, it seemed unlikely. He said something to the soldier, who translated for me.

'Why were you carrying a radio?'

'In order to get assistance for the children once we reached Albania,' I replied.

'Who do you work for?' translated the soldier.

'A British aid organisation.'

'Where is your identification card?'

'I only carry a passport but this is the organisation I represent,' I said, pointing to the Operation Angel logo on my T-shirt. 'We brought aid to the state hospital in Pristina. You can check with Mrs Todorović and Velko Popević of the Yugoslav Red Cross. They know me, they know my organisation. We brought several tonnes of medical supplies and equipped the baby unit with incubators. We even had the support of the mayor in Pristina. In fact, we were supposed to return there last month but at the last minute our visas were refused. If you have access to a computer you can look on our website.'

If he bothered to check out the website, he would see that I was telling the truth, for there were numerous pictures of our convoy being escorted across Kosovo by the Yugoslav Red Cross. The interrogator was quiet as he absorbed this information, then he rose and left the room.

'Would you like some more coffee?' asked the interpreter.

'No thank you, my head hurts and I feel a little strange. Some water might help, though.'

He ignored me and continued staring intently at the wall.

When the interrogator returned, he was accompanied by the Yugoslav (or as some states, including the US referred to it, the Serbia and Montenegro) Army officer. The interpreter left the room without looking in my direction and the officer took his place.

'What were you doing with a radio?' he asked.

I told him that most of the aid workers carried them, to keep in contact with one another.

'Describe this mission,' he said.

I explained how we'd arranged to return to Kosovo with a second convoy, but a week before departure our visas were refused.

'We decided to deliver the aid to the refugees and health centres in and around Tropojë on the Albania–Kosovo border.'

'What were you doing in Kosovo?' he demanded, impatiently waiting for the officer to translate.

'No aid is reaching the villages and there are sick children in desperate need of help.'

'You entered illegally. Why didn't you wait for permission?'

'I told you, our visas were refused. Sometimes desperate situations call for desperate measures.'

There followed a heated discussion between the two men, and then, scraping his chair noisily on the floor, the interrogator stood up and left the room. I massaged my temples, trying to ease the constant throbbing, and when I looked up the officer was staring at me.

'Sally Becker,' he said softly, 'you are a very brave woman.'

I couldn't think of anything to say, and we just sat there in silence until the interrogator returned.

'I feel very sick,' I told him, not sounding particularly brave. 'I really need some air.'

'First you will answer my questions,' said the man, glancing at some notes in his hand.

The interrogation continued for hours. Sometimes he'd ask a question and before I could even reply, he'd ask another. At one point he told me that he knew I was connected to the terrorist organisation known as the KLA. He believed that I was spying on their behalf, or on behalf of the West.

'You were travelling with a group of soldiers who were smuggling arms in order to kill innocent Serbs!' he cried. Of course I denied it, but he looked at me with disdain and said quietly, 'Your friend Hane is the wife of Nik Hiseni, who's wanted for terrorist activities. He's a murderer.'

I thought of Nik, so quiet and unassuming, and then remembered what Hane had told me.

'But he lives in Switzerland,' I said.

'No!' he shouted, again banging the table with his fist, 'He's here in Kosovo, planning the execution of our policemen. He's a terrorist!' He then seemed to calm down again before continuing. 'As a British citizen you should understand. You suffer the same problem with the terrorists in Northern Ireland.'

His words reminded of a similar comment made by Milisav Paić, a diplomat who worked at the Yugoslav embassy in London. I'd been asked to attend an interview regarding our first application for visas to Kosovo, and after a lengthy discussion Paić sat back in his chair.

'You're Jewish,' he'd stated, his hands clasped in front of him. 'Therefore you should understand our situation better than most.'

I looked puzzled, wondering where this was leading.

'You have a similar problem with the Palestinians. The Israelis declared Israel to be a Jewish state, but the Arabs don't accept it. They attack your people through terrorism, and therefore they have to be controlled, for the security of your citizens.'

I was worried that by contradicting him I might forego the permission I needed to enter Kosovo, but I couldn't agree.

'I'm British, not Israeli, and just because I'm Jewish doesn't mean that I support the way some Israelis treat their Palestinian neighbours. Oppression breeds violence. Discussion and compromise are the only way to secure a lasting peace.'

The official's eyes narrowed slightly as he leaned across the desk.

'The terrorists don't need to fight for Kosovo. The Albanians already make up 90 per cent of the population, and they breed at such an alarming rate that within a few years there won't be room for any Serbs.'

He then strode briskly out of the room and I thought I might have ruined our chances. Instead, much to my surprise, the visas were issued later that day.

Around the time of my interrogation at the army barracks, Nik Hiseni received a message from the Serb authorities informing him that they had his wife and children in custody. They warned him that if he didn't come forward, they'd be executed. Fortunately, he was familiar with Serb tactics and refused to comply.

My interrogator repeated his questions for a while until he must have finally realised that he was getting nowhere. I was now slouched in my chair, barely able to pay attention and afraid that at any moment I was going to collapse. I desperately needed to lie down, but he just kept asking the same questions over and over again. It was only when I slumped forward, my chin on my chest, that he finally gave up and left. The officer helped me to get outside and told me to sit down on the grass verge. I watched him walk away, wondering if I'd ever see him again.

I noticed that a television crew was setting up nearby, and Hane was brought out to be interviewed. To my horror, they'd placed the camera film, slides and the radio in front of her on a bench. With a great effort of will I forced myself to stand up and marched over to remove the items out of range of the cameraman.

'These are nothing to do with her!' I declared angrily.

At first they just stared in amazement, and then the cameraman turned his camera on me and proceeded to ask me some questions.

'I need a doctor,' I said, ignoring him. They tried to film me but I just kept turning my back to them. Eventually a man wearing a white coat with a stethoscope dangling from his neck appeared and offered to examine me.

I tried to explain how I was feeling and he placed his hand on my forehead. 'No problem,' he said straightaway. 'You're fine.'

It suddenly occurred to me that perhaps the coffee had been drugged. This could account for why I was feeling so sick, light-headed and strange. I remembered how quickly they'd refilled the empty cup, and yet weren't interested when I asked for water.

'So what are you doing in Kosovo?' the doctor asked, and I noticed he signalled for the cameraman to start filming. The journalists' equipment had now been moved and placed in front of me.

'You aren't a real doctor, are you?' I said.

'Of course I'm a doctor – but what are you? Are you a spy?'

This time I turned and spoke directly into the camera. 'These are not mine,' I said, pointing to the equipment. 'I'm not a spy; I'm a humanitarian aid worker trying to save the lives of innocent children. This is Serbian propaganda.'

This obviously wasn't what they wanted to hear, and without any warning I was grabbed roughly from behind and my wrists put in handcuffs that were so tight they cut into my flesh. I was then thrown into the back of a car and driven away from the barracks at top speed.

27

Driving through the centre of Gjakova, I could see people staring into the car and some of them smiled or waved. Gjakova was predominantly ethnic Albanian and I was hoping that someone might recognise me and report that I had been captured. We pulled up outside a police station and I was taken inside and ordered to sit on the floor in the corridor. I was concerned for Hane and the children, having assured her that I wouldn't leave them.

My presence was causing a stir, and a group of armed men dressed in the purple blue camouflage uniform of the Serb para-military police appeared in the corridor. They were known to be the main perpetrators of brutality against the Albanians, many of them being untrained civilians who'd been given arms and authority by Milošević when he first revoked the autonomy of Kosovo in 1989.

Sitting on the cold tiled floor with my back to the wall, the steel handcuffs biting into my wrists, one by one they swaggered past me, spitting and hurling abuse. My ankle throbbed and I had a pounding headache, so I leant my head back against the wall, closed my eyes and tried to shut out the sound of their voices.

Sometime later I was escorted along the corridor and into a room where the handcuffs were finally removed. I rubbed my sore wrists, which were ringed with bloody welts. There were two men in the room, one a policeman, the other a soldier. The policeman was holding Bill's radio and he told me to sit down, pointing to a chair near the door.

'Who's on the other end of this?' he asked, examining the walkie-talkie. He depressed the talk button, causing it to bleep.

'Probably one of my volunteers,' I replied.

'Why isn't it working?'

'The battery's dead.'

The soldier gave me a penetrating look. 'You were spying for the terrorists, weren't you?'

It was more a statement than a question, so I just sighed. After placing the radio on the desk, he came towards me. Bending down so that we were almost nose to nose, he whispered the word 'terrorist' in my ear. I struggled to avoid the sour odour of his breath.

'Where did you get the radio?' he asked.

'We all have them,' I replied, as he leaned in closer.

'To whom does the radio belong?' he asked gently.

I shook my head and sighed, wondering what to say. My ankle was aching and, hoping to change the subject, I asked for some painkillers. He told me to show him where it hurt, then slowly and deliberately he began to crush my foot beneath his heavy boot. I tried to push him off but he slammed me back into the chair. Just as I thought I might pass out from the pain, the policeman intervened. I don't know what was said, but a moment later my arm was almost wrenched from its socket as I was pulled from the chair and pushed back into the corridor.

Hane was sitting on the floor with Drita and Doruntina, and I was ordered to sit against the opposite wall. Hane raised her finger to her lips, warning me that we weren't supposed to speak. I was in a great deal of pain but I didn't want them to know that I'd been hurt. Instead I focused on Doruntina as she toddled around in front of me. Drita's eyes were red from crying, but now she just sat there quietly, staring into space. I wanted so much to reassure her, but even if I could have spoken their language, I didn't dare talk for fear of causing more trouble.

Hane held up her wrists and crossed them to show that she too had been in handcuffs. I was relieved to see that she wasn't marked but I was outraged that they'd done such a thing, especially in front of the children. Three of the men I'd seen earlier came back down the corridor to glare at us and one of them slid his forefinger across his throat, causing his companions to laugh aloud. Fortunately, Drita hadn't seen the gesture but Hane had, and I saw the fear flicker across her face. After a while we were taken upstairs and told to sit on a bench on the landing. Hane asked for a carton of milk for the baby, which was delivered.

We remained there until sometime in the early evening, when Hane's aunt came to collect the children. She told me that she lived close by and would be taking care of them until Hane was released. After they left, I was taken back downstairs to the reception area.

I was ordered to sit inside a glass enclosure on a broken chair, and the only way to prevent it from falling was to balance using my feet. An old policeman sat opposite me in the cramped space. He was tall and stooped, with thinning grey hair, and some of his front teeth were missing. When I asked to use the toilet, he sent me limping down the hall. They'd given me the rucksack containing my toiletries, so I was able to have a wash at the small sink. My foot was swollen and bruised, and when I gingerly began to clean the blood off, three of my toenails came away. I was very dehydrated, so I drank water from the tap before returning to my seat in the small office.

I spent the rest of the night and the whole of the following day balancing precariously on the broken chair. There was no sign of food and the only water available was from the tap in the toilet. I thought of Hane and hoped that she at least had somewhere to lie down. A German-speaking policeman had replaced the old man but apart from asking me where I was from, he largely ignored me. During the evening I returned from the bathroom to find another man in his place. He was in his mid-twenties, with short-cropped blond hair and blue eyes, and as soon as I sat down he began to ask questions in a mixture of Serbian, English and French.

Most of the questions were related to politics: my opinion of Milošević, how come I didn't help Serb children, why were Clinton and Blair supporting terrorists? I answered as best I could, but if he didn't like my answer he kicked the chair so I toppled over. After a while we were interrupted by a commotion in the hall. Some of the soldiers from the previous day were pressed up against the glass, jostling for position. Behind them was a big man with dark hair and a straggly black beard. He was wearing a bandanna tied around his head and a long knife dangled from his belt.

'You were on television this evening,' he said in English, after he'd pushed past the soldiers and entered the room. 'They say you were spying for the terrorists!'

I explained that I was an aid worker on a mission to help some children, but he sneered and demanded to know why I was carrying a long-wave radio.

'You had pictures of the terrorist Haxhiu. You also had film of women and children, and you were calling for NATO to help them.'

It became apparent that the video tape I was carrying had been broadcast on television, so I didn't bother defending myself, knowing it was pointless when the evidence was so obviously damning.

'You were filmed leaving Junik with the terrorists!' he shouted.

The soldiers began to mimic a chant used by Albanians in support of the KLA: 'UChK! UChK!'

The crowd increased until there must have been over a hundred men surrounding the glass enclosure, and they all joined in the chant. Some carried RPG launchers on their backs and grenades hung from the webbing on their chests. They were wearing black jumpsuits and many had long hair and beards. One of the men was carrying a Heckler & Koch machine gun and looked as though he'd kill me given the chance. They might have been Arkan's volunteers – he was rumoured to be operating in Kosovo. Arkan was the nickname of Željko Ražnatović, the notorious leader of the Tigers, a paramilitary force who were alleged to have committed atrocities against the Muslim population in Bosnia (and later proved to have done so).

'All those children died on the mountain because of you,' he said.

At first I thought I'd misheard him, but he said it again. 'They were all killed because of you.'

I sat there, my heart crushed by his words, and when some of the other men began to crowd into the office I hardly noticed. The man with the bandanna jabbed his gun into my stomach, calling me a spy, and although it was painful, I was not scared and in fact would have welcomed the bullet.

After a while they grew bored and gave up, leaving me alone. I removed the last cigarette from the pack I carried in my waist-coat and closed my eyes as I inhaled. Tears were running down my face. I couldn't stop them, and didn't try to.

Sometime later I was on my way to the washroom when I saw Hane sitting alone in the corridor and hurried past, hoping she hadn't noticed my swollen eyes. I was physically and mentally exhausted, and leaning against a table, I rested my head in my arms. Suddenly there was a resounding crack close to my ear. Looking up, I saw that the young policeman had smashed his stick across the table.

'No sleeping!' he cried.

I sat there all night long, and whenever I inadvertently dozed off I was woken by the crack of his stick on the Formica close to my ear. I had an unbearable headache but was forced to stare into the neon strip light overhead, feeling wretched and wishing I could stop the thoughts that threatened to overwhelm me.

The old policeman was back on shift again the next morning and he seemed concerned by my appearance. I asked him whether I could have a cigarette, but he didn't smoke and asked a colleague for one on my behalf. A few hours passed before I was taken upstairs and told to pick up the phone. Watched by two men in civilian clothes, I was put through to David Slinn, a diplomat at the British embassy in Belgrade.

'We've been trying to find out what happened to you, Miss Becker,' said Slinn. 'Are you all right?'

'Do you have news of the people I was trying to evacuate?' I asked him. 'I've been told they were killed.'

'That's not true. A call was made by a journalist who'd been with your group, and apparently they're all safe and well.'

At first I was unable to speak.

'Are you sure?' I eventually said.

'We received a message from an Italian news service that everyone is fine. No one was hurt.'

'Thank you,' I said. 'Thank you so much!'

'There was a family with you. Do you have any information about them?'

I told him they'd been brought to Gjakova with me and that the children were staying with their aunt.

'Their mother is still downstairs,' I said. Once again he asked if I was all right, and I told him that apart from some pain in my legs I was fine.

'It's possible you'll be moved from there soon, but don't worry, we'll find you. I'll try to visit you tomorrow. Do you have a message for anyone at home?'

I asked him to tell them I was fine and not to worry. We ended the call and I headed for the door. Hearing they'd all survived, all the guilt and remorse that had weighed so heavily on my shoulders was suddenly gone, and I practically floated down the stairs.

The old policeman had brought me a pack of Serbian cigarettes; the tobacco was rough and they had no filters, but I was very grateful and thanked him profusely. He didn't speak any English but he made it clear that I shouldn't say anything.

That afternoon, Hane and I were ordered into a car with two policemen and were driven through the town at high speed, as though they were expecting an attack. As we drove through the busy streets, I told Hane that Dede was safe. She didn't know whether to believe me and I couldn't speak enough of her language to explain how I knew. The car stopped outside a small café where people were sitting drinking coffee in the sunshine, and I found it strange to see life going on as normal.

We were ushered into a small office where a young woman sat typing while another woman, middle-aged with dyed red hair, was dictating to her. She reminded me of Rosa Klebb, the evil colonel in the Bond film *From Russia with Love*. The policemen joined us and we all sat down. I was asked if I wanted a drink from the café and, taken aback, I tentatively requested a cappuccino. I began to relax for the first time in days, sipping the delicious foamy coffee and smoking a Marlboro Light given to me by the one of the policemen. They were chatting to Hane in Albanian and I asked how come they spoke her language.

'We're Albanian,' one of them said.

'*Shum mir!* [very good],' I said.

They laughed but Hane looked slightly uncomfortable, her eyes darting towards the woman with red hair. I was given a piece of paper to sign that I couldn't read as it was written in Cyrillic, but a pen was passed to me and I was ordered to put my signature at the foot of the page. At first I hesitated, but seeing that Hane had complied I thought I'd better do the same. The woman made a short speech, and when I looked to Hane for an explanation she began to cry, placing one wrist across the other.

I immediately tried to make the woman understand that Hane was innocent and offered to serve double my sentence if they'd release her. To my surprise the redhead nodded and made a short speech. Glancing up at me, she then said, '*Trideset dana!* [thirty days]'.

Hane looked shocked, but at the same time she thanked me, explaining that they'd agreed to accept a fine for her release so she'd not be going to prison after all. I'd been tried and sentenced in a foreign language without the presence of a solicitor, and although I was unhappy at the idea of being locked up for a month, I was very relieved that Hane would now be free to join her children. We were driven back to the police station and I just had time to touch her hand before we were parted.

A short while later I was pushed into the back of a jeep alongside two soldiers and a civilian driver. We drove south across the lush green landscape towards Prizren, a large, picturesque and historic city, taking the long route to Lipljan prison to avoid KLA-controlled areas. (Most of the majority Albanian population was forced or intimidated into leaving the city during the Kosovo war.) One of the soldiers dropped his heavy rifle on my foot during the journey. He apologised, so perhaps it was an accident. It was nearly three hours before we arrived at our destination, which to my amazement looked nothing like a prison at all.

The place resembled a hotel complex, with neat lawns and flowerbeds. The officer who came to collect me from the main gate had dark, wavy hair and a surly face. Her uniform was blue, she wore a pale blue shirt and a navy cap, and a shiny black baton hung from her belt.

'I saw you on television,' she declared triumphantly as she escorted me along the path.

I kept quiet, thinking that for once it might be wiser to say nothing, and as we approached the main entrance I could feel the hot sun beating down. Birds were singing and the air smelt of roses. But appearances can be deceptive.

28

15 JULY 1998

By the time I began my sentence, a lot of small towns and villages had been surrounded by Serb forces. The recent offensive had resulted in many deaths and a quarter of a million people had now been displaced. The KLA, although still active, were losing territory, and despite a call from the international community for Milošević to halt the offensive, Junik was about to fall into Serb hands.

We entered a reception area leading to the women's block. Opposite the entrance was a staff room manned by two prison officers. Along the corridor was a washroom comprising a sink area, a small room with a plastic bowl for laundry and a Turkish-style toilet, which also doubled as a shower. There were two dormitories, one to the left of the washroom and the other directly opposite, but the majority of the prisoners were housed upstairs.

I was ushered into the staff room where a woman in her late thirties began to register my details. She was quite officious while my surly escort was present, but as soon as she left the atmosphere changed completely. I was to find out later that she was Albanian, one of only three still employed by the prison. The rest of the staff were Serbs.

Selima, who was pregnant, had worked at the prison for the past fifteen years. We communicated in my limited Serbo-Croat as she took down my name, date of birth and so on. I had to hand over my earrings, a ring and some of the items from my sponge bag, such as my razor, perfume bottle and scissors. They already had possession of my passport and money, and the walkie-talkie, plastic cameras, videotape and some of my papers had been confiscated by the police.

I was shown into the first dormitory, where among the row of beds was a child's cot. As I proceeded to unpack my spare T-shirt and underwear, the grim-faced officer returned and told me I had a visitor. I was escorted across the grounds to a larger building near the main entrance and was shown into an office where a pleasant-looking Englishman rose to shake my hand. He introduced himself as David Slinn, First Secretary at the British embassy in Belgrade, the man I'd spoken to on the phone. He was tall and good looking, with dark hair and glasses, and I guessed him to be around thirty. I was relieved to see him, and it was a pleasure listening to his refined British accent. Beside him sat a young woman employed by the prison to monitor our conversation, and Surly also stayed with us throughout the visit.

'So, how are you?' asked David.

'All the better for seeing you,' I replied. 'Thank you for coming.'

Although I'd been held since Thursday, he told me that it was not until Saturday that they learned of my arrest. As soon as the news came through, Colonel Crossland, the British defence attaché in Belgrade, had raced to Junik in a diplomatic car.

'We were led to believe you were being held by the KLA, although that didn't make much sense,' he said. 'When the colonel stopped to pick me up from my hotel in Pristina, a reporter from Sky suddenly announced that you were actually in the hands of the Yugoslav police. We tried very hard to get further information but it wasn't until Sunday that I was able to make contact with you in Gjakova.'

I'd spoken to Colonel Crossland back in March when I was trying to obtain visas for the first convoy to Kosovo. I'd agreed to deliver a large number of shoeboxes filled with aid that had been collected by his local charity, and although he was very helpful, he'd voiced his doubts about our securing permission to enter Yugoslavia. Shortly after we returned from Kosovo in April, having successfully delivered aid to both sides of the conflict, I received a fax from him with the words 'Well done!' scrawled across the page. I asked David to send him my regards.

'Actually, he drove me here and is waiting outside in the car.'

We proceeded to discuss what had happened to me following my arrest, and he assured me that my treatment in the prison would not be on a par with the brutality of the paramilitary police. He told me that one of the Italian journalists had informed their TV station in Italy about what occurred on the mountain. They'd received the call from a satellite phone in Junik the day after we were ambushed, and he again assured me that none of my group had been hurt and all had been accounted for. He also told me that he'd spoken to Duncan and my family, who sent their love.

'Your arrest and imprisonment have been broadcast internationally, and the fact that you were convicted without a proper trial and without an interpreter or lawyer present, may give you the right to appeal if you wish.'

I assured him that I certainly wanted to appeal; I had another convoy arranged for September and therefore a great deal of work to do. I also wanted the chance to highlight the situation in Kosovo and to begin tracing the families who'd managed to cross the border.

'How are you physically?' David asked. I told him I was OK apart from some pain and swelling in my legs.

'I'll have a word with the prison governor before I leave,' he said, 'and I'll visit you again as soon as possible. You'll also get a visit from Bob Gordon, the British consul in Belgrade. He'll bring a list of lawyers for you to choose from.'

'How will I pay for a lawyer? My work has always been voluntary so I don't have an income.'

'Your father said that he'll cover any costs incurred. Please don't worry. By the way, I've been asked to do an interview for Sky television tomorrow morning, so I'll be able to confirm that I've seen you and that you're well. Is there anything else I can do for you? Do you need anything brought in?'

I asked him for some clothing and a few books to help pass the time. He said that Bob Gordon would bring them on his visit, and with that he stood up and prepared to leave. We shook hands and I thanked him, before being led away.

I returned to my room in the women's' quarter to find that I was being moved into the dormitory across the hall. Although the room was large there were only four beds, two at either end. Plate-glass windows overlooked the front of the building, and although the windows weren't barred, wrought-iron railings were fixed to the exterior walls to prevent anyone from escaping.

I was told to collect supper from the hallway, where a large vat of soup was set on a table alongside several hunks of bread. The soup was watery and a vague reddish colour, with a piece of fatty meat floating on the surface, but I was starving, having had nothing to eat for three days. I returned to the dormitory and sat down at a long wooden table in the centre of the room. Dipping the dry bread into the soup, I ate while studying my surroundings. There was a stack of lockers against the wall, and hanging beside them was a long list of prison rules written in Cyrillic, which I couldn't understand.

When I'd finished eating, I returned my bowl and spoon to the hallway, surprised that my door remained unlocked. A short while later I was joined by my cellmate, a woman called Zoya. Although she was Albanian she spoke a little Serbo-Croat, so we were able to communicate. She spoke slowly, using her hands a great deal, but we had to whisper because one of the rules was no talking. Zoya was in her late forties, short and solid with a large and shiny round face, dark eyes, pale skin and a mane of long, straight black hair. She spoke with a slight lisp as her two front teeth were missing, and as we talked she kept glancing nervously at the door.

She told me that she was serving a five-year sentence for manslaughter. Her husband had been violent towards her, and eventually she snapped and killed him with a knife. She spoke about it quite calmly and without any shame. Her two children, both in their twenties, were living in Saudi Arabia.

'Only three years left and then hopefully I'll join them,' she said, proudly handing me a photograph of her grandchild.

Opening her locker, which contained a couple of shirts, a pair of leggings and some toiletries, she pulled out a box and invited me to help myself to her stash of biscuits, chocolate and boiled sweets. I asked her where she got them, and she explained that once a week the prisoners would make a shopping list and order things from the local shop. Having already sampled prison fare, I welcomed this news.

At precisely 10 p.m. an officer came to the door and told us to get ready for bed. I quickly used the wash room opposite and climbed into the bed I'd been allocated. After a few minutes the officer returned and, wishing us goodnight, closed and locked the door. I noticed that Zoya was very friendly and polite to the officers, almost deferential, and I wondered whether she genuinely liked them or whether it was just fear. I had many more questions to ask her, but straight after the lights went out she began snoring heavily on the far side of the room.

I lay awake for a quite a while, listening to the drone of military aircraft flying overhead and the distant thump of explosions. Having spent time with the people of Kosovo, seeing how they were living below ground in fear of their lives, I was able to visualise them all too clearly, imagining their anguish as the planes flew overhead, the children wide-eyed with fear. I thought of Marigona and the others, wondering how they were. I hadn't slept since leaving Junik, and this was the first time I'd been able to lie down, so it wasn't long before I fell into a deep, exhausted sleep.

At 6 a.m. an officer banged on the door, which gave us an hour to wash, dress and prepare for the day ahead. Breakfast arrived in the form of two hard-boiled eggs, a hunk of bread and a cup of incredibly sweet syrupy black tea. Zoya didn't want any breakfast. She worked in the staff canteen over in the main building and would eat there. At eight o'clock someone came to collect her and she padded out of the room, her open sandals clacking on the floor.

I could hear some of the prisoners cleaning the washroom and hallway. One of the women smiled nervously as she passed my open door and I returned her smile, making the symbol for 'free Kosovo'. She looked delighted, and after checking to make sure the officers weren't watching, she returned the salute. She then disappeared into the washroom to tell her companions. There were five of them, ranging in age from seventeen to forty, and they all began to wave at me from across the hall.

I wandered across to the window and saw a group of male prisoners dressed in blue overalls. They passed by in single file, their heads bowed, but when one of them suddenly looked up I caught a glimpse of his face. He was battered and bruised, and I noticed he was limping badly. There was an angry shout and he quickly averted his gaze.

The temperature was already rising rapidly despite the hour, and the sun, magnified by the glass, was increasing the oppressive heat inside the room. I had just opened both windows to let in some air when an officer appeared at my door shouting in anger. I couldn't understand what she was saying, but guessed she wanted me to move away from the window so I quickly complied.

She pointed to one of the chairs that were placed around the table. 'Stay there,' she barked as I sat down.

Sitting on the hard wooden seat, I wished I had a book or something to occupy myself. After about an hour, by which time I had studied every detail of the room, the officer reappeared and took me into a courtyard at the rear of the building. To my surprise I was left alone, so I had a look around. Lipljan prison housed both male and female inmates in separate two-storey buildings overlooking a central courtyard. Neat flowerbeds lined the perimeter of the courtyard, which was enclosed by a high wall. I went and sat down on the grass, making the most of being outdoors. The sun shone brightly and I could hear birds singing overhead. The smell of the freshly watered flowers hung in the balmy air, and once again I found it hard to believe that I was actually in prison. I could see the women waving from a window on the upper floor of the building where I slept, and I waved back. An officer came out and made it clear that this was forbidden. She beckoned me back inside and handed me a broom, a bucket and a washcloth, and told me to clean the other dormitory.

I swept and cleaned the floor as best I could until an officer came to inspect my work. She was in her early twenties, her short fair hair framing a baby face.

'Again,' she said in English. 'This is no good.'

I began to sweep the floor for a second time while she stood over me. I didn't know what I was doing wrong, but she became angry and began to shout. I held my hands out palm upwards to show that I didn't understand what she was saying, but she suddenly took hold of the broom and shoved it against my chest. Her attitude annoyed me and I shook my head and leaned the broom against a wall. She seemed a little surprised as I strode past her, and when I entered my room I could hear her complaining loudly to someone in the office.

There was no clock in the room and my watch had been confiscated, so it was only when I was told to collect a bowl of soup and the inevitable bread that I guessed it was lunchtime.

The day dragged on as I had nothing to do, nothing to read and no one to talk to. It was only six weeks since I'd been at Windsor Castle meeting the Queen.

During the afternoon the senior officer appeared at my door to announce that I was being taken to visit the doctor. The officer, a woman, took me to another building where the surgery was based. I was told to undress but as I did so, I noticed that there were two male officers watching me from the doorway. The doctor, ignoring my protest that the examination should be conducted in private, listened to my breathing and checked my blood pressure. He then examined my ankle, which was badly swollen. As he poked and prodded at the site of the bruising, I flinched.

'Where did this happen?' he asked.

'At the police station,' I replied, which didn't seem to surprise him nor, for that matter, to bother him unduly.

A middle-aged woman wearing a white coat entered the room. She smiled broadly and said that she'd be coming to see me the following day. I was given some painkillers and escorted back to the women's quarters.

The medication had to be left in the office, but Selima assured me that it would be available when required. While I was there, I remembered Zoya telling me about the shopping list. I told Selima I'd like to buy some things, and she agreed to take my order, which included two cartons of cigarettes, a box of matches, some fruit and two bars of chocolate.

The next morning I had a visit from Dragan, the chief prison officer. He wasn't much older than me and we were about the same height, To my surprise he spoke perfect English.

'So, how are you?' he inquired. 'Are they treating you well?'

I shrugged and nodded.

'If you have any complaints, please don't hesitate to say.'

I told him that I was unimpressed with the prison doctor allowing people into the room while I was undressed. He seemed embarrassed and assured me that it wouldn't happen again. I asked him whether I'd be allowed to contact anyone in the UK, and he told me I could write a letter or a fax, which would have to go before a panel of judges. He then stood up, shook my hand and left with the senior officer following behind.

I ate supper – more soup and bread – at about seven that evening. Later I was joined by Zoya, who'd finished working in the kitchen. She was bursting with excitement, and as soon as it was safe to talk, she told me that news of my arrival had spread all over the prison.

'You're famous!' she cried gleefully. '*Engjëlli i Mostarit.*' She stood gazing at me in disbelief. 'You're on television and radio. Serbs call you "The Terrorist" and Albanians call you "Daughter of Mother Teresa".'

She suddenly stopped talking and leapt to attention as two officers appeared in the doorway. Both had dark curly hair and were a little overweight, and I thought they might be twins until I was told that one was Serb and the other Albanian.

'I saw you on television,' said the Serb with an ironic smile.

The Albanian looked a little uncomfortable. She noticed some crumbs on the floor beneath the table and told Zoya to clear them up. Zoya immediately ran to get a dustpan and brush, which I tried to take from her as the mess was from my own supper, but she insisted on doing it herself and the officers didn't object. After they left, I asked her why she was so afraid of them, and she mimed being beaten. I asked her if she'd ever been hurt by any of the officers, and she said no, she never disobeyed orders. We continued to talk softly until it was time for bed and one of the twins came to lock us in for the night. It was the Albanian woman, and as she said goodnight she smiled warmly before softly closing the door.

Hours passed before I was able to sleep. The room was hot in spite of the open windows and the mosquitoes made a meal of me. As I scratched at the maddening bites I recalled a quote by the Dalai Lama: 'If you think you are too small to make a difference, try sleeping with a mosquito.'

I lay there listening to the loud snores from across the room and worrying about the forthcoming convoy scheduled to leave Britain in September. There was so much to organise. We had to find sponsors to cover the costs of insurance, fuel and ferry crossings, and there were interviews to conduct with prospective volunteers as well as funds to be raised to buy medical supplies. I had no idea whether Duncan would realise that I still intended to proceed with the mission, and these thoughts spun round and round in my head until I finally fell asleep.

In the morning when Zoya left for work, I was told to wait until the other women prisoners had showered and taken exercise before I too could wash. Preferring not to use the open toilet as a shower, I filled the plastic washtub with water and stripped off my clothes. Having also washed and dried my hair, I felt clean and fresh, and while the women came in to do their chores, I was taken outside. Several male faces were pressed up against a window that overlooked the courtyard. I held up my fingers in the victory salute and was rewarded with a dozen smiles.

I had no idea how long the prisoners had been at Lipljan, but since 1989 many within the adult Albanian population in Kosovo had at some time been arrested and detained. Some of them may well have been sentenced for criminal behaviour, but I suspected that the majority were political prisoners or jailed as members of the KLA.

Hour upon hour was spent in the room, where I was made to sit on one of the hard wooden chairs, staring at the walls. I'd have preferred to lie down on the bed where it was a lot more comfortable, but that was forbidden. The hours passed slowly, with nothing to break the incredible monotony. I was wondering if I might go crazy with boredom when an officer came to tell me that I had a visitor.

Bob Gordon, the British consul, was waiting for me in the annexe near the staff room. He was sitting between his interpreter and a male prison officer, and I was invited to join them. He was of medium build, with short grey hair and spectacles, and I guessed him to be in his late forties. He was more reserved than David Slinn, and after inquiring about my health he showed me some press cuttings from British newspapers that referred to my arrest. These stated that I'd been in the process of smuggling a refugee family across the border, but there was no mention of the fact there were many other children with me, some in urgent need of treatment. When I pointed this out, he said he'd inform the press.

'But why hasn't it been mentioned? David Slinn certainly knew what happened, as he's the one who told me the others had escaped. In fact, he said he was going on Sky News to talk about it.'

Bob shrugged. 'I've also been on Sky,' he said, 'and BBC Radio. So have your partner Duncan Stewart and members of your family.'

'Well, it would help if they at least knew the facts,' I said. 'Mike Mendoza is the spokesman for our charity – please tell him, and he'll deal with it.'

He gave me a pen and paper on which to write the number and then handed me a pile of books. Not one of them would have been my chosen reading material, but I was grateful for something to while away the time.

'David said he'd get me some clothes,' I said. 'I only have one pair of jeans and two T-shirts. Did you manage to bring anything?' I asked hopefully.

'Sorry,' he said, 'I forgot but you can have them next time.'

He asked my size but I wasn't sure, having lost quite a few kilos. My belt had been confiscated and my jeans were slipping down over my hips. He passed across two names he explained were lawyers the embassy recommended. I asked their nationalities, and was told that one was a Serb and the other Albanian.

'Well, I think I'd prefer to be represented by an Albanian under the circumstances.'

'That's up to you,' he replied. 'They're both very good.'

'When will I meet him?' I inquired, hoping it wouldn't be too long. I really didn't know how I'd cope with sitting on a chair doing nothing hour after hour, day after day.

'Within the next few days, I'd hope.'

I asked if he'd leave the cuttings so I could read them properly, but he said he didn't have permission, putting them in a folder, which he slipped back into his briefcase. We shook hands again, and he assured me that he'd return soon.

I was taken back to my room and told to sit on the chair, but at least I could read. However bad the books were, it was better than staring into space. I opened the most interesting of the three and lost myself until Zoya returned later that evening.

I'd received the items requested on my shopping list and signed a piece of paper that would allow them to take the money. I had $400 that had been confiscated by the police and returned with my passport, plus £50 that my father had sent through the British embassy. I gave Zoya some chocolate, bananas and a carton of cigarettes. She was thrilled and immediately put everything into her locker. I asked whether she'd any money to buy things, but she said she didn't. She hadn't had a single visitor since her arrest two years ago.

'How do you cope?' I asked.

'I don't think about it, I just do it.'

We feasted on fruit and chocolate and chain smoked until bedtime.

One evening I heard a dreadful scream from the room above. I looked at Zoya for an explanation, but she placed a finger to her lips. The screaming continued for about twenty minutes, interspersed by a constant rhythmic thump. The screams were heartrending, and although I couldn't understand the words, it sounded like someone was begging for mercy. I knew that it might be dangerous to interfere, but I couldn't bear the thought of doing nothing. Zoya tried to stop me but I shrugged her away and crept out into the corridor. All of a sudden the screaming stopped and I could hear the sound of footsteps descending the staircase.

There wasn't time to return to my room so I hid beneath the staircase as Baby Face and a big broad officer appeared in the hall. They were red-faced, sweating and breathing heavily, and in their hands were the long black truncheons they usually wore on belts. I realised that they'd shared the task of beating the prisoner and from the sounds we heard, they'd obviously put in a great deal of effort. As soon as they entered the office, I slipped back into the room to find Zoya in bed, feigning sleep. Lying awake that night, I imagined I could still hear the poor soul screaming.

The following morning when I opened my door I saw a young woman shuffling towards the washroom, her legs a mass of purple bruises. She was obviously the victim of the beating we'd heard the previous night, and I saw her eyes widen with fear as an officer appeared in the corridor. The technique they'd used is known as *falanga*, which involves a series of blows to the soles of the victim's feet, causing severe pain and swelling, which can lead to kidney failure. I desperately wanted to help her, but I knew that it would only make things worse. It was horrible, knowing there was nothing I could do. I toyed with the idea of sending a letter or fax to Amnesty International, but I realised it would be pointless as the letter would never be sent.

That afternoon I was told that I had a visitor. I was shown to the alcove directly opposite the office where a man sat waiting. He was about fifty, with greying hair and dark eyebrows. A young woman was with him, holding a notebook and pen. The man introduced himself as Azem Vllasi, a lawyer who'd been appointed as my legal representative. He told me that he'd decided to represent me free of charge for he admired and supported my work.

Azem, an ethnic Albanian and one-time leader of the League of Communists, became president of Kosovo in 1986 but was toppled in 1988 and replaced by appointees of Milošević. The local population responded with a series of demonstrations and strikes, and a state of emergency was declared. As a result, the newly appointed leaders were forced to resign, but under threat of force, Kosovo's legislature passed an amendment allowing Serbia to assert its authority over Kosovo. Azem was arrested by the police and charged with 'counter-revolutionary activities'. He remained in prison until 1990.

When Azem spoke to me I detected a twinkle in his eye, and I supposed that from a politician's point of view I was an interesting case. He asked me to recount my experiences of the last few days in order to ascertain exactly why I'd been arrested. I had to provide some background information in order to explain my reason for crossing into Kosovo without a visa, and while I spoke the woman took notes. Only when I reached the point where I was sentenced did Azem interrupt me.

'You weren't put on trial. This will give us the grounds for an appeal. Don't worry – you'll be out of here shortly.'

As they rose to leave, I told him about the woman upstairs who'd been so badly beaten. Although I saw concern in his eyes, he merely nodded. It was clear that this was nothing new.

A few days later Azem returned, but this time to my surprise and delight he was accompanied by Marta of the Mother Teresa Charity. I hadn't seen her since our mission to Kosovo in March, and I could hardly believe that she was now here, inside the Serb-run prison. As we hugged each other, I noticed Azem was carrying a newspaper, which he spread open on the table. I could see my name and recognised the words 'Engjëlli i Mostarit', but the article was written in Albanian so I wasn't able to read it. Marta translated, but as I listened to the words I was filled with dismay. The article was a gross exaggeration of what I'd actually said to Azem on the previous visit, and when I complained,

Marta explained that the woman who'd accompanied him was a journalist.

My words had obviously been twisted for political purposes, and I was livid. Marta reached for my hand and tried her best to reassure me, but her sympathetic tone and gentle touch seemed to dissolve my self-control. Hot tears pricked my eyes and trickled down my cheeks as the intense stress of the past couple of weeks finally took its toll. She pulled me close and held me as the tears streamed down my face. Finally, when I felt able to speak, I turned to Azem.

'How could you let this happen? It's bad enough knowing that my mission has been the subject of propaganda by the Serbs, but to see the Albanians doing the same ... It isn't right.'

Azem tried to assure me that it wasn't as bad as it seemed, but I was sure there would be repercussions.

'Please, just do your best to get me out of here. It's terribly frustrating, being shut away like this. People are suffering and there's nothing I can do about it.'

He nodded and patted my arm. 'We'll soon have an appeal date,' he said.

An officer came to announce that the visit was over and I gave Marta a quick hug.

'Stay strong,' she called after me as I was led back to the room.

That night, and most nights thereafter, I could hear the sound of jets roaring overhead and the sound of distant explosions as the bombs found their targets. I imagined the women, children and elderly huddled together in the damp cellars, cold, hungry and frightened.

I was visited by the Serbian minister of justice, Dragoljub Janković, who was accompanied by a number of journalists, which came as a shock. When they entered my room, I was ordered to sit down while he and the others remained standing. Speaking to me through an interpreter, he wanted to know whether my treatment in the prison was satisfactory. I nodded, and he asked whether I regretted my decision to commit an illegal act by violating the border without official permission.

I explained that I'd applied for permission but this had been refused, and I also reminded him that 15,000 refugees had crossed the same border within recent weeks. He became agitated, and I realised that his questions were for the benefit of the press – yet another attempt at propaganda. I decided to take the opportunity to get my own position across. I went to stand up, but Surly, who was directly behind me, forced me back down onto my chair, keeping a restraining hand on my shoulder.

'I'm sick of hearing the planes flying overhead to bomb innocent civilians. I'm not eating and I'm not drinking in protest against this war!'

As my words were translated I saw the minister's face darken with anger, and he quickly left the room, dutifully followed by the journalists.

Refusing to eat wasn't difficult, especially as watery soup and bread seemed to be the staple diet, but the daytime temperature had now reached 44°C, so refusing liquid was harder. Within the first two days I began to suffer from dehydration and my legs started to swell, but without a newspaper or radio I had no idea whether I'd managed to get my message across. In fact, the protest had been broadcast round the world and there were reports that I was in danger of imminent circulatory collapse.

A couple of days later I was handed a letter from Duncan faxed from Britain. He was extremely concerned by my decision to refuse liquid, and warned me that without water my body could suffer irrevocable damage and I'd die within days.

Bob Gordon came to visit me for a second time that week. He brought some more newspaper cuttings, which again failed to convey the facts. I asked him why it was still not clear that my mission involved more than one family and that there were other children who were also in need of treatment. He shrugged as though this was an unimportant detail, making me wonder whether the disinformation was deliberate, although I couldn't imagine its purpose. He tried to persuade me to stop the protest, insisting that I'd achieved my aim.

'But Milošević hasn't withdrawn his troops and I can still hear the planes flying overhead,' I said. 'Why hasn't a ceasefire been enforced?'

Dragan, the chief prison officer, came to see me again, but this time he was alone. He inquired about my work and we had quite a long discussion about the war. He seemed genuinely interested in my views, and we spent at least an hour in deep conversation. He talked about his family and how keen he was for the war to end. When it was time for him to go, he asked whether I had any complaints about my treatment.

'I'd really appreciate being able to move around more, and perhaps to lie down occasionally,' I said. 'Sitting for so many hours on a hard wooden chair is pretty uncomfortable.'

'You may do as you wish. I'll inform the staff immediately.'

As he was leaving he handed me a letter with 'OSCE' printed at the top. It was from Bill Foxton, and after I read it I felt a great deal better. He assured me that my protest was being heard around the world, and he wanted me to know that he and the rest of his team were immensely proud of me.

That same afternoon I was visited by the prison nurse with dyed orange hair. She explained in broken English that I must allow her to take some blood. She wasn't overly gentle when it came to the needle, but she made me laugh and I grew quite fond of her over the next few days. She was concerned that I was suffering from kidney damage and wanted me transferred to hospital, but I assured her that I was fine. I'd lost a great deal of weight but apart from a constant ache in my lower back, I felt OK. Zoya did her best to persuade me to drink, not really understanding my reasons for the protest. I appeased her concern by offering her the remaining fruit and chocolate, which she promptly deposited in her locker with a gleeful smile.

David Slinn came to see me, accompanied by a young woman. Bukurie, who called herself Bili, was an ethnic Albanian from Kosovo who worked as an interpreter for the British embassy. She was incredibly beautiful, tall and willowy with dark wavy hair. It was rumoured that she had ties with the KLA, but then so did most Kosovo Albanians. The two of them visited me regularly, trying to convince me to stop the protest, but I didn't yet feel I'd accomplished my aim. Towns and villages across Kosovo were burning and innocent people were still dying.

29

On the fifth day of refusing food and water, I was returning from the washroom when I collapsed. The prison doctor was called and he came to the room, accompanied by the nurse. He told me that if I didn't drink immediately I'd be evacuated to hospital in Pristina where I'd be force fed. Ignoring him, I addressed the nurse instead.

'I really am fine,' I assured her. 'I was exercising in the yard this morning and probably overdid it.'

She took my blood pressure and the numbers caused some concern, so she advised me to lie down and rest. The doctor left the room, muttering under his breath. David and Bili arrived, and both seemed concerned by my appearance.

'Sally, you're very important to the Albanian people,' said Bili, taking my hand. 'If you continue with this protest you might die.'

'Your people are dying all the time,' I said, 'because nothing is being done to help them.'

David pulled up a chair beside the bed. 'If you really want to help, you need to stay well.'

I collapsed again later that day, and this time I awoke to find myself attached to a saline drip. The doctor was standing beside me, and although it might have been my imagination, I thought I detected a smirk on his face.

The following day I was visited by Brian Donnelly, the British ambassador, who was able to talk to me alone in my room. I

proceeded to tell him about the violent attack on the female prisoner, but he pointed to the ceiling light that hung overhead – I
guessed he was concerned that the room might be bugged. He
informed me that my father was on his way to the prison. He and
Duncan had applied for visas at the Yugoslav embassy in London,
but although Duncan's application was refused, my father's had
been accepted.

I was surprised that he should want to come. My father wasn't
a staunch supporter of my work and never really understood why
I was prepared to take risks for people I'd never met. He'd
assumed that when my work in Bosnia ended I'd return to being
an artist. Instead I'd gone to Chechnya to try to help people
trapped in the war-torn city of Grozny, and by the time I turned
my attention to Kosovo he'd given up trying to dissuade me.

When he entered the room, tears pricked my eyes, but he wasn't
a sentimental man, so I bit my lip and gave him a quick hug.

'You've lost weight,' he said. 'You look a bit gaunt.'

He was holding two bags, one filled with clothes, books and
letters from friends, the other containing six large bottles of
water.

'Why have you brought the water?' I asked curiously.

'Duncan said you're in danger of severe dehydration and
kidney failure. You have to drink lots of water.'

I smiled. 'Dad, there's plenty of water here. That isn't the problem. I was protesting against the war!'

My father, almost six feet tall and well built, sat down heavily
on one of the chairs.

'Never mind all that,' he said impatiently, 'just drink the
water.'

I asked him why Duncan's visa had been refused.

'I have no idea,' he replied, 'though to be honest I think he was
somewhat relieved.'

His comment did not surprise me. Being a doctor with a very
large practice, it was difficult for Duncan to take time off. He'd

have to rearrange appointments and quickly find a locum, which was never easy at short notice.

'Bob Gordon picked me up in Belgrade last night and drove me down to Pristina,' he said. 'I'm staying at the Grand Hotel.'

I smiled wryly. Duncan and I had stayed at this rundown concrete construction in April with our volunteers. The rather imposing hotel, built by Albanians but used mainly by Kosovo Serbs, was rumoured to serve as a base for Arkan's paramilitaries. While we were there we had to watch what we were saying as apparently all the rooms were bugged.

My father looked tired, and he told me that artillery fire had kept him awake all night. In order to bring the bags in, they first had to be inspected by the prison governor. My father had bought him a bottle of Chivas Regal, and as he handed him the box, he asked whether I was a good prisoner.

'You see that list,' said the governor, pointing to a sheet of paper on the wall. 'Those are the prison rules and your daughter has managed to break every one of them.'

Nevertheless, he allowed all the items through without even checking them.

'What a nice chap he is,' said my father, 'and what a lovely place!'

Aware now that the room was probably bugged, I didn't bother to shatter his illusion.

He left a short while later, promising to return the following day. I noticed that among the letters from friends and family, there was another from Duncan. Unlike the previous one, which had been curt and to the point, this letter contained words I'd always treasure. He wrote how pleased he was to hear that I'd allowed myself to be rehydrated, assuring me that this would not lessen the impact of my protest. He also told me how much he loved me – something he hadn't said for a very long time. That night as I lay down to sleep, I realised that for the first time in two weeks there were no planes flying overhead.

The following day I was escorted to a secluded rose garden close to the main gates where my father was waiting. We were seated at an elegant table and served with coffee in china cups. Bob Gordon appeared, together with the senior officer, and told us that a film crew from the BBC were waiting at the gate because the governor had apparently given permission for them to interview me.

'Yes, of course,' agreed my father, until he saw the look on my face.

'I don't think it would be appropriate in this setting,' I said abruptly.

'Why? What do you mean?' he asked.

'There are similarities to Theresienstadt,' I replied, knowing that he'd immediately understand.

My father, an authority on the Second World War, had once told me about a particular Nazi concentration camp in Czechoslovakia where the conditions were terrible and only one in eight prisoners survived. When the Red Cross requested permission to inspect the camp, the Nazis agreed, but they delayed the visit for several months. In the meantime, Jewish labourers were ordered to transform the edifice from a dirty, dingy camp to a bright, sunny, cheerful Jewish 'town'. The prisoners planted flowers and cleaned and painted so that when the Red Cross representatives eventually toured the camp, they passed playgrounds, gardens and newly painted dwellings.

'This place, it's not real,' I said, gesturing around the idyllic setting. 'The sweet-smelling roses, the coffee and cakes served on delicate china. The prisoners are actually fed on watery soup and suffer brutal beatings. Some of them have been here for years without a trial. If I agreed to be interviewed here, I'd be endorsing the worst kind of propaganda.'

'I didn't realise,' said my father.

Bob went to tell the governor that I had declined the interview and when he returned he was smiling.

'You have been pardoned by Milan Milutinović, the president of Yugoslavia,' he declared. 'You'll be released this afternoon, as soon as they've arranged transport to the Macedonian border.'

I could hardly believe it.

'But the appeal … it hasn't been settled yet. How come they're letting me go?'

'They obviously realised that the sentence was unjust,' said my father. 'Anyway, what difference how or why? Just be glad you're getting out of here.'

Bob explained that I'd have to be escorted to the border by police because I was being deported. There was only one flight from Macedonia every day, so we had to hope I'd reach the airport in time. We sat there waiting anxiously for around two hours while Bob made endless calls on his mobile.

When the final permission came through, I was rushed to my room to pack my belongings. I gave most of the new clothes to Zoya, for although they wouldn't fit her, she'd promised to hand them on to others. I also left her some perfume and writing paper, make-up and toiletries, and by the time we were finished her locker was overflowing. As I said goodbye to her, large tears rolled down her cheeks and I gave her a hug, wondering how she'd survive another three years in that place.

Before I left I went to the office where Selima and the other Albanian officer were on duty. They were surprised but obviously delighted to hear the news that I was leaving. I asked them to transfer the remainder of my money to Zoya's account.

The senior officer arrived to escort me to the gate, and as we left I looked up at the windows where the female prisoners gathered to watch my departure. Letting the officer overtake me, I quickly turned and waved to the faces pressed up against the glass.

The officer walked me to the main gates where Bob and my father were waiting. It all felt unreal. Dragan and other members of the staff were standing in line to say goodbye, but Bob hurried me along. He told me that there wasn't much time before my flight was due to leave and we had a long drive ahead. He sat beside me in the back of the police car while Bob followed in a jeep. Our driver and his female colleague didn't seem to speak English, so I chatted to my father throughout the journey. We drove at top speed along narrow country roads and several times we almost crashed as oncoming vehicles passed us with only inches to spare. When we finally reached the Macedonian border we were both very grateful to get out.

Bob came alongside us and lowered his window to tell me that I had to walk through customs and meet him up ahead. I handed over my passport to the customs official, who stamped it. Across the top I saw that I'd be denied entry into Kosovo for the next three years. As my father attempted to join me, he was stopped at the checkpoint by the passport official.

'If you step across this line you'll enter Macedonia,' declared the man.

'But I'd like to accompany my daughter to the airport,' said my father, a little confused.

'Well,' said the man, 'that's fine. But you'll need a visa to return to Kosovo.'

'How long will that take?' my father asked, explaining that he'd left his suitcase in Pristina and his return flight was from Belgrade.

'Three months.'

We had no choice but to say goodbye on the spot, so keeping his feet firmly in Kosovo, he leaned across and kissed me good-bye. I watched him return to the police car, and as soon as he got inside it sped off down the road.

Bob was concerned that time was running out, so I began to hurry, not wanting to spend the night in Macedonia. My face had been all over the news, and for Serbs I was currently public enemy number one. Bob also drove very fast but much more safely, and we arrived at the airport with minutes to spare. He hurriedly escorted me to the check-in desk, where I thanked him profusely for all his help.

There was no direct flight that day, so I'd have to change three times before touching down in London. I was still quite weak, and the journey was long and tiring. Family and friends were waiting to greet me at the airport, but first I had to negotiate my way past the television crews and newspaper journalists. I hugged my mum, who was crying, and then I saw Duncan, his blue eyes twinkling as he smiled.

'Welcome home, Miss Becker,' he said.

My father had been whisked back to Pristina, where he'd been told to wait for Bob Gordon. As the police car pulled up outside the Grand Hotel, the woman addressed him for the first time since picking us up from the prison.

'What did you think of his driving?' she asked, nodding towards her colleague.

My father was so surprised that she spoke English that he was actually lost for words.

30

I awoke to find that Mary Banks had sold her story to the press. The *Daily Telegraph* wrote:

Mary Banks, a coach driver with the expedition convoy, said: 'We are worried stiff that she might take other convoys to Kosovo. If she does, volunteers could end up getting killed. She is a very foolhardy woman. When we came home and later saw her on British television after her so-called jail ordeal it just stuck in our throats. She unnecessarily put our lives at risk.'

And on it went. An article, titled 'Carry On Kosovo', was spread across two double pages in the *Daily Mail*. It was basically a send-up of the whole mission and included further quotes from Banks, who again implied that I'd taken the convoy into Kosovo. A similar story was repeated in one form or another by most of the British media, and a cartoon appeared across half a page of one of the broadsheets in which I was depicted swinging from a rope while figures tumbled into the ravine. Mark Cutts was quoted as saying, 'It was one of the most inexperienced groups I have ever found in a situation like that.'

He conveniently omitted to mention all the work we'd done on behalf of the UNHCR. He also stated that the UN had been forced to organise a special evacuation for Dawn, Alyson and

Jenny. Many of the volunteers were angered by the allegations and made statements to the contrary. Pat Bravington said:

> We are very distressed at the allegations being made against Sally. She took care of us to the best of her ability. She never put us in any danger and she had even arranged for the chief of police to escort our vehicles over the mountains.

Towards the end of August I was invited to appear on *HARDTalk*. The studio in which the interview took place was designed in the style of an interrogation room and was very intense. Tim Sebastian was a seasoned interviewer who'd challenged presidents, prime ministers and kings, so it was daunting to be sitting opposite him with a camera in my face. The programme was made for BBC World, so this was my chance to highlight the war. I was therefore frustrated when Tim raised the subject of Mary Banks; it seemed to be a terrible waste of airtime.

I was also asked to appear on the BBC's political programme *Breakfast with Frost*. Huw Edwards was hosting the programme, and with me on the sofa was Milisav Paić from the Yugoslav embassy in London. He disputed the evidence of atrocities committed by the Serbs and refused to accept that there was a continued offensive against ethnic Albanians. I talked about the suffering of women and children living in cellars beneath the rubble of their homes, but he simply denied it was happening.

Early one morning someone called me from BBC Radio 4's *Today* programme to set up an interview straight after the news. As one of Britain's most respected radio programmes – practically revered by the middle classes – I thought this would enable me to talk about Kosovo. Instead, Mary Banks came on the line.

While I was forced to defend myself against the allegations, I was prevented from talking about the things that really mattered. In addition to this, the British embassy in Belgrade had never corrected their mistake, leaving the press to believe that I had crossed the border to help one family. There was no reference to the fact that Junik was surrounded by Serb forces, nor any mention of the women and children I'd been trying to help.

I was hoping to try to find them during our next mission to Albania, and John Cox – who'd already done one mission with Operation Angel, having joined us when we took aid to Kosovo in April – had already started recruiting volunteers. We received a number of calls from production companies who wanted to make a documentary about my work but, disillusioned with the press, I turned down all the proposals. Following a meeting with Belinda Giles, the founder of Soul Purpose Productions, Mike Mendoza suggested I reconsider. He assured me that she was sympathetic to our cause and intended to make a serious film about my work.

The producer was Paulette Farsides and she was accompanied by her co-producer Juliana Ruhfas, a young woman with a slight German accent. Over lunch at Victoria Station I told them of my plans to trace the children and how I was hoping to bring them to the UK for medical treatment. Paulette told me that the film would be commissioned by *Witness*, a series on Channel 4; knowing that this show dealt with important world issues, I agreed they could join us.

I was invited to attend a demonstration against the war in Kosovo that took place in Trafalgar Square, to speak alongside Vanessa Redgrave and Bianca Jagger. The event was attended by about five thousand people, mostly ethnic Albanians who waved flags and carried banners bearing the words 'FREE KOSOVA'. Corin Redgrave and I led the march to Downing Street, where we delivered a letter to the prime minister Tony Blair.

While I'd been away, some of the volunteers had virtually taken over our house, which caused Duncan a great deal of stress. In addition to this, he and I were at odds on the subject of children. I was hoping to have a child of my own one day, but

Duncan already had two grown-up daughters and wasn't planning on having any more. The constant publicity that surrounded my work was also beginning to intrude on our personal lives. Although we were both loath to admit it, we eventually agreed that our relationship was no longer working and it was time to go our separate ways.

As the date of departure approached, I sent a fax to Bill Foxton, who was still based in Bajram Curri. The area had become more dangerous, so the aid organisations had pulled out, despite the recent influx of refugees. The volunteers were made aware of the situation, but this only seemed to make them more determined to help.

I flew to Tirana ahead of the convoy and was met by Pierre Maurer, a member of Bill's staff, who drove me to the Hotel Rogner in the city centre. Pierre was a bear of a man from Switzerland with a close-cropped beard. With his French drawl and his eye for a pretty woman, he had quite a reputation as a Casanova. As we booked in at the reception desk, he told me there had been a serious incident in Bajram Curri and for the moment our mission was on hold.

The brother of Fatmir Haklaj, the local clan chief, had been stopped in Vlorë with a car filled with arms and ammunition. He was arrested, and as a result the OSCE staff were being held hostage at the hotel. They were told that they would be killed if they tried to leave, and negotiations were currently taking place between the OSCE in Tirana and the Albanian minister of justice.

Haklaj, who was head of the Rapid Deployment Unit in Bajram Curri, had been chief of police until he was demoted for killing nine people in revenge for the assassination of one of his brothers. He killed one man for each of the bullets he found in his brother's body; blood for blood, as expounded in the Kanun, an ancient set of laws observed among the tribes of northern Albania.

Waiting for me at the reception desk was Hili Krasniqi and Nik Hiseni, but I didn't recognise them at first as they were dressed in civilian clothes. Somehow they'd heard I was coming and had brought their families to see me in Tirana.

'Where are they?' I asked, desperate to see them all.

Hili smiled and took my arm, and the three of us left the hotel. We crossed the main road and walked through a spacious park where there was a large café. As soon as we entered, Marigona ran towards me and leapt into my arms, where she remained all afternoon. I remembered Drita trembling in fear as I tried to protect her from the bullets, yet she and Dede gave me a hug and thanked me for helping them. I'd spent the past two months feeling entirely responsible for what happened on the mountain, but they obviously didn't feel the same.

Dede told me how he'd searched for us after the ambush, and how when he found my dog tags on the grass he assumed we'd been killed. They'd hidden in the forest overnight while the Serbs continued to search for them with dogs and helicopters, and as soon as dawn broke they made their way back down the mountain. When Hane was released they attempted the journey again, but this time they had Hili and Nik to help them. Upon reaching Albania they were taken to a refugee camp in Shkodër run by a local priest.

I offered to buy them all lunch, insisting they order anything they wanted. Valbona clutched my hand in hers, and every now and then Hane would give me a hug. We spent a wonderful afternoon together, watching the children eating, laughing and running around in the park. Although they were still pale and thin, they were much more relaxed, no longer living in fear of their lives.

Hili told me that his house had been destroyed when the Serbs attacked their village. He showed me photographs of the devastation and tried to describe how it had looked before.

'When the war is over, we'll go home and I'll rebuild it,' he said.

When the time came for us to leave, I explained that I was trying to arrange a medevac for the children. Duncan had managed to convince the Nuffield group of private hospitals to provide treatment for up to fifty patients. In addition, a local businessman had offered the use of a former hotel to house the families of the children for up to six months. As they said good-bye, I had to peel Marigona's arms from my neck and watched her squeal in anger as she was carried away.

I was telling the film crew about the refugees when a message came through that the hostage crisis was over. Haklaj's brother had been put on a ferry at Koman and had just arrived in Bajram Curri, so the OSCE staff had now been released.

That evening we were joined at the Hotel Rogner by Ismet Shamolli, who told me how worried he'd been when I was captured. We ate in the hotel dining room and were entertained by a group of musicians dressed in traditional ethnic Albanian costume – white caps and white shirts, red and black waistcoats, and black trousers tied with a sash. To my delight they dedicated a haunting song to me. Later we strolled past the opera house, where buses passed by, filled with pale-faced young men on their way to fight in Kosovo.

The film crew followed me to Durrës, one of the most ancient cities in Europe, where I was due to meet the convoy arriving from Britain. The port was filled with vendors selling cartons of Amita, the sweet cherry drink sold all over Kosovo. Others were peddling an assortment of nuts, cigarettes and cheap plastic toys. We were almost deafened by the sound of people shouting and cars hooting. While Rob the cameraman began to film the vehicles disembarking from the ferry, we were jostled by gypsies begging for a few lek, the local currency, and scruffy young men in search of a deal. Children with dirty faces and unwashed hair approached us for food, and I handed them some biscuits and fruit that I carried in my bag.

When the vehicles eventually cleared customs, I was joined by

Liz Dack in the Shogun. There were four 7.5-tonne trucks and a Mercedes minibus, a Carroll truck from Seaboard and Mary McDermott's trusty old campervan. Together, she and John Cox had catered for the volunteers as they drove across Europe. Coxy, who reminded me of the sailor that used to feature on Player's cigarette packets, was travelling with Janey and Rob Penny, his sailing companion. Sailing was Coxy's passion, and one time Duncan had joined him on his boat. They were happily sailing along the East Sussex coast when a wind whipped up, forcing them much farther than was originally planned. It was touch and go for a while, but eventually they were swept onto a beach and Duncan arrived home soaked to the skin.

While I'd been locked up in Lipljan prison, Coxy worked extremely hard, collecting aid and holding fundraising events at the Norfolk Arms in Steyning. The pub's landlord, John, was also on this mission. Coxy had recruited him, together with some of the other volunteers, including Bernie Sullivan and his wife Susie. Bernie worked for BSkyB, who gave him a satellite phone for the trip, enabling our convoy to be in direct communication with the outside world, even in places as remote as Bajram Curri.

Bernie and Susie shared the driving with Bill Parkes, a calm and softly spoken man who proved an asset to the mission. Roger Hall, a policeman, was travelling as Mary's co-driver in the campervan. We were also joined by Keith Carney from Dallas, Texas, who was Operation Angel's volunteer in the US. There was another American called Martha Grenon, a talented photographer who knew the region well. The group was smaller than on previous missions and therefore better organised, so this time I wasn't expecting any problems.

31

We headed straight to the border town of Kukës, 125 miles from Tirana. The streets in the town were lined with concrete buildings all sprouting satellite dishes on their façades. We were taken to a secure compound where the volunteers were finally able to rest. Night had fallen so it would be dangerous to continue as bandits operated in the area, eager to relieve the vehicles of the aid, and even in daylight we'd need an escort for the convoy. My vehicle was carrying very little, so it was agreed that Liz and I would continue on to Bajram Curri, from where we'd arrange an escort.

I agreed a price of $50 for two men armed with Kalashnikovs. They reminded me of the two villains in *101 Dalmatians*, their beady eyes scanning the road ahead. They told me to drive fast to reduce the chance of being stopped, but the road was very narrow with a sheer drop on one side. I did my best to keep control of the vehicle but it was extremely difficult around the hairpin bends, especially in the dark.

After a while Liz nudged me and pointed at some shadowy creatures looming up ahead. The bright headlights reflected in their eyes, and as we came closer we could see they were wolves. They ran alongside us, with the full moon shining overhead. They remained with our vehicle throughout the six-hour journey, then loped off into the night.

When we reached the Hotel Ermal, an armed guard opened his sleepy eyes and grudgingly gave us a key to one of the rooms. We carried our belongings upstairs and, exhausted from driving all day and most of the night, we slept fully dressed. The following morning we waited for Bill to return from a border patrol. Since the hostage incident the Presidential Guard had been stationed outside the OSCE office, and we had to show our ID before we were allowed to enter.

Pierre Maurer was there, and when I told him about the wolves he looked sceptical but said that perhaps they were sent to protect us. When Bill got back he greeted us warmly and ordered coffee, while I explained that the volunteers were still in Kukës. He offered to send his driver Durim to escort the convoy to Bajram Curri.

Durim was about six feet three. He wore a denim jacket and tight black jeans and carried a rifle and a Russian Tokarev semi-automatic pistol. He suggested he take along a friend, who turned up in a red Nissan Patrol. Curtains obscured the rear windows and as with many vehicles in the region, the number plates had been removed. The two men would drive to Kukës and escort the convoy back.

'Alessandra Morelli of the UNHCR is also in Kukës awaiting an escort. She's expected to leave there today, so your vehicles could tag along behind her,' said Bill. He made the necessary calls on his satellite phone, as there were still no landlines in Bajram Curri and mobile phones were useless.

In the meantime, he brought us up to date. With the escalation of the war, the international news media were flocking to Bajram Curri, and Fatmir Haklaj had organised, in the words of the *Guardian* journalist Julian Borger, 'the comprehensive fleecing of the foreign press corps as it has endeavoured to follow the KLA into Kosovo'. The BBC and others had, as a result, left the dusty town with only the clothes on their back. With most of the aid agencies now gone, the situation had deteriorated, and refugees were left wandering around desperate for food and clothing.

We had waited for several hours, giving Durim time to reach the convoy, when Alessandra Morelli made a surprise appearance. Her hair was a mess and she looked fraught, complaining that she and her staff had been forced to make the journey by themselves.

'All we had to protect us was an unarmed driver in a vehicle fit for the scrapheap!' she cried angrily as she marched around Bill's office.

When we judged it was time to leave, Bill sent two of his staff to accompany us. Armando Foresti, a local man, was slightly built with fair hair and a nervous disposition. The other man was Arben Miloti, a young man from Shkodër with thick, dark hair and deep-set eyes. The sun was still shining when we drove out of Bajram Curri, planning to drive for about an hour and meet the convoy halfway.

We'd hardly left town when two men wearing black balaclavas appeared from behind some bushes at the side of the road. They leapt in front of our vehicle, firing their guns into the air and forcing me to screech to a halt. Pulling open the doors, they tried to yank us from our seats, and I immediately realised they were after the vehicle. Knowing that our convoy would be approaching down the same stretch of road, I was desperate to warn them. As I reached for the radio one of the men hit me with his rifle. I saw a brief flash of light and found myself lying on the ground as the Shogun disappeared in a cloud of dust. Fortunately, I was still clutching the walkie-talkie and immediately tried to make contact with the volunteers.

'This is Angel One to convoy, I repeat, Angel One to convoy. Do you read me, over?' I cried, hoping the signal would reach that far.

While I waited for a response, a small car came chugging down the road and we waved for it to stop. Armando, still shaking with fear, demanded they take us to Bajram Curri.

Back at the hotel, I felt a little groggy and there was a large bump on the side of my head. While we were waiting to hear from the convoy, Bill insisted I go to the hospital to check for concussion. The doctor who examined me suggested I rest, but of course that wasn't an option. The convoy was on its way into town, although so far we'd not received any response to my messages. Bill had a superior radio with a much greater range, so he tried calling Durim.

'Yes, Oscar Charlie Bravo, go ahead, over,' a voice replied.

I spoke to Coxy and told him what had happened, but just as he relayed the information to the others we heard the sound of gunfire coming from the radio. I was panic-stricken, thinking someone might have been shot.

In fact, the shooting had come from the convoy's armed escort. Durim was walking ahead of the vehicles, firing his rifle in the air to deter any bandits that might be lying in wait. I sighed with relief at the news, but stood there watching anxiously until they eventually came into sight. The volunteers seemed largely unperturbed, but Paulette and Juliana looked strained and pale. They'd both obviously been traumatised by the event and went straight off to their room, while their cameraman joined us for a drink.

The volunteers had taken the rooms along the top floor, where I found Bernie preparing the satellite phone. It was in a small case, which he opened and attached to a laptop. Within a few minutes he'd transmitted a report to our webmaster, together with a number of photos. I was very impressed. Computers hadn't been around for very long, at least not in the public domain and of this size, and although I'd sent pictures before, it certainly hadn't been possible from such an isolated place.

After dinner we joined Bill on the terrace, where he regaled us with amusing stories. He had a very dry wit and would punctuate his remarks by waving the metal hook that he wore in place of his hand. Bill was unique in both looks and personality. He was a dreadful flirt, and although he wasn't exactly George Clooney, there was something very attractive about him. He told us that he had previously been married and had two grown-up children.

He'd been living with a German woman in Bosnia for the past three years, but she'd apparently ended the relationship because he wasn't prepared to commit.

The next morning I went to see the UNHCR, who'd scaled down their operation and moved their office to the Hotel Ermal. Only one resident member of staff remained, a local woman called Albana. I explained that I was trying to trace the children from the mountain in order to arrange their onward journey. She told me that most refugees were housed in the cultural centre opposite the hotel, so I went to see the man in charge.

After checking the names of the children, he informed me that they were already on their way to Switzerland, where they'd be reunited with their parents. Although disappointed that I'd only just missed them, I was delighted to know that they'd soon be together with their loved ones.

During the distribution of medical equipment to the local hospital, a tall, dark-haired man limped towards us with a small boy at his side. Just five years old, the boy had been seriously hurt when his home was destroyed by fire in Kosovo. His face and arms were badly burned, and although the wounds were beginning to heal, he couldn't use his fingers. Liz explained that the burns were causing his hands to claw; he needed plastic surgery or he'd soon be permanently disabled. We told them to come to the hotel where we'd collect all their details.

In the meantime, the OSCE had arranged for Pierre Maurer to escort us to the UN warehouse in Tropojë, which was still the central distribution point for humanitarian aid. Pierre had a PhD in political science from Bradford University and had written a book about Tito. He was very familiar with the Balkan region – as a research fellow at the School for Yugoslav Studies at Bradford University he was fluent in Serbo-Croat – and was a close friend of the famous Serbian film-maker Emir Kusturica. Pierre adored women, and it was impossible to have a serious conversation with him when a pretty woman was around. He was also a successful businessman, having introduced Swiss cigarettes to the Balkans, and as a result he knew all the major smugglers of the region and had experience in dealing with hard men.

As we drove along the muddy track, a call came through the walkie-talkie demanding the convoy to stop. I could hear raised voices and somebody mentioned a gun. Walking towards the rear of the convoy I saw Roger and Mary arguing with a man who was sitting in a car alongside the campervan. He was pointing his gun at Roger and looked angry enough to use it. According to the man, Roger had hit his wing mirror as they passed him on the narrow road. Pierre appeared and calmly suggested that I offer the man a few dollars for the damage. After a few tense moments, he grudgingly accepted.

Tropojë sits at the foot of a mountain called Shkëlzen, at 2,405 metres one of the highest peaks in the Albanian Alps. Since the escalation of the war there had been a tidal wave of refugees flooding into the town, which lay only ten kilometres from the border with Kosovo. Many of these were being housed by the locals, who were already living well below the poverty line.

When we pulled into the car park there was a large crowd of people milling around and I was concerned to hear that the warehouse had recently been targeted by looters. After a meeting, we decided to distribute the aid ourselves rather than leaving it in the warehouse. The refugees were told to form a line while Elizabeth and Riki wrote down their details. At the same time the volunteers started to rearrange the aid into individual boxes according to the refugees' needs. Each box contained a selection of clothing, food, cooking equipment and bedding.

Prenda Ismaili, formerly a local teacher, was employed as an interpreter for the UNHCR. Prenda tried to convince me that we should leave the aid in the warehouse but I refused. First, I didn't want the aid to be stolen, and second, I was reluctant to leave it with the UN.

Prenda started shouting, and Paulette quickly told Rob to start filming. Not wanting yet another public row with a UN official, I tried to reason with Prenda, explaining that we just wanted to be sure the aid reached the refugees. She continued to insist that we leave it in the warehouse, but as she had no real authority we began to distribute the boxes to the people on our list. During the distribution, a man came to see me and explained that he was responsible for the refugees in Bajram Curri, who were also in need of help. He gave me a list of their names and I told him we'd keep back some aid.

The distribution was difficult, with people pushing and shoving and doing their best to carry away more than their quota. Many of those waiting in line were desperate, for now that the aid agencies had pulled out, most things were scarce. One old woman staggered away with a huge container of goods, only to return for another. It was on her third trip that Liz noticed and confronted her. The woman shrugged and grinned, but still she didn't give up, sneaking round the back of a vehicle and helping herself.

Pierre and the local police were very helpful, holding the crowds back long enough for the bulk of the aid to be handed out before we prepared to leave. I was in the process of turning my vehicle around while the other drivers were closing their doors and revving their engines, when suddenly there were several loud gunshots. I turned round to see a group of men brandishing rifles, obviously intent on helping themselves to the rest of the aid.

'Angel One to convoy,' I called over the radio. 'Move out! Everybody move out now! Over.'

It was mayhem as several of the drivers began trying to manoeuvre their vehicles out of the car park and onto the road. Pierre and his driver had driven a few yards ahead, waiting for us all to follow. Guns were still firing as we sped off down the road, but no one was hurt and the vehicles were unscathed. Pierre, who seemed completely unperturbed by the drama, assured me they were just trying to scare us, hoping we'd abandon the aid. We returned to Bajram Curri and later I found the man from Tropojë with his list of refugees. By the end of the day we'd distributed all of the aid and the vehicles were now empty.

The following day I was sitting on the terrace when a shadow loomed over me and looking up I saw Rambo. He was dressed in a T-shirt and jeans with no weapons in sight, and he looked like any ordinary guy. As we sat there chatting in the afternoon sun, he told me that following the ambush he helped the families return to Junik. The widow could barely walk and had for the most part to be carried down the mountain on Rambo's back. He then rounded up some soldiers and went back to collect the others, who were waiting in the forest. Bekim was currently in a hospital in Tirana and would soon be discharged, but as a result of the gunshot wound he'd lost the use of his arm.

One afternoon I was walking through town when a man called my name. I turned round to see Chamed, the old soldier from the mountain. He took me to meet his family, who were living in an apartment block nearby. Over glasses of squash he told me that he'd remained in Junik for another three weeks until the town finally fell to the Serbs. He had two children in their teens, a son and a daughter. His son was hoping to study to become a doctor so I suggested that we send his details to the Sir Halley Stewart Trust, who might be able to help.

Having read of my release from prison, Hamez Shala arrived in Bajram Curri. He came to the hotel to remind me of my promise to try to help his two-year-old daughter Besa, and we suggested he fill out an application form, which we added to our growing list.

Shortly before the convoy was due to leave, Bill informed us that the chief of border security had organised a party on our behalf. Sheep were being slaughtered across Albania for the beginning of the Muslim festival of Ramadan, but I felt guilty at the thought of an animal being killed especially for us. Bill laughed and assured me that the one we'd be eating had slipped in a rocky gully and would have died anyway.

We drove for about two hours along a narrow dirt road running parallel to the River Valbona. The valley is bordered on both sides by spectacular mountains and some of the peaks were still covered in snow. We eventually stopped in a village situated high in the Albanian Alps and piled into a one-storey shack with a few tables and a bar, where we feasted and danced until dusk.

Security was getting tighter in Bajram Curri, and one day while we were having lunch a group of armed men rushed onto the hotel terrace. They wore uniforms and masks, and were part of the Rapid Deployment Team, brought in to impose law and order in the town. We were told to lie face down on the ground while they searched the building for a missing criminal, but they eventually left empty-handed.

Our volunteers had adopted a stray puppy, a sandy-haired mongrel that they named Angel, who now lived beneath the hotel terrace, much to the disgust of Halil. One evening a wedding was taking place, with the usual parade of vehicles around the town. As the party passed by the hotel, beeping their horns and firing rifles in the air, Angel went off to investigate.

One of the drunken guests was firing his rifle from the back of a truck, when suddenly there was a scream and a curse as he shot two of his own fingers off by mistake. Angel, who'd learned to take advantage of any opportunity for a snack, promptly ate them. The unfortunate wedding guest was rushed to the hospital, where the doctor suggested they try to locate the fingers. The dog was immediately taken to a vet and forced to vomit, but the chewed and partly digested fingers were no longer fit to be reunited with their owner; fortunately Armando had the foresight to get Angel out of the immediate vicinity before it was too late.

A short while later Paulette announced that she and the film crew were leaving. I was surprised, as they'd led me to believe that the documentary was about the evacuation of the children, which wouldn't happen until November. When I asked her about it, she said they were working to a deadline and needed time to edit the footage, but it seemed to me that all they'd filmed was a series of mishaps.

32

Médecins Sans Frontières and the International Committee of the Red Cross (ICRC) had pulled out, leaving many children without appropriate medical treatment. Having done what Daniel Enders suggested and arranged hospital beds in Britain, we sent word around that any children in need of medical help should contact Operation Angel at the Hotel Ermal.

In order to assess those who came seeking assistance, we had to convert one of the rooms in the Ermal. Liz was in charge of the assessments, and she examined each child before deciding who would be included in the medical evacuation. Those who could be treated in Albania would be referred to the hospital in Tirana.

Halili and his father arrived at the hotel, and while they proceeded to fill in a visa application, a nineteen-year-old boy arrived. He was tall and thin, with a shaven head and wild dark eyes. He told us that he'd been arrested and tortured in Kosovo where the police had sat him on a chair and interrogated him using methods that could only be employed by a sadistic madman. They'd driven a nail bit by bit into the back of his head and although the wound had now healed, he was obviously still traumatised by the experience and his mind wasn't functioning properly. Liz immediately prepared another application.

Choosing whom to help was not an easy task because some of the parents would exaggerate their child's problem in order to get visas. This was understandable, but as much as we wanted to help them all, we knew that our applications had to be restricted to medical emergencies and their families. Apart from the pressure caused by a constant influx of prospective patients, the psychological strain on Liz was immense; refusing treatment meant condemning the child to remain in Bajram Curri through the winter.

The details of those we accepted had been faxed to Duncan, who passed them on to the Home Office. The authorities wanted each medical case confirmed by UNHCR, so I told Alessandra Morelli of our plans and requested her support.

'We have nothing to do with medical evacuations,' she said in reply. 'You'll have to make a request to the ICRC.'

I promptly called the ICRC, who told me that medical evacuations were the responsibility of the UNHCR. I'd encountered this type of situation in Bosnia, and despite the fact that fifteen years had passed, it seemed nothing much had changed. I sent a fax to the British Home Office explaining the problem.

Many Kosovars came to the Ermal seeking information from the OSCE, one of the few organisations that retained a base in Bajram Curri. Among them was the widow who'd been with me on the mountain. She'd been reunited with her daughters and was hoping they could travel abroad, but I had to explain that we were only dealing with paediatric medical cases. I expected her to be angry; instead she shrugged and gave me a hug.

Liz and I were getting some supplies from a local shop when I spotted my Shogun on the main street. The vehicle had been sprayed with red paint but there was a small dent in the rear bumper that I recognised instantly. Before Liz could stop me, I approached the man sitting in the driver's seat, a local gangster called Petrit. He was a big, burly man with dark glasses. Around his neck were several very thick gold chains.

Leaning into the open window, I said, 'You're driving my car!'

He grinned disdainfully and gunned the engine, but just as I was contemplating grabbing the keys, Liz appeared beside me.

'Don't!' she hissed. 'He's probably armed.'

I chose to heed her warning and watched him tear off down the road in a cloud of dust. I had one more task to complete, which involved a trip to the British embassy in Tirana. Having received all the visa applications, the diplomats now wanted some of the parents to attend interviews. We arranged to travel with the OSCE and would meet Hili, Nik and the others in Tirana.

One at a time the refugees entered the room where the British consul waited to question them. When the interviews were over, he assured me that there would be no problem with regard to issuing the visas and we could expect to receive confirmation from the Home Office within a few days.

After the refugees returned to Shkodër, I went to meet my colleagues at the Hotel Rogner. Stephen Nash, the British ambassador, was having coffee with Demetrios Plaits, the Greek chargé d'affaires, and they invited me to join them. Demetrios was interested in hearing about the planned evacuation, and when I'd finished explaining, he offered the use of a Greek Air Force plane to take the children and their families to Britain. I was delighted, and could hardly believe my good luck when Daan Everts, head of the OSCE in Albania, offered to arrange the transport of our patients to Tirana.

Everything seemed to be falling into place, and back at home our volunteers had completely refurbished an empty, run-down hotel in Hove that had been donated to us for the duration of the mission. My brother Eddy and his friend had cleared out the old furniture while my mother and my aunt helped some of the volunteers to scrub and clean the place from top to bottom. Eileen, a woman with boundless energy, spent every free moment there until it was spotless. Windows and doors were fixed, and walls were painted. A new kitchen was installed, and Mari's husband put in new sinks and toilets. My cousin, who lives in Israel, donated money to buy enough food for six months, and we were given beds and covers, tables and armchairs.

Keith Carney had managed to secure visas for some of the patients to travel to the United States. He'd also arranged hospital beds and surgeons to carry out the operations; three of which involved open heart surgery. Besa Shala was on the list and she and her family were flown to a specialist clinic in Dallas, where she would be fitted with cochlear implants.

Bill's fifty-fifth birthday was on 2 November and he invited me to celebrate with him at a local restaurant. After a couple of large whiskys he decided to tell me what had happened on the night I was captured by the Serbs.

'We were at the border waiting for you to cross when we heard the sound of a fire fight and saw a helicopter hovering overhead. The UN and some EC monitors were there too, but after a while they left. I stayed there for most of the night, though, hoping to God that you'd eventually appear. When you didn't come I was devastated, thinking that you must have been killed.'

Bill then reached across the table for my hand and told me that he might be suffering from a condition commonly known as love. Before I could respond, the waiter appeared and Bill ordered a bottle of local red wine, which we drank with the meal. As we returned to the hotel later that night, Bill started to laugh. I wondered what had tickled him and he pointed to the large statue of Bajram Curri – the Kosovo-Albanian leader after whom the town was named – that overlooked the main square. In silhouette the rifle could be mistaken for something else, and I was laughing so much that I walked straight into the glass doors at the entrance to the hotel. This caused Bill to laugh even more, and as I rubbed my sore head he helped me up the stairs and into my room. I pointed out that we might wake the night watchman, who was asleep in the foyer. We crept past him and stumbled towards the stairs, both of us giggling like children. That night we became lovers, and although for Bill it was probably just another war romance, at the time I felt like I'd found my soulmate.

The day of departure approached and final preparations were put in place for the evacuation. The OSCE would ferry the children and family members to Tirana, where the British consul would issue the final documentation. The Greek ambassador had called to let me know that the plane was on standby to fly the children and their families to Britain, and I received confirmation that the St John's ambulances would be awaiting our arrival at the airport.

On the day of departure I was called into Bill's office. He looked completely bewildered as he handed me a fax from the British embassy in Tirana, and I'd just finished reading it when Liz entered the room.

'All visas have been refused,' I told her, hardly able to believe my own words. 'Jack Straw [the home secretary] has issued a statement to the press announcing that we've not fulfilled the necessary requirements.'

'But we've sent them all the medical histories, X-rays, doctor's diagnosis and all the rest. What more could they need?' asked Liz with dismay.

'Apparently each application should have been supported by the UNHCR, but Alessandra Morelli assured me in this very room that their support was not required. Straw also states that the cost to the British government would be £400,000, which is nonsense.'

'I'm going to my room,' said Bill, leaving me, Liz and two members of staff in the office.

None of the reasons given in the statement made sense. The Greek Air Force had offered to fly the patients to Britain and St John's Ambulance brigade would transport them to their destination. The medical treatment and aftercare would be carried out by staff at Nuffield private hospitals, meaning the NHS would incur no costs. The visa applications were for a maximum of six months, and we'd arranged accommodation, food and transport for the entire period. The cost to the British government would actually be nil.

The statement concluded with Straw saying, 'The British government has already made it clear to Ms Becker that the focus of UK aid for the Kosovo crisis is on winter supplies and health-care, channelling its funds entirely through projects based in the region.'

When Bill came back to the office he looked deeply upset. He told the staff to try to make contact with the people on our list to inform them that the mission had been cancelled, and without another word he went back to his room. Later he told me that it was the 'black dogs', a term he used to describe his depression.

I was called to reception, and descending the stairs with a heavy heart, where I found a small crowd of people waiting with their luggage. Among them were the children, smiling expectantly as I approached. Having to tell them that they wouldn't be leaving after all was one of the hardest things I've ever had to do.

That evening Liz and I went downstairs to the bar next to the hotel. Durim, Armando and a couple of friends were sitting around a table, and they'd obviously been drinking for quite a while. They invited us to join them and I ordered a glass of Skënderbeu, the local cognac, which I drank straight down, causing me to splutter. Durim told me that a Kosovar soldier had been admitted to the hospital following a border incursion by armed gunmen, who'd shot him in the chest.

'He's asked to see you,' said Durim.

I went to the hospital and found the soldier with his chest bandaged. He looked pale and very weak, but at least he was conscious. A woman moved aside so that I could see him.

'Thank you for coming,' he said, his voice just a whisper.

I saw that he was wearing a gold ring with a large red stone and realised it was Uli, the young man who'd entrusted me with his siblings.

'I wanted to thank you for helping us. The children are with our parents in Switzerland and they're very happy.'

I went to find the doctor, who told me that Uli would shortly be evacuated to Tirana, where they had better facilities.

'Do you think he'll survive?' I asked.

The doctor nodded. 'But the war is over for him,' he said.

The following afternoon Liz and I decided to write a letter to Tony Blair, appealing against the decision made by Jack Straw. We went to the Mona Lisa restaurant, a place where we'd often taken our volunteers. There were several men inside, and although it was not the done thing for women to go out alone here, they were used to seeing us around and barely looked up as we entered.

For two or three hours we sat writing and rewriting the letter, and when at last we were satisfied with our efforts, we decided to leave. With the curfew in place, it was forbidden to be out after dark, so we set off back to the hotel. It was pouring with rain and the street was deserted, but I caught a glimpse of Armando beneath an umbrella hurrying home.

Like everyone else we were tired of the hotel food, so we were all delighted when Bill was given permission to use one of the rooms as a kitchen. He'd scout around for whatever he could find locally and conjure up some tasty dishes. That evening we'd been promised roast lamb and all the trimmings, providing there was electricity.

As we approached the hotel car park, dusk was falling and the street lights came on, casting a warm sodium glow. This was a good sign as it meant the hotel had power. A man was standing beside a lamp post and I saw he was dressed in army fatigues, his face obscured by a black balaclava. He was holding a gun that glinted in the lamplight. As I threw myself into the shadows to get out of sight, there was a searing hot pain through my thigh.

When the man disappeared I gingerly touched my leg. It felt wet, and when I looked down I saw blood mingling with the rain.

I wasn't sure whether I was dreaming until Liz appeared in front of me, clutching the side of her face.

'What happened?' she asked, her voice trembling.

'It's my leg,' I said, my teeth gritted in pain. 'I think I've been shot'.

Liz rushed into the hotel to get help and eventually found Bill in the kitchen. He was holding a glass of whisky and when she rushed towards him crying, 'Sally's been shot!' it fell from his hand, shattering on the floor.

33

I was vaguely aware of voices, but they sounded muffled and distant. An army truck seemed to appear from nowhere and I thought I was hallucinating. Bill hauled me onto the back of the truck, and he and Liz leapt in beside me as the vehicle lurched onto the main street. We hit a pothole and I was thrown around, causing more and more blood to pour from my leg. I heard Bill's voice saying that the bullet might have severed the femoral artery, and if so, I only had minutes.

When we reached the hospital I was carried to the emergency room but there was no light, so someone was dispatched to find a bulb. As the doctor examined my leg, I heard Bill's voice again.

'Thank God, it's a "through and through".'

The bullet had passed through my thigh and come out the other side. An antiquated machine was brought to my bedside and an X-ray taken. The doctor then began to remove the debris from the wound, which caused me excruciating pain. I was given an injection of morphine, and as the medication started to take effect, Bill told me he was leaving.

'I have to send a report,' he said. 'Anyway, the dinner might be ruined.'

There seemed to be a great deal of noise around me so I hauled myself up to see what was going on. The room was filled with people.

'What's happening?' I asked, wondering again if I might be hallucinating.

The doctor smiled. 'They have come to see the Angel of Mostar,' he said.

That evening I was supposed to be attending a charity ball in London held by the Celebrity Guild of Great Britain. They'd decided to make a special donation to Operation Angel, and Duncan and my mother were there to receive it on my behalf. They were sitting in the banqueting hall surrounded by celebrities when a phone call came through to say that I'd been shot.

When the wound had been thoroughly cleaned I decided to leave the hospital – I was obviously a target and they had no security. The morphine had left me relatively free of pain, so I was able to make my way slowly down the stairs. Outside I found Durim waiting to drive me back to the Ermal. Liz was waiting in Bill's office with Andrea, a German woman who worked for the OSCE. Tall and athletic, with short blonde hair, she was studying to be a nurse. Liz helped me into a chair while Andrea was busy setting up a saline drip.

Liz's face was badly bruised and she had two loose teeth where a second man had hit her with his gun, but she insisted that she was all right. I sat down beside her and was listening to them speak when all of a sudden it felt as though my body were shutting down. Darkness was closing in and there was no way to let them know as I was unable to speak. My eyes were closing and I somehow knew that death was close, but I felt strangely calm. Liz happened to turn to me at that moment and immediately realised that something was seriously wrong.

'She's going into shock!' she cried, and they quickly tried to insert a canula into my arm. My veins had constricted and no matter how hard they both tried, they couldn't get the needle in. Andrea suggested they insert the canula into my neck, and when at last the drip was in place I immediately began to recover. If they hadn't acted quickly, my vital organs would have been affected and I would certainly have died.

Later, with the drip stand in tow, they helped me down the corridor to my room and as soon as I lay down on the bed I began to drift off to sleep, but was woken a few minutes later when Bill entered the room with a plate of lamb, potatoes and vegetables. When I realised it wasn't a joke, I politely suggested he take the plate away, for having just been shot, I really wasn't feeling very hungry.

During the night the pain in my leg intensified as the morphine began to wear off. Liz decided to increase the dose, but she explained that it would have to be injected into my buttock. I wasn't able to turn onto my side, so she went to ask Bill to help her. I caught a glimpse of him standing in the doorway and a moment later there was a sharp pain in my backside. But at least the deed was done.

I awoke the next morning to find two men standing beside my bed: one was the Albanian minister of health, the other a doctor. They asked if I minded them taking a look at the wound, and Liz removed the dressings from my thigh. Although the entry wound appeared relatively minor, no bigger than a ten pence piece, there was a large gaping hole where the bullet had exited, and the slight movement caused it to start bleeding heavily, immediately soaking the bedsheets. The men explained that they'd been sent by President Meidani, who'd arranged for a helicopter to fly me to Tirana.

'Can we take the children with us?' I asked.

'I'm sorry, no, that won't be possible,' said the minister, shaking his head. 'The helicopter is too small.'

'Then I'll have to decline your offer I'm afraid. I can't leave without them.'

Looking dismayed, he spoke to his colleague for a few moments before turning back to me.

'The doctor says that the wound is infected. You need specific antibiotics and treatment in sterile surroundings. In Tirana you'll have the best possible care.'

I told them that although I was grateful for their offer, I didn't feel able to leave without the children. 'I've promised to try to help these families, and if I go they'll think I've abandoned them. At least while I'm around they still have some hope.'

They eventually gave up trying to persuade me and politely said goodbye.

Bill called the British embassy and put in a request for antibiotics and sterile dressings. As soon as these arrived, Liz and Andrea started cleaning the entry and exit wounds in my leg.

We had a visit from the local chief of police, who wanted Liz and me to make a statement about the night of the shooting. His hair was cut like Elvis Presley, and he wore tight black bell-bottom trousers and platform shoes. We told him that our attackers were wearing masks and he wrote something down.

'Did you see what they looked like?' he asked, causing us to stare at him in dismay. Sherlock Holmes he was not.

Liz was prepared to remain with me in Bajram Curri, and although I'd have loved her to stay, I felt she'd done more than enough already. The OSCE had been inundated with calls from the media, so by going home she'd also be able to exploit the media interest to highlight the plight of the children. Bill arranged for Liz to be driven to Tirana, and as she prepared to leave we were both quite upset. We'd been through a lot together and I was going to miss her very much.

'I'll do my best to make them listen,' she assured me.

Mike had arranged a press conference upon her arrival in Britain, but although the coverage was widespread, it was not what we hoped for; the news media was more interested in details of the shooting than the plight of the children.

Back in Britain, the press had a field day. 'Nobody's Angel' and 'Fallen Angel', read the headlines. Lyndall Sachs, a spokeswoman for the UNHCR, criticised my attempt to arrange medical treatment for the children, saying: 'We are more concerned with building the infrastructure in Kosovo to benefit a greater number of people.'

Bill was inundated with calls from the press and he dealt with most of them on my behalf. I made an exception for Lorraine Kelly, because she'd been so supportive in the past, but she simply repeated the nonsense that had been published by the press and I was really disappointed.

Channel 4 broadcast the documentary they'd commissioned, and when Mike called me to say how biased it was, I decided to resign. I was fed up with the sniping and the constant criticism from the UN and the press. With my credibility at zero, there seemed little point in continuing to represent the charity. I'd continue my work alone.

34

In order to avoid infection, Liz and Andrea had cleaned and dressed the wounds in my leg several times each day. Now with Liz gone and Andrea busy patrolling the border, there was no one around to perform the regular surgical procedure known as debridement necessary for my leg to heal, so Bill Foxton offered to take over.

Five or six times each day Bill patiently dug away at the wounds with a knife. It was difficult for him to be gentle with a hook in place of a hand, but he carefully removed each remaining cotton thread from the trousers I'd been wearing that had been blasted through my leg on the point of the bullet. He also had to snip away necrotic tissue from the cavity to avoid the risk of gangrene. This was so painful that it made me grip the metal rungs of the headboard while gritting my teeth.

With Liz's departure, Bill insisted I move closer to the OSCE office where the Presidential Guard remained on duty day and night. My room was very small, containing just a single bed and a chair, and there was a strange smell in the air, though I was never able to identify the cause. At night I could hear the sound of mice scurrying across the floor.

Some of the children came to visit me, and among them was little Halili, the boy who'd been badly burned. He stood beside my bed and smiled, and as I looked around at their faces, so innocent and full of hope, it made me even more determined to stay.

One afternoon there was a loud commotion in the corridor and two men entered my room, both of them heavily armed. One was the infamous Fatmir Haklaj, tall and slim with curly fair hair and a bushy beard. He was dressed in camouflage and carried an Uzi submachine gun, a Makarov pistol and two RPG-7 grenades; his bodyguard, Feriz Kërnaja, a convicted killer, was cradling a rocket launcher. To my relief, Bill Foxton and Beni came in behind them. Fatmir started shouting and gesticulating while I lay there helpless on the bed, unable to understand a word he was saying. Finally, when he finished speaking, he turned to Beni and grunted.

'He says you're much respected throughout Albania and Kosovo for all you've done,' said Beni. 'He wants to assure you that no Albanian would take up arms against you, for you are the symbolic daughter of Mother Teresa.'

'Thanks,' I said, thinking it might be wise to leave it at that.

'You have his protection and his guarantee that you'll come to no further harm, and if you ever need his help, you only have to ask.'

I was just debating whether to tell him that my Shogun had been hijacked, when he turned on his heel and left, followed closely by the bodyguard.

While I was recovering, I received a fax from Bujar Bukoshi, the prime minister of Kosovo in exile in Tirana, wishing me a speedy recovery.

Although I was starting to move around more, my leg remained quite stiff and the slightest movement would cause the wound to bleed. Fortunately, the British embassy in Tirana continued to send a regular supply of dressings and antibiotics, so the treatment could continue.

It was snowing and the roads were icy but I wanted to visit the children, so Durim took me in his car. We stopped at a small house where Halili and his family were living in one room. I gave his father a few hundred dollars, thinking it would help them to get through the winter, but he decided he'd use the money to take his family abroad. A few months later I received a message to say they arrived in Britain and his son was having treatment.

With nothing much to do while my leg was healing, I spent a lot of time sitting in the office, the only room in the Ermal that was heated. The OSCE were now the only organisation using the hotel, and two new members had recently joined the team: a Pole called Krysztof, an authority on cinema, and a lieutenant colonel from Bulgaria.

Bill had managed to find a television and someone hung a satellite dish outside the window. Whenever there was electricity, we'd huddle around the gas fire and watch the news or light a few candles and talk late into the night. Nursing a glass of whisky, Bill would amuse us with tales from his army days, which began when he first left school. As soon as he was old enough, he joined the French Foreign Legion, serving in France and Algiers before escaping across the desert with a couple of friends; the journey was hell and one of his friends didn't make it.

In 1969 he enlisted with the British Army, serving with the Royal Green Jackets. He was brake man for the British Bobsleigh Team during the 1972 European Championships, and the following year he served as a company intelligence sergeant in Belfast, where he was mentioned in dispatches.

Later Bill joined the Sultan's Armed Forces in Oman, rising to the rank of major. He told us about an incident that happened during this period when he was returning from an operation with sixteen soldiers and two other Frontier Force officers. They were flying in a Short Skyvan towards the Raysut airstrip when at 4,500 feet the pilot collapsed. Grabbing the joystick, Bill, who happened to be sitting in the co-pilot's seat, took control of the aircraft while his two colleagues tried to revive the pilot. The pilot's legs were jamming the rudder and the aircraft went into a spin. The Balochi soldiers could see what was happening and started to panic as the aircraft descended. Warning lights were flashing, a siren was wailing and the officers tried to prepare everyone for a crash landing. Fortunately, someone thought to retract the flaps, so Bill was able to level out and fly towards a nearby airfield. Having never flown an aircraft before, he started to think very hard about how to land the plane, but one of his fellow officers managed to resuscitate the pilot, who took over at the last minute. Bill and his two colleagues were awarded the Sultan's Commendation for saving both the aircraft and all those on board.

It was during his time with the SAF that Bill lost part of his left arm when destroying an unexploded 60mm mortar round after a training exercise. Bill was eventually fitted with a prosthetic limb and he added various attachments. One, made of solid steel, he called his 'war arm'; another the Sultan of Oman ordered to be made for him by the jewellers Asprey. The hook was studded with diamonds and he used it for special occasions. After the injury Bill returned to duty as deputy force welfare officer, and he later received an MBE for services to disabled Omani soldiers.

When the war broke out in Bosnia he joined the European Union Monitoring Mission (ECMM) and spent two years in the Bihać pocket, which was often isolated by Serb forces surrounding the area. After the war he lived in Sarajevo and continued to work for the ECMM as a training officer. It was around this time that he crawled through a minefield to save a Serbian child in the Vrbas valley. Tony told me the story but when I asked Bill to confirm it, he simply smiled. Bill eventually transferred to the OSCE and in 1998 became head of office for northern Albania. It was rumoured that he also worked for British intelligence, but this was never verified, although the CIA were certainly very active in the region.

Bill had an en suite bathroom that he offered to share, and after weeks of using the Turkish-style shower/toilet on the floor below, this was a great luxury. One evening after the water went off, I was struggling along the corridor with a full bucket to pour into the sink. All of a sudden the lights went out and I could hear the sound of footsteps creeping up behind me. I almost jumped out of my skin as a voice suddenly yelled loudly in my ear and caused me to drop the bucket. Water spilled all across the floor and I slipped, yelping with pain as something sharp suddenly caught me from behind.

I heard Bill say, 'Oh dear, it's all gone wrong.'

After the electricity went off, he'd told the others to keep quiet while he crept out of the office to make me jump. His joke went further than he had intended, however, because as he reached out to stop me from falling he caught me with his hook. Andrea tended to the bleeding tramlines that ran down my back while Bill apologised profusely and tried not to laugh.

When I felt fit enough to travel, we drove down to Tirana. Bill and Andrea were on leave, so we booked ourselves into the Rogner and spent three days living in style. The beds were soft and comfortable, and the rooms were heated, unlike at the Ermal where they were freezing cold. In the evenings we ate in the palatial dining room, feasting on steak and sautéed potatoes and selecting mouth-watering desserts from the trolley. I'd forgotten how pleasant it was to eat off china plates and drink out of crystal glasses. Bajram Curri had been my home for over two months, so the break was much appreciated.

During the day I visited some of the embassies in Tirana and requested help for the children still awaiting treatment. The embassies of Czechoslovakia and Greece offered visas for the refugee families still waiting in Bajram Curri, and Liz Dack managed to arrange for a British paediatrician to travel to Albania to help those who could be treated at home.

I received a message from Keith Carney, letting me know that most of the patients who'd gone to the States were now undergoing treatment. Besa Shala was still waiting for the cochlear implant, but the device, surgery and subsequent speech therapy would be very expensive. Keith was doing his best to raise the moncy and in the meantime the family had applied for their visas to be extended.

On the day of our return to Bajram Curri we were driven to the ferry in Koman, which would take us to Fierzë in the north. A group of Albanian men were lounging around in a haze of cigarette smoke and they cast suspicious glances in our direction as we headed towards the stairs. I was feeling slightly dizzy as we climbed the rusted staircase and assumed that it was due to the long car journey. Moments later I felt myself falling and then everything went black.

Somehow Bill managed to get me to a cabin and I awoke to the chugging of the engines as the ferry made its way across the lake. He was nowhere to be seen, but sitting beside the bed was Prenda, the UN interpreter. I hadn't seen her since that unfortunate day in Tropojë. She hugged me warmly and apologised for what happened when we first met.

'If I'd known who you were, I wouldn't have interfered,' she said. 'I'm so sorry.'

I was surprised when she began to cry, and I took her hand and assured her that it didn't matter.

She pulled some papers from her bag and showed me an article she'd written in which she had likened me to Edith Durham, the remarkable and flamboyant Englishwoman who'd spent the early part of the 20th century travelling through the Balkans and championing the Albanian cause. I was flattered, as she was revered by many in the country.

My dressing had by now come off, leaving the wound exposed and bleeding. It was obviously infected, which wouldn't be helped by the fact I was lying on a dirty blanket stained with oil. With Prenda's help I hobbled to a covered enclosure on the deck where of all people I found Avdyl, the caretaker from the tent above Padesh. He greeted me warmly and, ever the gentleman, offered me his seat.

The ferry made its way through a series of spectacular gorges and interconnected lakes that were formed when the Drini valley was dammed in the 1970s. Passing between the high mountains, we occasionally caught a glimpse of some hardy peasants climbing the steep, half-hidden pathways to their solitary homes. Apart from the breathtaking scenery, it was a great pleasure to travel by water rather than by road across the rugged terrain.

Two hours later the ferry docked at Fierzë, where Durim was waiting to take us to Bajram Curri. Wagon and Trailer had cleaned my room, though it still smelled a little strange. The mice, perhaps in search of food, had relocated to the OSCE office, where the staff often ate.

Marigona and her family were still living in the refugee camp alongside Nik, Hane and their children. As Christmas approached, Coxy and Janey packed up all the food, clothing, bedding and toys that had been donated or bought for the hotel in Brighton and transported it all across Europe. When they arrived in Shkodër, the aid was distributed between the 150 refugees living in the camp.

Despite the daily debriding of the wound and taking large doses of antibiotics, my leg remained infected and Bill was concerned about gangrene. I was feeling constantly sick, which we put down to the antibiotics. Bill told me that his superior was being leaned on by the British government to get me out of the country and he explained that if I were to fall into a coma I'd be immediately evacuated.

Nik had family in Switzerland, and once he got exit visas for his wife and children he planned to take them there. Marigona was now four years old, and without an operation to remove the cataracts her eyesight would be irreversibly damaged. I decided to go to Britain and try to arrange things from there.

Duncan came to meet me in Tirana and we flew home together. Although he was now in another relationship, we remained very close and I knew he'd do everything he could to help Marigona.

My parents were waiting at the airport with some of the volunteers, and I hobbled down the walkway and gave my mother a hug. The press were there, as always, and a photo ended up in *Hello!* magazine.

The next day I went to the Sussex County Hospital and was examined by a trauma specialist. Although the wound in my leg was still infected, it turned out that the constant nausea was most likely due to the fact that I was pregnant. An ultrasound scan confirmed that despite large doses of antibiotics and painkillers, everything looked fine.

When I called Bill to tell him about the baby, he told me he'd be honoured to father my child, but he was actually married. He asked me to conceal his identity for the sake of his wife, which of course meant I'd have to bring our child up alone.

A couple of months later on Valentine's Day I received a dozen red roses and a small enamelled box. Engraved across the top were the words 'Forget Me Not' and inside was the flattened 9mm bullet that Bill had dug out of the pavement after I was shot.

35

We made a new visa application to the Home Office on behalf of
Marigona and included a letter from Christopher Lui, an ophthalmic surgeon who'd agreed to operate free of charge. It took some
time, but finally we received confirmation that she'd been granted
permission to come to the UK – on condition that she came alone.

Mike Mendoza had been commissioned to make a film about
the refugees in Shkodër, and although he'd been involved with
my work for many years, it would be the first time he'd be join-
ing me on a mission.

Shkodër is an ancient city on the shore of Shkodër Lake in
north-west Albania. An important cultural and economic area,
it's the centre of Albanian Catholicism and at the same time the
pre-eminent city of Sunni Islam in the country. The city was built
in the shadow of Rozafa Castle, which clings to the rocky hillside. A famous legend surrounds it, dating back to Illyrian times.

Three brothers had set about building the castle, but no matter
how hard they worked each day, when night came the walls
would fall down. A wise old man advised them to make a sacri-
fice so that the walls would remain standing, but they couldn't
decide whose life should be taken. Eventually they agreed that
whichever of their wives brought the lunch the next day would
be buried in the wall of the castle. They each promised not to tell
the women of their plan, but the two older brothers broke their
promise. Only the youngest man kept his word, and the next

afternoon, as the brothers waited to see who'd come, Rosafa, wife of the youngest brother, arrived with a basket of food. When he told his unfortunate wife that she was to be buried in the castle wall so that they could finish building it, she didn't protest. She agreed to be sacrificed on condition that they would leave parts of her exposed; her right eye so that she could see her infant son, her right hand so that she could caress him, her breast in order to feed him, and her foot, to rock his cradle.

Crossing the spacious square in the centre of the town, I noticed that the fountain was filled with tyres, though no one seemed to know why. We passed the Al-Zamil mosque, which stands in the shadow of a Catholic church, and making our way through the heavy traffic of old cars and bicycles we tried not to breathe in the diesel fumes and dust that polluted the spring air. In the older part of town we walked through narrow streets past colourful houses with fading façades and broken shutters. The shabby store fronts were virtually empty, and blowflies buzzed around the rotting fruit and vegetables displayed on the market stalls.

When we entered the refugee compound I could see Marigona playing with her sister in the mud. She didn't notice me at first as her eyesight had deteriorated, but as soon as I came closer she raced into my arms. With the children clutching my hands, we headed towards the unfinished building that had been their home for several months.

There was a terrible stench as the refugees only had two toilets between them all, and rainwater was leaking through the roof of the building, forming puddles across the floor. Marigona led me down the corridor to a small, dark room that was no more than ten feet by six. There were two sets of bunk beds against the exposed walls and the family's belongings were kept in bags suspended from a washing line. When we entered the room I almost stepped on Arbresha, who was playing on the concrete floor.

Valbona was delighted to see us and threw her arms around me, talking animatedly until she remembered that I couldn't speak Albanian. Miranda, proudly sporting her two new front teeth, was immediately sent to find her father, who appeared a few minutes later with Nik and Hane. More hugs were followed by coffee, and Nik told me that he'd finally managed to secure the exit visas for himself and his family.

Although they were concerned about Marigona travelling without them, Hili and Valbona decided she should go. Beni had offered to accompany us as her interpreter, and on the day we were leaving he joined us at the camp. Most of the refugees had turned out to see her off, and being so young I expected her to cry. Instead, she gave her mum and dad a hug and jumped straight into the car.

Within days of arriving in Britain, Marigona was admitted for surgery at the Sussex Eye Hospital, but she was naturally very frightened and kept getting out of bed. At one point she raced into the corridor, crying for her mother. My heart ached for her; she looked so small and vulnerable, and she'd already been through so much. With Beni's help we eventually managed to convince her to go back to her room, where she was given a pre-med and then wheeled into theatre.

The operation went well, and after two weeks of treatment she was ready to go home. Upon her arrival at the airport in Tirana she raced across the concourse to her parents, able to see them clearly for the very first time.

In the meantime, Serb forces continued to wage war against the ethnic Albanians, and NATO finally responded with a series of air strikes. The bombing campaign, which began on 24 March 1999, lasted ten weeks and involved 1,000 aircraft that flew over 38,000 combat missions. By the end of May more than 500,000 people had become refugees, but Operation Allied Force was deemed a success, eventually restoring peace to Kosovo.

Bill was awarded an OBE for his work and he wore his 'best arm' for the ceremony at Buckingham Palace. On 19 July 1999 our daughter Billie-Jo was born. Holding her in my arms, my sympathy for the mothers caught up in the war, forced to choose whether to place their faith in a stranger or struggle for survival amid the bullets and the bombs, was redoubled.

With a newborn baby to care for, I didn't have much time on my hands but I wanted to continue helping the victims of war. In September I returned to Kosovo to establish a centre that would provide counselling for women and children suffering from trauma.

In 2001 Slobodan Milošević was arrested and pleaded not guilty to charges of abuse of power and criminal conspiracy. He was put on trial at The Hague, where just a few months before the verdict was due he was found dead in his cell from a heart attack.

Ibrahim Rugova and Hashim Thaçi agreed to work on creating provisional institutions of self-government until Kosovo's final status was decided. Rugova was elected as president of the Republic of Kosovo, and he remained in office until his death from lung cancer in 2006.

That same year war broke out between Israel and Lebanon, and I travelled to the border to help. In between delivering aid to the frail and the vulnerable, I was based at Hanita, the kibbutz where I stayed in my youth. Once again I found myself dodging Katyusha rockets that were fired into Israel from just across the border and although thirty years had passed, it seemed nothing had changed. Upon my return to the UK, I was invited to become a Goodwill Ambassador for Children of Peace, a non-partisan children's charity dedicated to building trust, friendship and reconciliation between Israeli and Palestinian children. The charity was founded by Richard Martin, whose vision and inspired leadership has brought together many individuals and organisations who share his fresh approach to conflict resolution in the Middle East.

On 17 February 2008 Kosovo's parliament unanimously endorsed a declaration of independence from Serbia and thousands of people swarmed onto the streets of the capital Pristina. The city centre erupted with the sound of fireworks and celebratory gunfire as Hashim Thaçi, the prime minister of Kosovo, said in a speech, 'We have waited for this day for a very long time. From today, we are proud, independent and free.'

The following year I was watching the news when Bill Foxton's image appeared on the screen. We hadn't seen him since 2003 but he kept in touch by email. He was country director for a German NGO in Kosovo for several years and then he moved to the central Afghan province of Bamyan, where he managed humanitarian aid projects on behalf of Caritas. According to the news report, Bill, who was due to retire that year, had invested his life savings in two Austrian-based hedge funds, both of which had been closed and the funds reinvested with Bernard Madoff, the notorious American fraudster. As a result of the collapse of Madoff's Ponzi scheme, Bill was facing bankruptcy. On 10 February he set off to a small park near his home in Southampton carrying a semi-automatic pistol. Once there, he sat down on a bench and shot himself through the head. Bill was an incredibly brave man with an adventurous spirit who always lived life on the edge, and had he been killed by a bomb or a stray bullet in some war-torn country, I wouldn't have been surprised. But I was profoundly shocked that he had chosen to die by his own hand, alone on a park bench on the south coast.

PART III
Peace and Justice

36

I often wondered what happened to the children from Mostar. Senad Zukić, who was ten when he came to Britain as part of the Operation Angel mission in 1993, remained in the West Midlands and graduated from Leeds University with a master's degree in computer science. He created a website for me in case any of the children wished to find me, and I was working on my computer one day when I received the first message.

'Hi Sally, It's Selma!!!'

In between numerous operations, Selma had continued her studies and graduated from Pace University in New York. She was planning to move to San Francisco where she had been offered a job in human resources at Google and she'd recently got engaged. Billie and I were invited to her wedding.

There was a murmur of anticipation among the guests as they sipped champagne and waited for the bride and groom to appear. The doors opened and Billie squeezed my hand as the newlyweds entered the opulent ballroom. Selma was dressed in an ivory satin gown and her blue eyes sparkled beneath the glittering lights of a crystal chandelier.

'She looks like a princess,' said Billie, and Selma's mother caught my eye … and smiled.

Maja Kazazić graduated from high school and college, going on to gain a BA in psychology from St Francis University. She moved to Tampa in Florida, where she became a successful certified empathy life coach and amputee peer counsellor. Hanger, the company that designed her prosthetic leg, flew me and Billie to the States for a reunion. When we arrived at the airport I caught a glimpse of Maja striding towards us with a broad smile on her face. She took us to Disney World followed by front-row seats at the Cirque du Soleil.

Maja was a successful business woman and a motivational speaker but some years later she developed post traumatic stress as a result of her experiences during the war in Mostar, dealing with panic episodes that occasionally rendered her unable to function. She adopted Rosie, an amputee great Dane, on her clinician's advice, and the Hanger Clinic created a prosthetic limb for the dog, who joins her on stage when she gives talks. Two amputees changing lives and inspiring people around the world.

A couple of years later I received another message, this time from Lela, who was seven days old when she and her brothers were injured. She wrote, 'I am the baby you rescued.'

She told me that her family would love to see me, so I decided to return to Mostar for the first time since the war.

Wandering through the narrow streets, it was hard to believe that the snipers were gone, especially as some of the buildings were still pitted with shrapnel and bullet holes, incongruous among the colourful awnings of the sidewalk cafés and department stores. They were living in a house their father built on the outskirts of the city after the war, and after plenty of hugs and kisses, Sendzana handed out glasses of homemade pomegranate juice while her husband Mohamer talked about the war. He recalled the day when the anti-tank missile ripped through their fourth-storey apartment, injuring him and the children, and he spoke of their heartbreak at losing their eldest son. Elmir still bore the scars from the shrapnel but although he lost the sight in one eye, he was able to drive and was working as a car mechanic. Lela had grown into a beautiful young woman and was studying information technology.

Although Hafid had an apartment on the west side of Mostar, he rented it out, preferring to live on the eastern side of the city. We met outside Higijenski, the public health laboratory that had served as a makeshift hospital during the war. The brickwork was no longer painted red and the bullet holes were gone, but as we entered the compound I half-expected to see my old ambulance parked outside the door. Going down into the basement was like stepping back in time, and I stayed alone in the corridor for a while, recalling those who had died there. I could clearly see Medina's little face in my mind and the memory made me cry.

Dr Milavić, the anaesthetist, had left during the war, so Hafid had taken over as director of the hospital. I asked him whether he received any kind of recognition for his work – he and his colleague had carried out more than 1,700 operations over a period of eleven months, an astonishing feat – but Hafid shook his head. When he was asked to reflect on what he felt about the war, he said that because of the dreadful things that were done to the children, he still doesn't feel able to forgive.

Amel, the boy we called 'Hafid's miracle', was living with his family in a small house on the hillside above the city. Selma's father Mirsad, who was running a small antique shop in east Mostar, called them to ask if we could pay them a visit, and they immediately agreed. It was a miserable day and was raining quite hard as we pulled up outside the small house. Amel's mother greeted us warmly and invited us inside, where her son was waiting. She told me that he'd spent a year in the hospital before returning to Bosnia. He was now able to use a computer and as we were leaving, he asked if he could add me as a friend on Facebook. A few minutes later I received a notification that he was subscribing to my updates.

I'd tried without success to contact Zoran so I was delighted when he turned up at my hotel. He was living on the east side of Mostar near Žena BiH, the women's shelter that was founded by his friend Azra Hasanbegović. In 2011 he received the Duško Kondor Civil Courage Award, which was granted in commemoration of Professor Kondor to 'those brave people who risked their own lives by standing up to negative authorities and acting according to their own values'. Erna Danon became president of the Jewish community, which continued to work alongside their Muslim, Serb and Croat neighbours in an effort to reform and improve the unique relationships they had prior to the conflict.

I visited Stipe and Erna Rozić, and as we pulled up outside their apartment, Erna was leaning over the balcony just as she used to do almost twenty years earlier. Damir became a doctor and went on to specialise in nuclear medicine. When we arrived he was working at the hospital on the hill in west Mostar. He'd married a Croatian girl and they had three beautiful children.

Vava came to see me and, despite the passing years, he hadn't really changed much. We talked about old times and he recalled the first time we met.

'I wondered who was this mad woman so willing to cross a front line,' said Vava, laughing at the memory. He told me that after the war ended he returned to teaching children at primary school but he continued to write. He was also an artist and has had many exhibitions of his work. He arranged for me to meet Dr Ivan Bagarić, who was a member of parliament in the Croatian government.

As I walked along Bulevar, the street that runs north–south through the centre of the city, once Mostar's front line, I saw him coming towards me with his arms outstretched. He called out in English, 'My Angel!'

We talked about the divisions still in place across the region and he told me that the only way things would ever really change was if Bosnia-Herzegovina became part of the EU. He believed that was the only way to ensure a democratic process that would correct the present injustices and provide equality for all.

'This is vital, for without equality, the state of BiH will not survive and that will generate ongoing conflict in the heart of Europe.'

In Mostar there are graveyards where there used to be parks, and row upon row of headstones. I watched as a man laid flowers at the grave of two young boys, probably his sons. I visited Šarića Harem, the graveyard where five-year-old Damir Greljo is buried, and I placed a small bouquet of flowers at the foot of his grave. Etched into the headstone, which is fringed with daffodils, is a portrait of the beloved little boy.

Yet despite the damaged buildings and the graves, parts of Mostar are thriving and tourists now flock there in summer like in the old days. The narrow cobbled streets are straight out of a middle-European fairy tale, and people who once ran past the snipers in terror now wander through the shopping malls and linger over coffee in sidewalk cafés. Stari Most, the bridge destroyed by shelling in 1993, has been restored to its original magnificence, a symbol of unity in an otherwise divided city. As I strolled across the bridge the sun was shining and a young man prepared to dive into the river, just as his father might have done before the war.

*　　*　　*

At 18 minutes past midnight on 28 July 2012 Her Majesty Queen Elizabeth II declared the Summer Olympic Games open, and I jumped as fireworks exploded all around, stirring memories of war. We were told to start walking, and the rhythmic beating of the drum seemed to be in time with my heartbeat. I looked around, taking in the sounds, the smell, the amazing atmosphere, aware that I was walking with giants. As we tipped the flag towards the presidential box, our names were announced over the tannoy and I heard the words 'Sally Becker, Goodwill

Ambassador for Children of Peace, we salute her courage.'

Ban Ki-moon, secretary-general of the United Nations, had been chosen as my partner on the flag, and I did my best to keep in step with him. When our part of the ceremony was over and we went back inside, he took my hand and thanked me for all I'd done for the children, a moment I'll never forget.

I only heard about my role four weeks earlier when the executive producer of the opening ceremony arranged to meet me at Patisserie Valerie in Brighton. The spectacle would be called 'Isles of Wonder', directed by Academy Award-winning British film director Danny Boyle, and produced by Stephen Daldry and Tracey Seawood.

He explained that I was one of eight people who'd been chosen to carry the Olympic flag. The theme was 'Peace and Justice' and we'd all be dressed in white, but the content of the event was being kept secret so he wasn't able to tell me who would carry the flag alongside me.

When I arrived in London there was a tremendous sense of excitement in the air. The ceremony would feature children and young people in most of its segments, reflecting the 'inspire a generation' aspiration of London's original bid for the Games, and on the way to my hotel the cabbie told me that his daughter and other pupils at her school would be taking part in the show.

I was booked into the Corinthia, one of the best five-star hotels in London. I couldn't afford to eat in the dining room but it was only a couple of minutes' walk from Trafalgar Square, so I found a café and sat down to watch the world go by. The atmosphere on the street was amazing and many people wore T-shirts, hats or badges bearing the Olympic logo. It was a magical time for me, my only regret being that that there was no one to share it with me.

I'd received an invitation to attend a gala fundraising dinner at the Victoria and Albert Museum that evening. The event was hosted by Sports for Peace in honour of Muhammed Ali. Although best known as the three-time world heavyweight boxing champion, outside the ring his influence as a humanitarian, mediator in world conflicts, civil rights crusader and fierce opponent of the Vietnam War elevated his stature in the modern world.

I arrived alone and was seated at a table with a number of bankers. Looking around, I'd never seen so many celebrities in one room and I'd no idea why I'd been invited – perhaps my name had got confused with Boris Becker, who was one of the hosts. Turning slightly, I saw that Muhammed Ali was seated on the next table, and when the speeches started I was surprised to see him looking in my direction. He appeared to say something to his wife Lonnie while continuing to stare at me intently, but I'd no idea what it could be.

The following evening I was invited to drink champagne in the hotel bar with Shami Chakrabarti and Doreen Lawrence, who explained that they'd also been chosen to carry the flag for Peace and Justice, but none of us knew who else might be involved.

On the day of the opening ceremony we were taken by coach across London to the Olympic Park in Stratford. Key landmarks like Tower Bridge were adorned with the Olympic rings, creating a striking visual symbol of the Games. There were road closures and restrictions for regular traffic on key routes, and we travelled in a special lane that was reserved for athletes, officials and the media. We were not due on stage until later in the evening, so I was able to sit with my dear friend Heather James and her husband Simon for part of the show. The Isles of Wonder ceremony opened with idyllic scenes of a traditional British countryside, complete with live animals, maypoles and farmers. It was a spectacular event that celebrated British history, culture and creativity, and I found it quite incredible to sit there watching the amazing spectacle knowing that I'd soon be down there taking part.

When the runners came to collect us we were told to move quickly as the show was running late, and as we hurried along I almost bumped into the person in front of me who'd stopped abruptly. He turned around to apologise, and I realised it was Paul McCartney.

There were eight of us, each dressed completely in white, and I was partnered with Ban Ki-moon. The show was directed by Danny Boyle, and when I asked him during the rehearsal if he was aware of my history with the UN, he grinned.

We entered the stadium just after midnight and slowly made our way around the track, stopping in front of the presidential box to tip the flag towards the royal family, who were sitting alongside Michelle Obama and other dignitaries. We then made our way towards the model of Glastonbury Tor, where Muhammed Ali, also dressed from head to toe in white, was waiting to stand alongside us. My heart went out to him, as he looked so frail when he tried to grasp a section of the flag. His wife was urging him to wave but I could see the pain in his eyes as he tried to raise his arm. But the Olympics is about triumph of the human spirit and he epitomises that. As we stood alongside him people began chanting 'Ali, Ali', and the sound of their voices reverberated throughout the stadium.

The flag was then received by a colour sergeant from Her Majesty's Armed Forces and hoisted to the sound of Emeli Sandé singing the Olympic anthem. Eighty thousand people filled the stadium and 900 million people were watching around the world. I thought of the athletes who'd died in Munich in 1972; politics have no place at the Olympics, which is about nations coming together. On 17 October 1992 the UK sponsored a UN Resolution on the Olympic Truce entitled 'Building a peaceful and better world through sport and the Olympic ideal'. In an unprecedented show of support, all 193 UN member states signed up to the ideals of peace and conflict resolution, and the premise that individuals, not countries, compete against each other in peaceful competition without the heavy burden of politics, race and religion. There was ongoing conflict in Afghanistan, Syria was imploding, Israel was burdened by the constant threat of war and the Palestinians continued their struggle for a homeland. But for those fleeting and tremulous moments our nations did come together and manage to put politics aside, and for a while at least in the heart of London there was a sense of the way that things could be.

Around that time I found a small lump in my breast, but the radiologist who carried out the ultrasound decided not to bother with a needle biopsy and I was told there was no need to worry, that the changes to my breast were probably hormonal. The lump continued to grow, however, and the following year the medics decided to take it seriously. I returned to the clinic and had two mammograms and an ultrasound, which resulted in five core biopsies in which small tissue samples were removed using a needle. This was done in the same small windowless room where I'd been given the all-clear and been assured that there was nothing to worry about by the same radiologist the previous year.

After cleaning the conducting gel from the ultrasound device, he prepared to leave the room.

'Doesn't look too good, huh?' I said.

'No, I'm afraid not,' he replied. At least he had the decency to look slightly uncomfortable.

A few hours later I received a call from the clinic telling me that it was likely I had cancer.

A week later an MRI scan confirmed that I had an invasive lobular carcinoma and the tumour was 7cm. ILC is a condition that starts in the milk-producing glands and makes up around 15 per cent of all breast cancer cases. However, it is one of the most difficult cancers to detect, especially if the tissue is dense, as on routine mammograms it is often 'invisible', presenting more like a spider's web than a single lump. I was told that my breasts were very 'dense' for my age, making it hard to detect cancer at an early stage, but clearly had they carried out a biopsy eighteen months earlier when the lump was very small, I'd have been spared the ordeal I was now facing.

A cancer diagnosis is a major setback for anyone, but it was especially difficult knowing that had it been detected sooner, it would have meant far less aggressive treatment. The NHS do their best for women with breast cancer, but there's no doubt that mammograms fail to detect certain types of cancer and so anyone presenting with a lump should be given further tests. According to the National Institute for Health and Care Excellence, most patients are diagnosed through the triple assessment and it is 'best practice' to carry out these tests at the same visit. The cost would have been negligible and saved the NHS a much greater sum in the long run.

I chose to opt for a double mastectomy because, with this type of cancer, there's a higher risk of the disease appearing in the other breast. I opted for reconstructive surgery at the same time, so I had to wait two months, but the operation was successful and the margins around where the tumour had been were clear.

The day after I was discharged from hospital my father had a major heart attack. I travelled with him in the ambulance as they did their best to resuscitate him, but soon after we reached the hospital he died. Standing beside his bed, tears rolling down my face, I realised that he'd never actually told me he loved me. And then I remembered him travelling alone to Kosovo at the height of the conflict to bring me water, proving that sometimes actions speak louder than words.

A few months later I travelled to Israel in my role as Goodwill Ambassador to Children of Peace and visited some of the NGOs we support in Gaza and the West Bank. Amongst them was an organisation called Road to Recovery whose volunteers were ferrying children from Gaza to hospitals in Israel for vital medical treatments. One of the drivers was Uri Yogev, CEO of a company that was involved in the development of a new immunotherapy drug that harnesses the body's immune system to fight cancer and chronic viral diseases. The goal was to enhance or modify immune responses to target and eliminate harmful cells, while sparing healthy tissue. Trials were being carried out on patients with terminal cancer, and despite being unable to take part in the official trial, I convinced him to let me have the treatment. I injected the drug known as EF-022 twice weekly for around four months, and apart from a slight temperature following the first injection I experienced no side-effects at all. Sadly, the company was unable to get funding to continue developing the treatment and two years later they went into liquidation. I have no way of knowing whether this immunotherapy treatment was part of my cure, but eleven years have passed since my diagnosis and the cancer hasn't returned. Immunotherapy is now commonly used for various cancers and is being explored for treatment of HIV, tuberculosis and even viral infections such as Covid-19.

37

On 3 August 2014 members of the self-proclaimed Islamic State of Iraq and Syria, known as ISIS, swept into the Sinjar region of northern Iraq. This region is home to the majority of the world's Yazidis, whose religion, known as Yazidism, is thought to be older than Islam and Christianity. Yazidis believe in one God, who gave the world into the care of seven angels, the foremost of whom is Tawûsî Melek (Peacock Angel), a central figure in the Yazidi faith. Muslims and followers of other Abrahamic religions have erroneously associated and identified the Peacock Angel with the unredeemed evil spirit Satan, a misconception that has incited centuries of violent religious persecution of the minority Yazidi group as 'devil worshippers'.

ISIS militants rounded up the Yazidis into three groups: young boys who were to be indoctrinated as future fighters for ISIS, older males who were imprisoned or killed, and women and children who were kidnapped and sold. Tens of thousands fled, many to Mount Sinjar and the neighbouring peaks, where the militants surrounded them in the scorching summer heat. The US, Iraq, Britain, France and Australia flew in water and other supplies, and US air strikes kept ISIS at bay, but many died before they could be rescued.

Some of those who escaped subsequently found refuge in other countries, but most took shelter in the sprawling refugee camps of northern Iraq, where thousands of people were in desperate need of help. These included many women and children who were subjected to months of imprisonment and sexual abuse by their captors and were suffering from post-traumatic stress and depression. Healthcare was minimal and there was only one paediatric hospital in the whole region. Many of the women and children were traumatised and in urgent need of psychosocial support, but very few trained psychologists and counsellors were available.

Young women and girls as young as nine were separated from their families and sold as sex slaves or 'given' to the combatants, and in every case they were forced to convert to Islam. ISIS militants specifically targeted Yazidis because they believed that by degrading these women the whole community would be affected. 'They wanted to eradicate us,' said Nadia Murad, a former prisoner of ISIS who later received the Nobel Prize for her efforts to end the use of sexual violence as a weapon of war and armed conflict.

I was contacted by Ruth Purim, CEO of a successful staffing agency she founded in her mid-twenties after leaving school at just fifteen. On that day in August, along with the rest of the world, Ruth watched the siege of Mount Sinjar unfold. She remembered the vow she'd taken while visiting the gas chambers in Auschwitz in 2006, to never turn a blind eye to genocide. After reading an article published in the *Huffington Post*, Ruth tracked down a Yazidi community in the UK and had been working behind the scenes to highlight their plight.

Ruth had been told about my work helping children in war zones and set up a meeting for me with Yazidi diplomat Breen Tahseen, grandson of Prince Tahseen Saeed Bek. I arranged to fly to northern Iraq together with Scott La Stati, a volunteer from the US who wanted to use his current affairs platform to highlight the plight of the Yazidis. After stepping off the plane we were escorted to the VIP lounge, where we were introduced to Breen and two of his colleagues, Dr Shirzad Khaleel and Karim

Kamal. Over the next few days they took us around the internally displaced persons (IDP) camps in the Kurdistan region of Duhok.

We found numerous cases of children in need of specialist treatment. Two-year-old Dilbireen Muhsin's face had been badly disfigured in an accident in the Iraqi refugee camp where he was living with his family. In 2014, when Flosa Khalaf, Dilbireen's mother, was pregnant with him, ISIS attacked their village. Dilbireen's family fled their home to escape the bloodshed, eventually finding shelter among other displaced Yazidis in a refugee camp, where Dilbireen was born in January 2015. A year later, around the time of Dilbireen's first birthday, a fire started by a malfunctioning gas heater set his crib ablaze. Flosa was baking bread outside when her baby's crib went up in flames, and people nearby rushed to his aid. Dilbireen was severely burned on his face and feet, but a blanket protected the rest of his body from harm. Iraqi doctors advised the parents to get him treated outside the country.

In Kurdish, the young Yazidi boy's name means 'wounded heart'. Yet two-year-old Dilbireen, affectionately called Dili, remained cheerful and self-sufficient, cuddling his blanket and playing peek-a-boo, exhibiting more independence than many other children his age, from feeding himself to brushing his own teeth.

With help from Scott we managed to get Dilbireen and some other Iraqi children, medical care in Boston and Minneapolis, where Shriners Hospitals for Children agreed to treat him and other injured refugee children at no cost. The family had a plan: with the charity's assistance, Dilbireen and his father Ajeel would go to the US for the boy's first round of reconstructive surgery in October, while Flosa, who was pregnant, would remain in Iraq.

Together with Ajeel and Dr Shirzad Khaleel, our medical coordinator, I accompanied Dilbireen and three other severely injured children on their journey to the US.

Dilbireen's treatment went well, but the family's travel plans didn't unfold so smoothly. As Dilbireen was recovering from the first round of surgery in the States, Ajeel flew back to Iraq for the baby's birth, then planned to return with Flosa and their newborn so the family could reunite for the rest of Dilbireen's treatment. Flosa gave birth to their second child in November, and when it came time to name their new son, the family thought of the country caring for their first baby boy.

'America is helping us to do surgery on our boy,' Ajeel said in an interview from Iraq. 'We want to show our appreciation to America for what they are doing.'

They named the newborn Trump.

Ajeel and Flosa planned to join Dilbireen in time for his next operation. They already had visas to travel to the United States, but before Donald Trump took office, they submitted an application for a passport and visa for their newborn.

Their application was denied, and then the visas they already had were revoked. President Trump had signed an executive order to prevent refugees from entering the country for 120 days. Immigrants from seven predominantly Muslim nations – Iran, Iraq, Syria, Sudan, Libya, Yemen and Somalia – were included, and Dilbireen and his family, who counted as refugees, were among those impacted. The letter denying them entry stated that Ajeel and Flosa were unable either to sufficiently demonstrate strong ties to their home country that would compel them to leave the US at the end of their stay or clearly establish that their stay would be temporary.

Ajeel and Flosa quickly submitted new applications to the US consulate in Erbil, Iraq, but were refused entry to the US consulate itself. Dilbireen, who was starting to show signs of separation anxiety from his mother, could either remain in the US without his family or return to Iraq without undergoing any more operations.

'Though his injuries aren't life-threatening,' Shriners Hospitals said in a statement, 'Dilbireen will need ongoing surgeries to further improve the appearance and function of his face. The next step will be to work on scarring around his eyes, and to begin to reconstruct his nose.' Dilbireen's doctors advised that it was best to do these types of procedures while a child's face was still growing, so that scar tissue can be released, enabling as much normal growth and development to occur as possible. He was scheduled to have another operation in Boston on 25 January, but the appointment was cancelled as the doctors felt it would be too cruel to go forward without the emotional support that a toddler needs from his parents. Dilbireen's case was unique, so I was hoping that his parents' visas would be approved on compassionate grounds. If they were refused, it would mean I'd have to take the little boy back to Iraq without treatment, which was out of the question.

Fortunately, CNN Health had been covering the story from day one and with the pressure from the public, Dilbireen was eventually reunited with his family in Boston.

Upon my return to the UK I received a call from Yazda, a charity that had been set up to advocate on behalf of the Yazidi people. I was asked to help facilitate a meeting for Nadia Murad with Prime Minister David Cameron in the hope that the British government would recognise the genocide of the Yazidis in northern Iraq. Nadia had become a figurehead for her community after having been abducted alongside thousands of other Yazidi women and girls during the genocide carried out by ISIS in August 2014. She was taken from her home town of Kocho and held as a sex slave for three months before finally managing to escape. Since her release she'd become an advocate for the Yazidis, meeting with global leaders to raise awareness of the genocide against them.

David Cameron wasn't able to see us, but he arranged for us to see Richard Harrington, the minister with responsibility for Syrian refugees. I met Nadia in a small café in Westminster opposite the Home Office prior to our appointment with Harrington, and as I sat down, my heart ached as she looked so incredibly vulnerable. I'd bought her a small necklace with two interconnecting circles to symbolise infinity for her people, and as I explained what it meant she smiled the saddest smile I've ever seen.

During the meeting with Harrington and his colleagues we talked about the fact that over a thousand children, including many orphans, were now living in refugee camps just fifteen miles from ISIS-controlled territory. They were unable to receive medical treatment or psychological help for the trauma they had suffered and we were hoping it might be possible to bring some of them to the UK under the Children at Risk initiative. At the same time, Nadia asked Harrington if the British government would recognise the genocide of the Yazidi people, which could help protect them from further harm. Harrington explained that it would be a very long slow process and by the time we left his office I wasn't feeling very hopeful. It was shades of Bosnia all over again, with politicians wringing their hands while looking the other way.

In fact, none of the orphaned Yazidi children came to Britain and it wasn't until August 2023 that the UK formally acknowledged the atrocities committed against the Yazidi people by ISIS in 2014 as an act of genocide.

38

It was June 2017 and the battle for west Mosul raged. Iraqi government and US-led coalition forces advanced slowly under intense fire, house by house, in the dust and heat of the symbolic capital of ISIS, the last city in Iraq the group controlled. Each day we set off to the muster point in our 4×4 ambulance to collect the injured children, zigzagging around potholes and piles of rubble, burned-out cars and scores of corpses, some of them civilians, others ISIS fighters clad in black.

Survivors appeared out of the ruined buildings like ghosts emerging from the rubble, their faces telling of years of suffering and desperation. The occupation had resulted in massive damage to the city's infrastructure, with bridges, water facilities and power plants completely destroyed, so there was no electricity or running water. There had also been widespread torture and other human-rights abuses, and the death of many civilians who refused to abide by Sharia law.

East Mosul was now under the control of the pro-government forces, but the 100,000 civilians still trapped on the west side of the city were being used by ISIS as human shields, with those who tried to leave being targeted by snipers. The pro-government forces were met with fierce resistance from the ISIS fighters, and they relied heavily on wildly inaccurate and destructive IRAMs (improvised rocket-assisted munitions), wreaking havoc in densely populated areas and taking the lives of countless people.

As we drove through the labyrinthine streets, people held babies in the air and cried out for help. My job was to collect the injured children and drive them, together with their mothers and siblings, to our Trauma Stabilisation Point (TSP) housed in a small rundown building in Abar, close to Al-Yarmouk bridge.

There were twelve beds in the TSP, and four of these were assigned to our patients, the others belonging to the Iraqi Army and reserved for their wounded soldiers. Major Mohammed, an officer serving in the 9th Division, was tasked with the running of the TSP, although he was actually a veterinarian. While there appeared to be a mountain of dressings, bandages and other consumables necessary to treat blast injuries, there were no paediatric medicines or equipment. We'd purchased everything that we thought might be needed from a private hospital in Erbil and brought it with us in the back of our ambulance, planning to restock whenever we were able to make the 180-kilometre round trip from Mosul.

I was joined on the mission in Iraq by Dr Marino Andolina, an Italian paediatrician and immunologist from Trieste, and a brave young Canadian paramedic called Ryan Ahlgren. We also employed a driver called Lawned, a Turkman from Kurdistan who drove me to the muster point each day.

Marino was in his late sixties but he looked about forty-five, with thick greying hair and a neatly trimmed goatee beard. With his gravelly voice and a wicked sense of humour, he was always ready with a clever remark that would catch people off guard. He was the former secretary of the Italian Paediatric Immunology Group, a former director of the Bone Marrow Department in Trieste and the first paediatrician to perform a bone marrow transplant in Italy. Marino had volunteered in several disaster areas, including three earthquakes and a tsunami, and from 1989 onwards he volunteered his services in various war zones including Lebanon, the former Yugoslavia, Afghanistan, Darfur and Somalia. He is one of the bravest and funniest men I have ever met, but he is also a complete nightmare; every time we work together I swear, 'Never again!'

We partnered with a Kurdish NGO called Doctors Aid Medical Activities (DAMA), based in Erbil, whose CEO, Dr Nabaz, helped us purchase medical supplies and equipment, as well as camp beds for our team to sleep on. We were sharing the mission with a German NGO called Cadus, who sent six volunteer medics. They'd arrived a few days before us and in the garage – which would serve as our living quarters – they'd installed a generator. They'd also already set up their camp beds by the time we got there, and the only spaces left were near the back next to a car covered in a thick layer of dust. One of the medics warned us not touch the vehicle as it hadn't been 'cleaned'. He wasn't referring to the dust, though, but to the fact that it hadn't been checked for explosives. ISIS had a habit of setting up booby traps using IEDs before they abandoned a building, and the city was littered with unexploded ordnance.

Ever the gentleman, Marino had chosen the space closest to the vehicle. I was constantly worried that he might inadvertently roll over or reach out and touch the car in his sleep. Fortunately, he had a habit of sleeping on his back with his hands clasped across his chest like a recumbent medieval effigy, but he was always on call, and whenever someone from the clinic shouted his name he'd leap up off the bed, causing me to hold my breath for a few moments as I waited for the explosion.

There was a flight of stone steps near my bed, and at the top was a small concrete platform where someone had made an improvised toilet using a bucket filled with mud and a plastic toilet seat balanced on the top. We had plenty of bottled water, but it was 45°C outside so we were constantly dehydrated. Needless to say, I was strangely grateful for this, as perching on an unstable bucket with a 20ft drop below was not ideal, and I only went upstairs when it was absolutely necessary.

One evening as darkness was falling, Lawned suggested we

head back to base as there were was no one left at the muster point. As we pulled up outside the garage, an explosion suddenly ripped through the building across the street, rocking our vehicle. Someone shouted that ISIS militants had broken through the lines, so we quickly made our way inside. Black smoke blotted out the moon and we could hear bursts of machine-gun fire, indicating they were getting closer.

We were told to stay as quiet as possible and not to use our torches, to avoid alerting the fighters to our presence. I was horrified at the thought of being captured, having seen the propaganda videos of foreign aid workers in orange jumpsuits being beheaded. These acts were part of the broader campaign of terror aimed at spreading fear, intimidating enemies and gaining international attention. ISIS has targeted civilians, journalists, aid workers and military personnel in its propaganda videos, which were widely condemned for their graphic violence. As the sound of gunfire got louder, I sat there in the dark, imagining various horrible scenarios involving severed heads.

There was a large hole in the brickwork to the rear of the building, and I was informed that this would have to serve as our escape route if necessary, although I'd no idea where it would lead us. As we sat there wondering whether we'd actually make it out alive, the screen on my smartphone suddenly lit up. I realised I'd forgotten to switch it off, so I quickly moved further into the shadows. A photo of a large spider trapped inside a glass tumbler appeared on the screen with the words MUM HELP! The message was from Billie.

Not wanting her to worry about me, I told her that I'd be based in Erbil throughout the mission, so as far as she was concerned I was still there. She'd no idea we were in Mosul or of the danger we were in, and I didn't want to scare her, so shielding the screen beneath my clothes I wrote 'slide a piece of card under the glass then carry it to the window'. She texted back 'ok Mum, thanks x'.

The Canadian journalist Lyse Doucet was stationed in Mosul with the BBC and had come to interview me a few days earlier. I still had her in my contacts, so I sent her a private message asking her if she could connect me with someone who could advise us what to do. She kindly put me in touch with Michael Pregent, a former US soldier and security advisor, who wrote, 'You should leave immediately, the Iraqi Army is not good at holding cleared areas. Make contact with the military and have them secure your exfil.' He gave me the number of the commander of the Peshmerga, but after a couple of hours an Iraqi soldier came to the garage entrance and announced that they'd managed to push the fighters back and it was safe, for now. The next morning they brought a bulldozer to dig a large trench outside the garage to prevent further attacks. They also parked a Humvee with a mounted machine gun directly outside the entrance of the clinic.

On our way to the front line one morning I noticed what looked like a very large cloud in the distance and assumed it was dust thrown up by a convoy. A mother and two children with light shrapnel injuries had arrived at the muster point and were now seated in the back of our vehicle, but as we prepared to leave Lawned asked me if I could smell anything. I sniffed the air and told him it reminded me of the smell at a swimming pool. He looked horrified and shouted, 'Gas! We need to go!'

We had gas masks back at the garage but none in the vehicle, and he shouted at me to hurry up and get inside so we could leave. As I was about to open the passenger door, I saw a woman coming round the corner carrying a toddler who appeared to be badly burned. I couldn't just leave them, so I raced across the concourse and helped them to the vehicle.

By the time we got back to the unit my eyes were streaming and I couldn't stop coughing. Someone told me there were four soldiers in the clinic who'd been caught in a chemical attack released by a drone that morning. It was thought to be chlorine gas and they had the same symptoms as me. Marino was busy in the clinic and it wasn't until several hours later that he came into the garage and realised what had happened. By that time I was lying on my camp bed struggling to breathe. He checked my oxygen saturation levels with an oximeter and looked shocked as the reading was 87 per cent, which is quite low. There wasn't much he could do to help me, and he was needed in the clinic, so I just had to wait until the worst of the effects wore off. It took a couple of days before I was actually fit enough to work, and I still have saturation levels of around 94 per cent, which is probably a result of the damage to my lungs from the chemicals I inhaled that day.

Word soon spread that there was a paediatrician in the facility, so in addition to the injured children we were bringing from the front line, there was a constant queue of mothers with children outside the door. Most of them hadn't seen a doctor since ISIS insurgents captured Mosul in 2014, and it was clear that while many of their problems could easily be treated in normal circumstances, here in the midst of a war it was a very different story. Doctors and field medics often lack the specific training required to support children during critical events, and lives can be lost due to a lack of paediatric expertise.

Children have a unique anatomy and physiology, which, if not taken into consideration by the medical team, can lead to life-threatening complications in their treatment. For example, a child's ribcage is still flexible (made of cartilage instead of adult bone) and transmits any sudden impacting forces to the chest organs (heart, lungs, major vessels). Following a blast injury, even in the absence of any rib fractures, a child can sustain severe damage to their heart and lungs, requiring acute and lifesaving procedures such as placements of tubes directly through the ribcage to drain any blood or air.

In addition to this, when a child has suffered a burn injury or loss of blood, it's crucial to give intravenous fluids, although too much or too little can be fatal. Estimating the amount of fluid that's needed must be done immediately, based on the child's weight, without using scales and by a doctor trained in these calculations. Placing intravenous access (drips, lines) to give fluids and medications is much more difficult in children than in adults due to their smaller size and differences in anatomy, so guidance to find appropriate sites is needed. Shock can be difficult to recognise in children on account of their ability to compensate for fluid loss. This can create an illusion of stability, which, if not recognised and treated appropriately, will be followed by a precipitous deterioration and death.

In areas where the health infrastructure has been damaged, more fatalities occur due to disease and other factors than to battle. Children require treatment for all kinds of acute or chronic illnesses but without an effective healthcare system and dedicated paediatric care, common paediatric conditions can't be treated, and children die from curable diseases such as respiratory tract infections, diarrhoea, malaria as well as vaccine-preventable diseases.

Some of the children we saw needed specialist help so I spoke to Professor Eitan Kerem, head of the Department of Paediatrics at the Hadassah Medical Centre, who connected me with his colleagues via WhatsApp. Every time a patient presented with symptoms that required specialist advice, I'd upload the child's details, together with photos and videos, and we managed to help hundreds of children that way.

The battle for Mosul officially ended in July 2017, when Iraqi Prime Minister Haider al-Abadi declared victory. However, this came at significant cost, with large parts of Mosul left in ruins, a staggering number of civilian casualties, and thousands of homes, hospitals and historical sites destroyed. The liberation of Mosul marked a turning point in the fight against ISIS, significantly weakening their control in Iraq, but the city's reconstruction remains a long and ongoing process.

39

The battle to liberate Hawija, the last ISIS enclave in central Iraq, began in late September 2017. Iraqi forces, backed by the Popular Mobilisation Forces (PMF) and a US-led coalition, launched an offensive to recapture the town. It had fallen to ISIS in June 2014 and became a strategic and symbolic stronghold, due to its proximity to key cities like Kirkuk and Baghdad, and was used as a base for launching attacks in the region. The campaign involved ground forces, heavy artillery and air support aiming to clear the militants from their defensive positions.

As the offensive began, people were faced with the choice of remaining in the midst of the battle or braving the snipers as they tried to flee. The operation progressed rapidly, and by the time we arrived Iraqi forces were declaring they'd successfully retaken the area from ISIS control. Civilians who managed to escape the fighting had to travel through minefields to cross the river to safety. We parked the ambulance at the crossing point to provide emergency medical aid for children who were suffering from dehydration in temperatures of 35°C and above.

While we waited on the hillside, Brigadier General Dr Kamal Kirkuki arrived and suggested we set up a paediatric unit at Dibis, a transit camp for refugees on the outskirts of Kirkuk. The camp was in the compound of the Kurdish security and intelligence services, known as Asayish, and was made up of hundreds of UN containers that could in total accommodate up to four thousand women and children. When the trucks transporting refugees arrived, the men were separated from the women and children and taken into the Asayish headquarters.

Dr Nabaz, the CEO of DAMA, had sent a small truck with general paediatric supplies and equipment as well as a couple of camp beds and an electric kettle. We also had medicines provided by MedAir, who also supplied a nurse to work alongside Marino for a couple of days a week.

Mothers queued outside our door day and night, desperate for their children to see a doctor. Some of the children had walked barefoot across the mountains and had snake bites and scorpion stings, some had shrapnel wounds and burns, but most were suffering from throat infections, scabies, or dehydration and malnutrition.

Among the refugees were some blond- and red-haired children with blue or green eyes who could have been Yazidis. Children who were kidnapped by ISIS in 2014 were later sold to local Sunni families in Tal Afar before the fighters fled to Syria, and some of these families ended up in Hawija. It was also possible they were the children of foreigners who came from Europe to join the Caliphate, but there was no reliable way to tell. I took a few photos that I emailed to the UNHCR and Yazda, an organisation founded by Nadia Murad's brother Murad Ishmail. Organisations like Yazda and the Kurdistan regional government created centralised databases to track missing individuals, and these included details like names, ages and photos. DNA testing was used to identify children who were unable to recall the names of their families or their origins, but this was only possible if the family member was able to identify the exact location of the child and made a claim. Within a few days the children I'd identified as possible abductees were herded into buses late at night and taken to IDP camps set up for ISIS-affiliated families. I was told the names of the camps were Leylan, Haj Ali and possibly Jedaa camp, which held thousands of individuals, mainly women and children associated with or related to ISIS members.

Hundreds of suspected Islamic State fighters had fled towards Kurdish-held lines and surrendered to avoid summary execution at the hands of vengeful Sunni tribesmen and Shi'ite Muslim paramilitaries trained and armed by Iran. Our container, which served both as a clinic and our sleeping quarters, was situated directly opposite the building belonging to the Asayish, and each day we saw trucks arriving in the compound carrying hundreds of men with long dark hair and bedraggled beards. I was standing outside when the latest truckload of prisoners arrived, and I noticed that one of them was staring down at me with intense hatred. He couldn't possibly know me, so I guessed he simply hated the fact that I wasn't wearing a burka. Given the brutality and violence these men had inflicted on anyone who crossed their path, I found his piercing stare quite chilling.

Every time I wanted to have a wash or use the toilet, we had to enter the building close to where these men were being held in tightly packed cells. Marino would march ahead of me holding a toilet roll aloft so the guards would understand that he was accompanying me to the roof, where the bathroom was situated. We had to step over the legs of some of the prisoners who were sitting on the floor in the corridor waiting to be 'interviewed', but the only other option was to use one of the portable toilets at the rear of the camp. Apart from the long queue to use the facilities, the lack of adequate cleaning, water and proper waste-disposal systems meant the smell was overpowering, so I preferred to take my chances with ISIS.

By the end of the first week we were seeing up to a hundred children every day, with many of them coming to us for help in the middle of the night for although Médecins Sans Frontières clinic was close by, the staff had to close for security reasons at around 5 p.m. every day.

We spent about three weeks in the camp in Dibis, and during that time we treated over two thousand children. Some of the children were suffering from scabies, and it wasn't long before

Marino became infected. He was scratching himself constantly and was unable to examine the patients for fear of infecting them, so instead he'd simply lie on his camp bed and call out instructions. He treated himself with ivermectin, which in England is used to treat infestations in animals, but I was very relieved when it worked, for sharing such a confined space with someone who's continuously scratching himself like some kind of mad dog is far from ideal.

One day we received a text from Dr Nabas warning us that al-Hashd al-Shaabi, also known as the Popular Mobilisation Forces (PMF), were approaching Dibis. Al-Hashd al-Shaabi were formed in 2014 as a response to the rise of ISIS, with the goal of defending Iraq from the group's advances. Many of the Shia militias within al-Hashd al-Shaabi were well-established groups with close ties to Iran. Some of these militias tended to engage in sectarian violence, particularly against Sunnis, and there were reports of widespread human rights violations. Sunni civilians were often accused of being ISIS sympathisers or collaborators, leading to extrajudicial killings, torture, detentions and destruction of property. We were told to pack up and leave the camp immediately, but most of the refugees had left by then anyway, transported in buses to UN camps in Kurdistan or northern Iraq.

We'd arranged to move our mission to Sinjar in northern Iraq, where the Yazidis were starting to return home. They were in urgent need of medical help as none of the major aid organisations had deployed there yet. First, though, I needed to return home for a break and to see Billie. When we arrived at the checkpoint on the outskirts of Kirkuk there was a long line of vehicles waiting to pass. Word had spread that al-Hashd al-Shaabi were on their way and people were desperate to leave. We were worried that if we didn't manage to leave now, we could end up stuck there indefinitely as the checkpoint was about to close. We handed over our passports to the soldiers and Marino explained that we'd been helping children fleeing from ISIS, but they were not impressed. I suddenly remembered that I was carrying Brigadier General Dr Kamal Kirkuki's business card, so I handed it to them and showed them photos of Marino and me with the general when we met with him in Dibis. They looked at each other, then waved us through.

Within hours of arriving at our headquarters in Erbil I began to feel quite ill, so I was relieved when Lesli, our field coordinator, managed to book the last seat on a flight from Erbil to Baghdad. International flights from the city had been suspended, so the only way to get a flight home was via the Iraqi capital.

I landed in the early hours and the airport was virtually empty. My flight to London was several hours later and I spent most of the time in the toilet with terrible stomach cramps. By the time I arrived in the UK I was very weak and dehydrated, and it transpired that I'd contracted dysentery. I also noticed that I had developed an angry red rash on my chest that was itching constantly and realised I had scabies. Fortunately, Marino thought this might happen and had given me a course of ivermectin tablets just in case.

40

Following the three-year battle against ISIS, the Yazidis began returning to their homes in Sinjar, but much of the infrastructure such as water and electricity had been badly disrupted. The general health of the population was extremely poor, with malnutrition responsible for many chronic illnesses.

Children were suffering from a range of health issues, largely due to the lack of healthcare, displacement and poor living conditions. Many of the families had been living in temporary camp shelters with inadequate ventilation and no heating, leading to high rates of respiratory infections such as bronchitis and pneumonia. The lack of clean water and proper sanitation led to the spread of waterborne diseases, especially diarrhoea, which tends to be life-threatening in malnourished children.

I'd posted online about the urgent need for medical help in Sinjar and a wonderful woman called Sarah Griffin, based in the United States, offered to help. Sarah was a lawyer, but she'd taken time out to care for her two little boys and was keen to do whatever she could to help the children in Iraq. She introduced me to Laura Webster, an investment analyst who worked for her husband's company, Coltrane Asset Management, and these two women, together with Heather James, became the backbone of our charity, helping to fund the numerous missions that would have been impossible without their help.

Marino had a short break in Italy before meeting me at the airport in Istanbul on the way to Kurdistan in February. We were joined in Erbil by our fixer Lesli, who was working as a volunteer for a Christian NGO providing support to Yazidi women who'd escaped from ISIS. Originally from Minnesota in the US, Lesli was now based in Erbil and had proved herself to be a godsend during our previous missions in northern Iraq so I was delighted when she offered to accompany us to Sinjar. Lesli was very tall and softly spoken. She had a wonderfully calming influence, especially on Marino. When asked to describe her he said, 'Our angel is a model of evangelical fundamentalism'.

On our way to Sinjar we stopped off in Duhok, where I'd arranged to meet with Mourad, a Yazidi from Sinjar with a narrow face and soulful dark eyes. He had managed to escape when ISIS invaded and lived in one of the many IDP camps that were housing Yazidis in Duhok. When the town was liberated he began working at the hospital and had offered to be our coordinator. He introduced us to Dr Kifah, the director of Sinjar General Hospital. Following the Kurdish independence referendum, Sinjar became particularly volatile on account of the complex dynamics between the Kurdish forces, the Iraqi government and the various militias, and many NGOs left the area because of the closing of checkpoints and problems between local warring factions. Dr Kifah, a Kurdish Muslim, was accused of collaborating with ISIS and had received death threats, and despite being the director of the hospital he hadn't returned to the town since ISIS left. There was an urgent need for medical supplies and equipment, and I explained that we were hoping to establish a paediatric unit in Sinjar to help bridge the gap until the major NGOs were able to take over. First, however, we'd need his approval.

The landscape bore the scars of intense fighting and occupation. Many of the buildings had been reduced to rubble or were pockmarked with bullet holes, and the streets were filled with debris, with abandoned vehicles rusting at the side of the road. Fields and farmlands were neglected, overgrown or destroyed, and many areas were unsafe because of landmines and unexploded ordnance. The haunting absence of people was one of Sinjar's most striking features. Once a thriving community, many residents had either been killed, kidnapped or had escaped. Some of the families who'd been living in makeshift camps in Kurdistan had started to return home, but entire neighbourhoods had been levelled or heavily damaged by bombing and shelling by coalition forces. Sinjar General Hospital had been damaged, with only a few of its rooms now able to be used. ISIS fighters had looted vital medical equipment, everything from operating tables and scanners to consumables like syringes, dressings and drugs. A charity called Bring Hope provided some basic drugs and equipment, but most of the medical staff had departed, and those who remained were living on the premises and working 24/7.

There was only one emergency doctor, a young Yazidi called Hussein. Although he was on permanent duty, Dr Hussein hadn't been paid for months. We offered to employ him, together with three nurses who were also working without any pay. Next to the main hospital was a one-storey building that had also been damaged, with no glass in the windows and a large black hole in the wall used as an ISIS machine-gun nest. ISIS imprisoned some of the kidnapped Yazidi girls in the building, and they were either killed or abducted when the group fled across the border to Syria.

This building was freezing cold, with no electricity or running water, but there were many children in need of help and no paediatricians available, so Kifah had suggested we use it as a temporary paediatric unit. We began by setting up a clinic in one of the smaller rooms and within a few hours over a hundred children were queuing with their families in the corridor. Many of the patients were suffering from common childhood diseases such as asthma and eczema, chickenpox, bronchiolitis, diarrhoea and vomiting. Most of them had missed routine vaccinations due to the instability in the region, leading to outbreaks of preventable diseases like mumps, measles and diphtheria.

Like other populations with a history of isolation and endogamy who don't marry outside of their community, Yazidis tend to have a higher incidence of congenital diseases. There were a number with children with serious blood disorders such as beta thalassemia, a condition that requires regular blood transfusions, as well as those with neurological disorders and congenital deformities like cleft lip and cleft palate, scoliosis and heart defects. A few of the patients presented with historical injuries such as burns and blast injuries. One fourteen-year-old boy had lost his left arm and had his right arm severely damaged when an ISIS fighter threw a grenade at him, shouting 'Catch!' We referred him to our paediatric team via WhatsApp, and one of the specialists advised us to arrange a scar release z-plasty to release the tension in his damaged arm and give him some mobility.

We also received a lot of babies. One little girl, just six months old, was diagnosed with hydrocephalus and was now presenting with symptoms of meningitis. Dr Hussein was advised to insert a shunt to release the fluid, but the child's head circumference was increasing and she had a fever that was causing convulsions. Our remote emergency specialist suggested treating her with vancomycin and referring her to the nearest neurological unit as a matter of urgency. We had a two-week-old baby who presented with a respiratory infection associated with severe cyanosis. He was being treated for pneumonia but an ultrasound revealed that he had a congenital heart problem.

We also came across several cases of leishmaniasis, a parasitic disease caused by protozoa from the genus *Leishmania*. It's transmitted to humans through the bites of infected female sandflies and can lead to skin ulcers or sores at the site of the bite that can develop into open wounds, which often take months to heal. In some cases the children were covered in multiple sores; Marino treated these with paromomycin, which was highly effective.

Because it was so cold in February and our generator was broken, whenever Marino used the mobile ultrasound device that we'd brought with us he had to be very quick as we couldn't remove our patients' clothing for more than a few minutes. We worked using flashlights for the first few days while we arranged for the generators to be fixed. In the meantime, Jane Arraf from NPR radio in the United States had come to Sinjar to do a story. She was travelling with her colleague Cecilia Uddén, a foreign correspondent for Sveriges Radio in Sweden. They needed somewhere to stay so we offered them a room in our apartment. We ordered some wonderful local dishes like biryani and kubba mosul, a meat pie made of bulgar dough that's mixed with spiced ground beef and stuffed with ground lamb and fresh onions. During dinner Marino, a notorious lothario, who basically adores women, used his Italian charm to great effect. This wasn't the case with me, though. In fact, when we first met at the airport in Turkey on our way to Iraq, he looked a bit disappointed and said, 'Oh, I'd hoped you were blonde – and perhaps a bit younger!'

The next day they came to the hospital to interview us about our work with the Yazidi children and the fact that we were using telemedicine for remote consultations with paediatric experts.

Before they left they brought us two heaters that they paid for out of their own pockets. This enabled Marino to examine his patients more thoroughly without worrying about the cold. A couple of weeks later the generator arrived and was soon providing power to the paediatric unit, as well as several houses close by who somehow managed to connect to our system. In spite of the lack of basic supplies and equipment, we treated hundreds of children, uploading the details of around a third of them to our remote paediatric team for advice on the rare forms of leukaemia and other types of cancer, cardiac problems and kidney disease that we encountered.

Word soon spread among the other aid agencies, and we were visited by teams from Médecins Sans Frontières and the ICRC, who told us that they were planning to set up their own clinics in the area. At first this seemed like great news, until we realised that it would take about six months before they could actually begin their operation. This meant we'd continue to be the only clinic specialising in paediatrics, so I returned to the UK to raise some funds towards the refurbishment of our building. With funding from United to Assist Refugees UK and Coltrane Asset Management, Mourad was able to employ a builder and a decorator to repair the holes in the wall and ceilings and replace the glass in the windows. He found some volunteers to paint the interior, as well as an electrician to repair the wiring and install spotlights in the corridor and the wards. We also equipped the wards with hospital beds and vital equipment such as oxygen concentrators, and within a couple of weeks the unit was completely transformed. Hearing that there was a working paediatric unit in Sinjar, more families began returning home from the camps in Duhok, and during those few months we managed to help thousands of children.

41

The faces of the children I saw among the refugees from Hawija haunted me and I contacted the UNHCR to see if they could manage to trace any of them, but they were unable to help, explaining that I'd need a family member to come forward with a letter from a local judge. Of course, I wasn't able to locate a family member without knowing the name of the child so it seemed I'd reached a dead end.

I contacted the abductees office in Duhok and discovered there were 2,800 missing women and children on their list. The Yazidi community relied heavily on family members and tribal networks to exchange information about missing persons, and survivor testimony provided clues to the whereabouts of children, helping search teams narrow down potential locations. The DNA techniques to help find missing people that I described in Chapter 39 were developed by the International Committee for Missing Persons, and I was put in contact with a Yazidi called Ali who worked with them. He explained that they were mainly focusing on identifying bodies that were found in mass graves so he couldn't really help, but he suggested I contact a group of men known as the 'smugglers', who would act as brokers between ISIS and the Yazidi families.

A man called Khalil came to my hotel and told me that most Yazidis were scattered across Syria, Iraq and Turkey. Getting them back would cost around $20,000 per person in ransom money, which families often didn't have, but the Kurdistan government had arranged to pay part of this and the family would pay the rest. While we were together his phone never stopped ringing, as Yazidi families would contact him to ask for help finding their relatives When I showed him the photographs of the children I was searching for, he told me we'd need their names and location, which of course I didn't have.

Hearing of my efforts to trace the missing children, Lyse Doucet offered to accompany me to northern Iraq with a film crew to highlight the situation, as the more people who knew about the children, the more likely it was that some might be found. I called Breen Tahseen, the Yazidi diplomat, who put me in touch with Hadi Baba Sheikh.

He was the brother of Baba Sheikh Khurto Hajji Ismail, the spiritual leader of the Yazidis, who, following the genocide in 2014, had declared that all Yazidis, women, girls, men and children who were captured by ISIS and forced to convert to Islam should be accepted back into the community. In 2017 Baba Sheikh was honoured by the Iraqi parliament and the United Nations for his critical role in supporting Yazidi survivors of sexual violence and facilitating their recovery and reintegration into the community. After drinking tea with the charismatic leader at his headquarters in Shekhan, I was invited to Hadi's office and showed him photos of the children I'd seen on the hillside. Hadi explained that it would be difficult to do anything without some form of proof that they were Yazidis, and to do that we'd need to match them with their families. He told me how difficult it was to trace children, as many of them had been taken to Syria by the militants to be trained as fighters.

Ali told me about a family he'd interviewed who were searching for five family members: their mother, father, elder brother and sister, and the youngest child Sabir, who was just fifteen days old when they were captured. The family were taken to Tal Afar, a town on one of the strategic routes between Mosul and Syria.

Most of the residents were Shia Turkmen, many of whom had fled after it was seized. The town was finally liberated by the Iraqi Kurdish Peshmerga forces in August 2017, but as the militants fled, the younger children (250 of them were under nine years old) were distributed among local families.

I showed Hadi a photo of Sabir that had been posted on a Facebook page by a Yazidi policeman who'd tried to match children with their families.

Hadi had worked tirelessly to try to find missing Yazidi children, and he sometimes received calls from local police if they suspected a child might be Yazidi. On one occasion he was told about a group of fifteen children who'd been brought to the Centre for Unaccompanied Children in Hamam al-Alil to the south of Mosul run by Save the Children. Their job was to try to reunite the children with their families, and those who couldn't be traced were sent to orphanages in Mosul or Baghdad. Hadi told me that he had driven straight to the centre but on arrival at the gate he was told that the deputy director wasn't there and he was ordered to leave. Fortunately, the policeman who'd contacted Hadi had filmed and photographed the children, and was the one that posted their images on Facebook. After Sabir's sister recognised her brother, her uncle received a letter from the judge in Dohuk but was told that he'd need permission from the court in Mosul before contacting Sabir. He went to the court to ask the judge to help him but was immediately thrown out of the session. He then went to the UNHCR office, and one of their advisors got permission for him to go to the orphanage in Mosul. When he got there he was told the boy had been moved to Baghdad.

I showed the video to Hadi, who pointed at two little boys and said they were brothers called Rasul and Josef Muhammed. ISIS members would usually give the kidnapped children Muslim names, so this was no surprise, but I knew that Sabir only had one brother, a thirteen-year-old boy who was still missing and believed to be in Turkey.

I'd arranged to meet with Lyse Doucet at her hotel in Duhok and the following day she and her crew accompanied me to Dawudiya camp, where Sabir's sisters were waiting to meet us. The three youngest girls were aged one, three and five when they were kidnapped. Silvana, who was now seven, had recently been reunited with her family after being traced to Turkey. She was found when police raided a hospital where a doctor was preparing to remove a kidney. This was becoming common practice, with many children being trafficked for their organs; these would sell for between $50,000 and $60,000 apiece, often to the to buyers in the Arab Gulf states.

I showed them the video of the children, and Asia immediately identified Sabir. She was the one who took care of him while they were in captivity, and it was only during the liberation of Tal Afar that they were separated.

After the meeting I contacted Mubarak Maman, the international head of child safeguarding at Save the Children, who immediately authorised an investigation but he was told that there was no records of Sabir or the boy called Josef ever having been there.

We managed to get someone to identify the Yazidi policeman and talked to him on the phone. He was clearly quite scared, and before he would talk we had to assure him that we wouldn't reveal his name. He said that while he wasn't sure about the boy they called Josef, he was adamant that Sabir was a Yazidi. I decided to launch a campaign on Twitter, and after a few weeks I was contacted by Nafiseh Kohnavard, a BBC journalist who was a making a documentary about the Yazidis. She'd heard about my search for Sabir and told me that she'd actually accompanied these children to the centre together with the police in 2017. She'd filmed their arrival at the camp, and she shared this video with me. Sabir and Josef were found in a building together with a group of Shia children. They were being used as human shields by ISIS, who abandoned them as Iraqi forces closed in.

They were moved to the Save the Children centre in Hamam al-Halil, where they were interviewed by the Yazidi policeman. He asked them their names and where they came from but Sabir, whose head was bandaged, didn't respond at all and looked a bit dazed. He was being cared for by one of the girls, who said she thought he was a Yazidi.

I sent the video to Mubarak, who confronted the staff again and this time they managed to find the missing documents confirming that the boys had indeed been there, and they were able to provide some details. They told Mubarak that a man had turned up at the centre with a reunification order and claimed that he was their father. The order was issued by the judge in Mosul, the same official who'd refused to help Sabir's uncle and had him removed from the court.

When we finally traced Sabir, the man who claimed him refused to have a DNA test. I asked Mubarak how it was possible for the staff to allow a man to enter their premises and remove two children, and he explained that the reunification order was granted through a court of law. Of course, this didn't account for why in July 2017 Hadi was refused entry to the camp, or why eighteen months later the staff were able to produce a list of all the children apart from these two boys. When I asked Mubarak what could be done to prove that the boy was indeed Sabir, he suggested that I contact the judge and ask him to issue an order demanding a DNA test be done. It took several months, but we eventually managed to locate the judge, who insisted there was no record of any court order for these two children.

I was contacted by the Kurdish president's office, asking how they could help with this investigation, so I sent them all the relevant information, including the name of the man claiming to be the boys' father. I was hoping that they could deal with this and be the ones to take credit for bringing Sabir back to the family, as this would greatly help improve the level of trust between the Kurdish government and the Yazidi community, which had been under strain since the Kurds had failed to protect the Yazidis from ISIS.

Mubarak has given me details of the man who had claimed the two boys, and although we weren't able to contact him directly, a colleague of mine found him on Facebook, where he'd posted photos of himself with his two 'sons'. Prior to July 2017, when he'd turned up at the centre with the reunification order, there was nothing to indicate that he had any children. After checking further, we discovered that he was actually a Kurdish officer serving in the Iraqi Army. If this were correct, then it would account for all the secrecy and why we kept coming up against dead ends.

Human rights lawyer Amal Clooney, who was representing one of Sabir's relatives in a case against her abductors, offered to help, and we also had a representative from both Yazda and Nadia Murad's charity Nadia's Initiative. A local lawyer agreed to take on the case pro bono, but after several weeks it became clear that he was worried about the potential repercussions and we didn't hear from him again.

We'll never know who exactly was involved in this case or why. Was it a conspiracy between the judge who issued the order giving custody of the two boys, and the member of staff at the centre, who simply handed them over? The boys were only at the centre for a few days when they were claimed. Did money change hands between those who were involved? I'm guessing that this must have been the case, but we had no way of proving it, so we finally had to give up.

Sabir was three years old when they found him in Mosul. 'Sabir' means 'patience' in Arabic, but being too young to remember his real name or where he came from, I don't suppose he'll ever be reunited with his family. I often wonder how many more of the 1,138 children who are still missing will ever know who they really are.

42

The war in Syria began with an act of youthful defiance that ignited widespread unrest. In March 2011, during the early days of the Arab Spring, a group of teenage boys in the southern city of Daraa scrawled anti-government graffiti on their school walls. Inspired by uprisings in neighbouring countries, they wrote slogans like 'Your turn, doctor,' referring to Syrian President Bashar al-Assad, who trained as an ophthalmologist.

The Syrian government's response was swift and brutal. The boys, aged between ten and fifteen, were arrested by security forces and reportedly tortured in detention. Their families' pleas for their release were met with disdain, sparking outrage in Daraa. Large-scale protests erupted, initially demanding the boys' release and broader reforms.

When security forces responded to these protests with lethal force, killing several demonstrators, public anger escalated. The demonstrations spread to other cities, transforming into a nation-wide movement calling for Assad's resignation. Over time, the protests evolved into a full-scale civil war, with multiple factions and foreign powers becoming involved.

This small act of rebellion by children became the spark for a devastating conflict that would engulf Syria for over a decade.

In March 2019, five years after ISIS militants invaded Syria and Iraq, a US-backed coalition of Kurdish-led Syrian Democratic Forces (SDF) surrounded the town of Baghuz in Deir ez-Zor province, the last ISIS stronghold in Syria. The ISIS leader Abu Bakr al-Baghdadi had recently decreed that ISIS families should leave the area, but Yazidis were forced to remain imprisoned underground. Hostages were being used as bargaining chips, and families were getting phone calls from the smugglers offering to release their loved ones in return for thousands of dollars in ransom money. At the same time, some of the ISIS fighters were offering to release their female prisoners in return for safe passage to Turkey. After a ten-day truce to evacuate thousands of women and children, fighting resumed, with ISIS snipers, suicide bombs and rockets preventing the SDF from taking the town.

During the battle, the building housing some of the younger children was hit by a mortar, and twelve-year-old Zainal, kidnapped from Sinjar in 2014, was badly injured. He was thrown outside the compound and was later found lying on the road, clutching a red blanket. His leg was fractured in several places, he had shrapnel in his back and his chest, and he was suffering from hypothermia. Zainal's parents were missing, believed dead, but we managed to connect him with his elder brother Ahmed, who collected him and brought him to a hospital in Duhok. Apart from Ahmed, the family were all in Canada, having been accepted in a survivor programme by the Canadian government the previous year. Ahmed was refused a visa due to the fact that he'd 'taken up arms' to defend his people when he was twenty-one. I was asked if I could help reunite him with his family, so I arranged to visit them at the hospital on my way back.

I travelled to Syria with Jane Arraf, who was planning to do a report for NPR radio on my efforts to find Yazidi children believed to be hidden among ISIS families in the al-Hawl camp in northern Syria. We were accompanied by Sangar, her fixer, who played a key role in developing some of the most important news stories in the region since 2014. Things didn't quite go to plan, though, as it turned out the person who could identify the Yazidis was the wife of a prominent ISIS fighter who would need to be taken out first. I couldn't agree to smuggle an ISIS wife into Iraq, so the mission had to be aborted. Instead we headed to the Yazidi safe house in Al-Hasakah, where eighteen of the Yazidis who'd already made it out of the camp were waiting for permission to travel to Sinjar. While I knew it was unlikely that the children on my list would be among them, I was hoping that the women and children in the safe house might recognise some of them from photos that had been sent to me by relatives via Facebook. A girl recognised a friend of hers who'd died several months earlier and one of the women recognised her nephew, but he was older and had been sent to fight.

Solana, whose arm had been broken in three places when she was beaten for stealing food by an ISIS wife who 'owned' her, told us, 'They called ISIS the state of religion, but it was not so. It was the state of slavery and tyranny. Our men were killed, we were raped and our children were their slaves.'

Inside the safe house, a teenage girl with shrapnel wounds was stretched out on a mattress. She looked terribly sick, and I wondered if she'd be able to survive the journey home. Beside her a young woman, just twenty-two, was cradling her five-year-old daughter, who could not stop crying. She was also holding the hand of a little boy called Ibrahim, who was going to be left behind because he was the son of the ISIS fighter who enslaved her. 'We've never been apart since he was born,' she said. 'I love him but my parents won't accept him.'

They'd tried to leave that morning but got turned back at the border. When they returned to the safe house her son ran towards her with his arms outstretched. As she was telling us her story she began to cry, and the other women in the room were crying too. Families who accept an ISIS child were shunned by their community, as children of ISIS men are regarded as Muslim and seen as a threat to the ancient religion. Consequently, many women chose to remain in Syria rather than be separated from their children. She had spoken to her mother on the phone and begged her to let her keep her son, but her mother wouldn't let her. 'I have many friends that have two or three children whose families won't accept them,' she said. 'My parents told me that no one brings any of these children back.'

There were problems getting permission for the group to cross the border to Sinjar, so I tried calling the Kurdish prime minister's wife to see if she could help. She immediately offered to arrange for them to travel on the ferry to Kurdistan, but when I offered to accompany them to the vessel, the person in charge of the safe house told me they wouldn't be going that way. The Yazidis believed they'd been betrayed by the Kurds, whose army fled from Sinjar when ISIS invaded, leaving the Yazidis with no protection. He told me they didn't want to give the Kurdish government an opportunity to use the rescue mission for propaganda purposes, so the next day they'd once again make the long journey to the Iraqi border instead and hope that this time they'd be allowed to cross. That night I called Hadi Baba Sheikh, Dr Shirzad and Karim Kamal and asked them to do everything possible to ensure these people were granted safe passage across the border.

The group left at around six o'clock the following morning, and that afternoon we received a call to say they'd arrived. Solana wasn't sure how her husband would cope after everything that had happened, but when he saw her he immediately swept her up in his arms and carried her to their house. Ibrahim stayed behind in the safe house, and we were told he'd be taken to an orphanage run by Kurdish Syrian fighters, where he'd eventually be adopted by a local family. The Yazidis have suffered in every way possible – having been separated from their families, forced into slavery, and sexually and physically abused – but after everything they've endured, one of their cruellest fates is that the women are forced to make a choice between keeping their children or going home.

That evening I stayed in my hotel room writing my report, and because one of the panes of glass was missing from the window it was very cold. It was also incredibly noisy as the SDP soldiers had finally taken Baghuz and they were driving in convoy through the streets, firing their machine guns and rifles in the air in celebration. Jane was staying in Qamishli to report on al-Hawl camp but Sangar had kindly arranged a car to take me to the border the following morning. The floor of the seven-seater vehicle was covered in artificial grass and plastic flowers adorned the dashboard, and it all felt rather surreal as we drove at high speed across the flat landscape. Apart from me and the driver, the vehicle was empty, so I stretched across the back seat and slept all the way to the ferry that would take me across the River Tigris to Faysh Khabur in Kurdistan.

I arrived in Duhok to find Ahmed worried that the hospital caring for Zainal was demanding payment for his treatment and they were recommending surgery to remove a piece of shrapnel that was apparently lodged in the upper pole of one of his kidneys. The family had no money, so I settled the bill and we moved Zainal to Shekhan hospital, a medical facility that treated many children from Sinjar free of charge. They performed an ultrasound and assured us that the shrapnel was not in his kidney and could be left indefinitely in his body without causing any harm.

Zainal was deeply traumatised and, having been separated from his family when he was just seven years old, he suffered from severe separation anxiety, so each time Ahmed had to leave him he'd cry constantly. Ahmed's young wife was heavily pregnant so it was incredibly difficult for him, torn between his traumatised younger brother and his wife who was due to give birth to their first baby any day. I discussed the problem of separation with his doctor, who said that once Zainal's infection was under control, he would arrange for him to go and stay with his brother in the Sharia refugee camp, provided that I could arrange for a private nurse to change his dressings every day. Zainal had spent five years living with his captors, suffering profound and multifaceted trauma stemming from both physical and psychological abuse.

Many of the Yazidis who'd been released from ISIS captivity had undergone experiences that left a long-lasting impact on their mental health, development and ability to reintegrate into society. ISIS exposed children to propaganda, coercing them to adopt extremist ideologies, and they were forced to witness executions, torture and other brutal acts, desensitising them to violence. I bought Zainal an iPad, and when I turned it on he immediately typed in the link for a website that he'd visited before. I held my breath for a moment, worried about what we might see, but to my delight it was a video of some Yazidi girls singing a song. This gave me hope that now he was back in his own community, surrounded by people who loved him, he might eventually forget the horrors inflicted on him in the past and be able to move forward. On 29 March, my birthday, Ahmed became a father, and to my delight they decided to call their baby Sally.

43

Having seen how many children we helped through our WhatsApp group, I wanted to expand the project and create a solution that would transcend borders and reach besieged or remote communities where children are dying due to a lack of paediatric expertise. This was the motivation behind the creation of the Save a Child charity and our telemedicine app.

We'd already proved the concept in northern Iraq, where hundreds of children benefited from doctors having remote access to our team of paediatric experts, but knowing how expensive it would be to create a bespoke programme I decided to explore other possibilities. We worked with experts on every aspect of the programme, with health innovation knowhow from the LEO Innovation Lab, a Danish organisation committed to creating healthcare solutions through innovation. Christina Kirk, director of entrepreneurship and innovation at LEO iLab, which managed and implemented digital transformation projects, was assigned as our business development manager.

LEO iLab's developers assisted us with the design of a digital platform, and we collaborated with Professor Richard Wootton, a prominent figure in the field of telemedicine, recognised for his contributions to improving healthcare delivery in underserved areas. His organisation, Collegium Telemedicus, was helping people who wanted to use telemedicine networks to deliver healthcare in remote or low-resource settings. Working with

Richard and his partner Barry O'Kane, who founded HappyPorch, a B Corp company that specialises in digital product development, we designed a mobile app that would enable doctors in besieged or remote areas to refer cases to our team of paediatric experts.

Emergency care in conflict zones tends to rely on aid organisations, but their access is often limited by safety concerns and restrictions on movement of personnel, leading to a lack of paediatric expertise in the field. The cost of recruiting specialists for international placements is quite high in terms of travel, accommodation, insurance for working in high-risk areas and other considerations, and doctors are often only stationed on site for a limited period of time. The Save a Child telemedicine app is designed for areas with poor infrastructure and employs technology that is optimised for use in resource-constrained contexts. At the core of what we offer is the fact that our paediatric specialists join as remote, unpaid volunteers responding to cases whenever they have the time. This enables us to provide specialist support while incurring none of the costs normally associated with the physical placement of medical staff.

Pernille Richards, a mother of three with considerable experience in digital technology, contacted me to offer her help and became our project development manager on a purely voluntary basis. In between school runs, swimming clubs and working for her husband, an oncologist, she spent much of her time helping me to expand our paediatric network. To assist with the implementation of the programme, we appointed an eminent board of advisors, led by Evelyn Peng Ong, consultant paediatric hepatobiliary and transplant surgeon at the Birmingham Children's Hospital. Evelyn was able to secure formal approval from the Birmingham Women and Children's NHS Foundation Trust to recruit paediatric specialists willing to volunteer their time free of charge. Ashish Desai, who took over from Evelyn as honorary secretary of the British Association of Paediatric Surgeons (BAPS) in 2020, introduced me to the president of BAPS, who agreed to partner with Save a Child.

On 29 January 2020 the first confirmed cases of COVID-19 in the UK were reported, involving two Chinese nationals in York. Community transmission began to be detected and the UK government issued early advice, such as the benefit of handwashing, but didn't yet enforce significant restrictions. Cases surged, prompting the government to announce its first nationwide lockdown on 23 March. Schools, non-essential businesses and public venues closed, and people were instructed to stay home except for essential reasons. The UK saw its first major wave of infections and deaths, with deaths peaking at over a thousand a day in April.

By the end of 2020, the UK had reported over 2.4 million confirmed cases and more than 72,000 deaths, one of the highest per-capita death tolls in the world. Travel was restricted, so we used this period to further develop our paediatric network, and in October 2021, with help from a local man called Ehsan Faisal, we launched our first paediatric telemedicine programme in Afghanistan. According to the WHO, there are currently only two doctors, five nurses and midwives, and less than one pharmacist per 10,000 people in the country. The Afghan public health system is clearly compromised, and there are enormous difficulties in ensuring even basic levels of healthcare.

On account of security challenges and lack of resources, most healthcare facilities where specialists are based are limited to larger towns and cities, so patients with complex conditions and other chronic illnesses living in remote areas often need to travel long distances across difficult terrain to receive specialised medical care. Many of these outlying communities struggle with retaining and attracting a qualified health workforce, and they are sometimes served by just a single frontline healthcare worker with limited training. Many of these healthcare workers are isolated and lack the type of professional support found in urban areas. Poverty and restrictions on movement can also prevent families from accessing medical diagnoses and treatment advice.

Ghor Province in central Afghanistan is an area that's especially affected by a lack of healthcare access as a result of both geographical and political factors. In the winter months roads from the urban centres of Kabul and Herat are blocked by snow, while bad weather also impedes travel between the provincial capital and smaller towns and villages, restricting the movement of healthcare workers and medicines. The Hazaras, a Persian-speaking ethnic group predominantly practising Shia Islam, make up 39 per cent of the population and are among the poorest and most vulnerable people in the country, with the majority of the community living in extreme poverty. During the first period of Taliban rule in the 1990s, thousands of Hazaras were persecuted and killed. When the international coalition invaded Afghanistan in 2001, the Hazaras supported democracy, but with the return of the Taliban to power in 2021, they again faced systemic discrimination, preventing them from fully accessing societal benefits such as healthcare. The region where they live is both mountainous and isolated, with numerous communities living far from any healthcare facilities.

Some of the children referred to our specialists have cancer diagnoses and are in urgent need of specialist treatment, but oncology services are limited and most hospitals lack the necessary equipment for advanced diagnosis and treatment. A few private clinics in the country provide cancer care, but these are expensive and way beyond the reach of many Afghan families. Dr Hadi Mohseni-bod, Save a Child's chief medical officer, who has worked as a volunteer in numerous conflict and resource-limited settings, contacted his colleagues at MAHAK, a charity dedicated to helping Iranian children with cancer. He convinced them to accept a twelve-month-old baby who was referred to us with cancer, and she was admitted to their hospital in Tehran.

This was followed by many more referrals from Save a Child, and there's no doubt that had it not been for the doctors at MAHAK, these children would not have survived.

In 2023, with funding from our partner, international law firm Clyde & Co, we launched our first mobile paediatric telehealth unit in Ghor Province, consisting of a local doctor, a skilled midwife and a driver. The medical staff incorporate our mobile app as part of their medical toolkit, which has proved to be a critical lifeline for both healthcare providers and patients, offering a level of expertise and care that's normally unavailable in this remote region.

We now operate two of these mobile units, which visit families in areas where many of the children have never seen a doctor. If the staff come across children with complex cases they upload the details to our medical coordinator and will usually receive a response from one of 300 paediatric specialists within an hour or so. If they require specific tests that are not available locally, we arrange to send them to Kabul.

Afghanistan has some of the highest infant mortality rates in the world and what we do is a drop in the ocean, but our neonatal specialists are helping to save the lives of newborn babies on a daily basis, while our oncologists advise on appropriate tests and then offer a diagnosis. Our orthopaedic specialists advise doctors treating children with bone deformities and blast injures, and our neurologists help them to manage patients with complex and debilitating nervous system disorders. Liz Dack has joined our network as a medical coordinator helping to allocate cases to the appropriate specialist and Marino is always on call to respond to children in need of a general paediatrician. Our ultimate goal is to make the app available to clinicians helping to save the lives of sick and injured children in areas affected by conflict or disaster across the globe.

44

Although several countries required proof of vaccination or negative COVID-19 tests for entry, the travel ban was finally lifted and we were able to start travelling abroad. When Russia invaded Ukraine in February 2022, we partnered with EUPSA, the European Paediatric Surgeons' Association, who wanted to offer their support to doctors treating children on the front lines

I flew to Rzeszów in Poland where Joel Bennett, an extremely resourceful man, had agreed to accompany me to Poland as our fixer. Joel had some amazing contacts who'd be able to help us source the medical supplies we planned to bring to Ukraine. We stayed in a local hotel before setting off to the station in Przemyśl, where I was catching a train straight across the border to Lviv. On our way to the station I received a call from Pernille, who told me about a man called Steven Carr. He was a member of a group of Hibernian FC football fans who'd set up a charity called Dnipro Kids after visiting Ukraine for a football match in 2005 and had appeared in a BBC report asking for help to bring some orphaned children to the UK.

Pernille passed on my details and Steven emailed me to say that he was on his way to Żnin with some children, but there was another group currently on a train to Lviv who'd also need help with transport to Poland. I told him that I was on my way to Ukraine and asked if there was anything we could do to support his mission. He explained that they needed help to pay for the transport to Poland, so I agreed to transfer £3,500 to cover the cost of a coach and two drivers.

The station at Przemyśl was filled with women, children and the elderly, all of whom had decided to leave Ukraine before it was too late. Men of fighting age remained in Ukraine, as the imposition of martial law required them to stay and defend the country. The concourse was crowded with people carrying suitcases, backpacks and carrier bags bulging with their possessions. Many had brought their pets with them: dogs on leads, cats in baskets, and guinea pigs and hamsters in cages. Some of the women were traumatised, having been separated from their husbands and now facing an uncertain future.

I queued for several hours prior to boarding the train, which was filled with men returning to fight for their country. Joel waited with me for a few hours until I finally went through. I found a space in one of the carriages alongside a young couple who were on their way back. On arrival in Lviv I was struck by the architecture, with its Polish, Austrian, Jewish and Armenian influences. Located in the west of the country not far from the Polish border, Lviv had now become a key hub for refugees, humanitarian aid and logistics. All the hotels were full, but Steven had arranged for me to spend the night with his colleagues, a Russian woman called Lisa and her husband Peter, who was Ukrainian. They told me that the children would arrive from Dnipro by train the following day and we'd meet them at a refugee holding centre.

During the night I heard the sound of an air raid siren, for while Lviv had remained relatively secure compared with the war-torn regions in the east and the south, it remained under threat from air strikes targeting critical infrastructure. My hosts quickly ushered me to the bathroom. This had no windows and was therefore the safest room in the apartment block, and they said it would be a good idea to remain there until they got the all-clear, which would be texted through an app on our phones.

The next morning Lisa took me to a temporary shelter for displaced persons where we waited for the children. She explained that Ukraine had been transitioning away from institutional care towards family- or community-based alternatives such as foster care and small group homes, usually run by a husband and wife. Before the war, Ukraine had one of the highest numbers of institutionalised children in Europe, with 100,000 children in orphanages or other state-run institutions. Many of these children were not true orphans but came from families unable to provide adequate care due to poverty, substance abuse or other social issues. After a couple of hours we were joined by twenty-two children, ranging in age from two to fifteen. They were accompanied by Oleksandr and Mareena, a married couple who were foster carers for ten of the children, and two other women who were carers for the rest of the group. A very cute three-year-old girl with shoulder-length red hair and wearing a stripey T-shirt, pink leggings and pink boots raced over to where I was sitting and climbed onto my lap. She made it clear that she wanted food, so we ordered pizzas for the whole group, then settled down to wait for the coach that would return to Lviv that evening with the same two drivers.

The coach had around sixty seats but there were only twenty-six of us altogether, so there was plenty of room. When we reached the border numerous buses and cars filled with people desperate to leave the war zone tailed back a long way. While we waited, I called Steven to make sure the children could be accommodated at the hotel in Żnin, and he told me that the Lena Grochowska Foundation, which was funding the mission through the Arche Hotels Group, had agreed to house them temporarily but would soon need the rooms for other guests. He told me that he hadn't made any plans beyond getting the children to Poland, so I asked if he'd like me to explore the possibility of bringing them to the UK, to which he texted back, 'That would be amazing!' Together with the group already waiting in Poland, there were forty-eight children in all, so I immediately started to make some calls.

Richard Harrington had recently been appointed as minister of state for refugees, working across both the Department for Levelling Up, Housing and Communities and the Home Office, and he obviously had particular concern for the situation in Ukraine. I still had his number in my phone, so I texted to let him know that I was about to cross the Ukrainian border with a group of orphaned children and wondered if he could help. He replied immediately.

I messaged Joel to update him and to ask if he could help, and he called his colleague Dan Burger, CEO of Magen David Adom, who happened to be friends with Shai Weiss, CEO of Virgin Atlantic. Joel also called Rob Rinder, a well-known TV personality and barrister best known for his role in the reality courtroom series *Judge Rinder*. He'd been reporting for ITV on the refugees arriving at the Polish border and he offered to do whatever he could to highlight our mission.

When we finally reached passport control, the driver collected all the documents and handed them to the customs officials. About fifteen minutes later one of the officials climbed onto the coach and demanded to see Oleksandr, who was escorted into the building without any explanation. Eventually another official came to tell us that although Oleksandr was claiming to have joint responsibility for ten of the children, only his wife's name was on the official document. As a man of fighting age, he'd need a letter proving that he was exempt from fighting and could therefore leave Ukraine. Without it, they couldn't let him cross the border and he'd have to return to Lviv.

Oleksandr was clearly in shock and Mareena started crying, insisting that she wouldn't leave without him. I tried to reason with the customs officials, but they insisted that these were the rules. They said he'd need to return to Lviv and ask the authorities to issue the necessary exemption certificate. While we were talking, Mareena went to get her children from the coach and ordered the driver to start unloading their baggage. It was after midnight now and bitterly cold. The children, who weren't dressed very warmly, gathered around their 'mother', shivering and confused. The youngest child, who was only two, began screaming for Dad, meaning Oleksandr.

I didn't speak Ukrainian, and no one in our group spoke English, but using Google Translate I managed to convince Mareena that if she was willing to leave with us, I'd do absolutely everything I could to bring her husband to Poland as soon as possible. It took some time to persuade her, but finally she agreed, and the children, shivering from the cold, were able to climb back onto the coach.

As we drove across Poland I could hear the children coughing and sneezing, and I asked the driver to turn the heating up as it was terribly cold. He explained that the heater was broken and there was nothing he could do. I was sitting near the front of the coach trying to keep warm, when one of the girls called Snezhana, squeezed into the seat beside me. 'I'm cold,' she said in English, so I pulled my coat around her and she immediately fell fast asleep.

It took thirteen hours to reach Żnin, and by the time we arrived we were all exhausted. Steven was waiting for us outside the hotel with some of the children from his group, and I could see that he had a great relationship with them. They were older than the children on my coach and the Hibernian group had been supporting them for years, taking the kids on trips and for birthday outings.

Mareena and the two other women in charge of our group weren't really sure what was happening as they'd simply been told to board the train to Lviv, so with one of Steven's volunteers translating, I told them that we were hoping to get permission to bring them to the UK. They were clearly delighted. Lisa had texted me earlier to let me know that Peter was going to help

Oleksandr to get the papers he needed, and if all went well he might be able to join the group in a few days.

Joel arrived, and we had dinner with Steven and his assistant Duncan McCree. Steven told us that he was flying home the next morning as he needed to work, but he assured me that Duncan would take care of the children together with a Ukrainian woman called Natalia, who'd accompanied them from Dnipro along with their carers, and who was now both translator and coordinator for the group. The hotel had assigned two floors to the refugees. It gave them all breakfast every morning, and the women were given food so they could prepare lunch and dinner for everyone in in a small kitchen on their landing.

The next day we dropped Steven Carr at the airport before I headed back to Lviv, where Lisa had arranged for me to meet with the director of the Children's Hospital. We arrived soon after curfew, so the streets were completely empty, and I managed to get a room for the night, then met up with Lisa the next morning. The director promised to share details of the Save a Child telemedicine app with colleagues across the region, but he also told me how desperate they were for medical supplies like trauma packs, which could be used to help victims of blast injuries in areas where there was heavy fighting. Within three hours of calling Joel with the request, he was able to arrange the delivery of seven hundred of these packs to Ukraine in the next few days.

While Steven was in Britain he appeared on various TV and radio programmes alongside Scottish National Party leader Ian Blackford, who was supporting our efforts to bring the children to the UK. The issue of the orphans was raised during Prime Minister's Question Time at the House of Commons, but their predicament was still looking fairly bleak, so I called Richard Harrington, who assured me that everything would be OK, and that he and his colleagues were working urgently with Poland to ensure the children's swift arrival to the UK.

In the meantime, Shai Weiss was preparing to send an aircraft to Warsaw to collect the children. Virgin Atlantic had no flight arrangements with Poland and would need special permission to enter their airspace, but Tiggy Thiagarajah, head of operations at the company, told me that once they had the flight manifest containing the names of all of those who'd be travelling, he'd submit it to the Polish Civil Aviation Authority. I was amazed at how quickly it was all coming together, and it was clear that although no longer part of the EU, the UK wanted to show solidarity with its European neighbours, who'd opened their borders to millions of displaced Ukrainians.

Lisa told me that Oleksandr wouldn't be able to get his papers in time for the flight and was on his way back to Dnipro to see if the local authorities could help. Now that Joel was able to confirm delivery of the trauma packs and Oleksandr couldn't leave Ukraine for at least two weeks, I had no reason to stay in Lviv. I managed to secure a seat on a bus from Lviv to Przemyśl and was relieved to note that the bus actually had a working heater, as I'd developed a cough and was running a fever. Later I discovered that some of the children who'd travelled with me on the coach from Lviv had tested positive for Covid.

Joel was late arriving at the station, and by the time he turned up I was shivering uncontrollably, so we went straight to the hotel. He told me that Virgin Atlantic couldn't start to make arrangements for the flight until they had written confirmation from UK Border Force that the children would be allowed to land in Britain. It took a few more days, and a lot of emails and phone calls, before we finally received confirmation that the visas would be granted.

The only problem we could now foresee was the issue of biometrics. I talked to Crispian Wilson, political counsellor at the British embassy in Warsaw, who assured me it wouldn't be a problem, provided each person completed an application form and had their biometrics done. The visa hub was in Warsaw, so this was going to be impossible logistically as the children were well over three hundred kilometres away in Żnin. Fortunately, Crispian was very keen to help, so he arranged for his team from the embassy to travel to the hotel where the children were staying and complete the applications on site. As far as I know this had never been done before, so it shows how smoothly things can proceed if those in authority decide to think outside the box.

When the day of departure finally arrived, Aneta, who was representing the Lena Grochowska Foundation, sent a fifty-five-seater coach and a nine-seater minibus to take us all to Warsaw, where they'd arranged lunch at one of the Arche hotels. As the children glimpsed the tables laden with food and queued up at the buffet, their eyes wide with anticipation, I received a message from Pernille. She was waiting at Heathrow Airport together with Dan Burger, Steven Carr and Ian Blackford, as well as two British doctors who Joel had engaged to accompany the children on the plane.

While they were waiting, they were told that the children's flight from Warsaw had been cancelled, but nobody seemed to know exactly why. It appeared to have something to do with the Polish authorities, who stated that they couldn't issue exit permits for the children unless the Ukrainian Social Affairs Office agreed. I sent a flurry of messages to Harrington's office, who confirmed there was a hold-up related to the fact that some of the children's parents would need to give official authorisation for their children to travel to the UK. We'd already explained that the assigned guardians had the right to make decisions on behalf of the children in their care, and we sent the documentation to prove it. The British government, however, was told that the Ukrainian Ministry of Social Affairs needed to confirm directly to the Polish Ministry of Families that they were happy for the children to leave Poland, with the Polish ministry then needing to issue that permission.

A lot of people were involved on a political level, including the Ukrainian ambassador to Britain, and Harrington's private secretary assured me they were putting pressure on the Ukrainian authorities. To my relief we finally heard that the Ukrainian ambassador had written to the Home Office stating that the Dnipro Administration and Ministry of Social Policy said that no additional permission was needed, as all the children were from foster families or family-type children's homes.

This message was passed to the Polish authorities, and although it was now too late to fly them out as planned, Tiggy told us that they'd try to arrange another slot in about three days. In the meantime, we had nowhere to accommodate the group of sixty-four women and children, but I mentioned this to Aneta who made a couple of calls and a short while later the manager of the Renaissance, a five-star hotel next to Warsaw's Chopin Airport terminal, came to collect us. After retrieving all our bags from the buses, he led us on foot to the hotel, where he quickly organised thirty rooms as well as access to the main dining room, where all our group could eat completely free of charge.

The day before we were due to fly, two young women aged twenty and twenty-two who were formerly from one of the orphanages turned up at the hotel. They'd arrived from Ukraine that day and were desperately hoping to join their brothers and sisters on the flight to the UK. I couldn't see how we were going to manage it as they were too old to be included, but I suddenly remembered that the Home Office had just announced a new scheme called Homes for Ukraine. The scheme was designed to provide refuge for those fleeing from the war, and British people could apply to sponsor an individual or a family. Upon their arrival in Britain, Ukrainians could apply for residency, which automatically gave them the right to claim benefits while they learned English and looked for work.

I asked Duncan McCree if he could try to find a sponsor, and he gave me the address of a colleague of his called Dougie, who responded immediately. Dougie spent hours on the Homes for Ukraine website that night, and finally in the early hours of the morning he obtained approval for both women to come to the UK. We only had a few hours left before the flight was due to leave, so I called the British embassy in Warsaw and spoke to Crispian. He told me to send the women to the hub first thing in the morning and they'd do their best, but he warned me that it was unlikely they'd be issued with visas in time for the flight. I called my daughter, who was on a break from university, and she immediately offered to fly to Poland and accompany them to the UK. I pointed out that it would mean travelling alone with two young women who didn't speak any English, but she insisted it would be fine, so I sent an urgent request to Tiggy, who kindly agreed to include her on the flight from Heathrow the following day.

Steven Carr had flown back to Poland the previous day so he could join the children on the flight to the UK, and as we all sat around waiting and wondering if it would all go to plan, some women from the British embassy came into the reception asking for me. They were carrying a very large stack of paper, which turned out to be the visas. They'd been incredibly helpful throughout the whole process, travelling for miles to the hotel in Żnin to do the children's biometrics, then rushing to get all the paperwork done in time for the flight. It was an incredible feat, as they'd somehow managed to bypass all the usual red tape in order to get the visas processed so quickly. As they handed them to me, I received a message from Pernille to say the plane had just landed in Warsaw. Billie was preparing to leave the aircraft as there had been no news regarding the two young women, so it looked like we'd have to leave her behind with them.

They were saying goodbye to their 'brothers and sisters', and they were all crying, but as we prepared to cross the road to the terminal building, someone arrived with the final two visas and I had the pleasure of telling them they were flying with us after all. It took some time to get everyone checked in and through passport control, but we finally reached the departure gate, where the crew were waiting to welcome everyone on board. The air stewardesses were waving Ukrainian flags as the children boarded the aircraft, their eyes wide in disbelief as they looked around at the spacious Dreamliner. The aircraft could seat two hundred and forty passengers but there were only around sixty-eight of us. A young woman called Bianca Sakol, the founder and CEO of a charity called Sebby's Corner that provides essential resources such as clothing, baby equipment, nappies, toiletries, buggies and other necessities for families living in poverty, had put together bags for each of the children containing things they might need on arrival in the UK.

This was the first time I'd actually met Pernille in person, although she'd been working with Save a Child for two years, so it was great to finally meet her and have her be part of such a wonderful mission. The captain came down the aisle with his arms filled with toys for the children, and then it was time to fasten seatbelts and prepare for take-off. The children's eyes widened when they discovered the movie screens on the back of the seat in front of them, but Billie noticed that Snezhana was looking a little scared. I sat on one side of her, with Billie on the other, and we held hands with her as the plane began rolling down the runway and then lifted smoothly off the ground.

As we flew higher the aircraft was filled with sounds of excitement, and as soon as the seatbelt lights went out the children were told they could move around. They were served with hot food and plenty of treats throughout the flight, and it was a journey none of us, including the flight staff, will ever forget. It was after midnight by the time we landed at Heathrow Airport. Two coaches were waiting to take them all straight to Edinburgh College, where they'd be housed in halls of residence and cared for by the local council. We watched as they all came down the steps of the plane, and there was just time to give some of the children from my own group a hug before they climbed onto the buses and disappeared into the night.

45

The mission to bring the orphaned children to the UK received considerable publicity, and I returned home to find four hundred emails in my inbox from people either offering to adopt them – which wasn't an option – or asking for our help to reach Britain.

One of the messages was from a woman called Sue Evans, who was hosting some Ukrainians. She told me that an orphanage in Kryvyi Rih was closing, and she was hoping we could help to facilitate the relocation of the children and their carers to the UK. Sue's sister-in-law was headmistress of Bruton School for Girls in Somerset, which was closing for the summer months. She offered to house the children in one of the school's boarding houses, until the government was able to provide something more permanent, and connected me with Ukrainian politician Lesia Vasylenko, who had initiated the request. Lesia, who was moving to the UK temporarily with her own children, told us there were ninety-one children and thirty carers at the Kryvyi Rih orphanage who were in desperate need of help. She in turn introduced me to a young businessman called Alex Ong, whose wife Svetia was Ukrainian. She and another Ukrainian woman called Iri were originally from the orphanage in Kryvyi Rih and they wanted to help.

I called Marino, who said, 'My bag is already packed'! We were also joined by Kenny, a forty-eight-year-old former bodyguard who specialised in risk mitigation, intelligence and logistics.

He told me that while he was in bed with COVID, he saw me on ITV News having just helped the orphans from Dnipro, and hearing that I was planning to go back for more children he decided to volunteer his services. We'd spoken on the phone quite a lot, but the first time we met face to face was at Stansted Airport. Alex and his wife, who'd just had a baby, were also there to meet Iri, and they offered to join us once the children reached Poland.

Security that day was exceptionally busy and extremely slow, and we were worried that we might miss our flight. I got stopped for a routine bag search so I urged Kenny, who was already through security, to go on ahead to the departure gate and ask them to wait for me. It was a long way, and by the time he got there he was out of breath but managed to explain our mission to the chief purser. The purser called the captain over a walkie-talkie, then told Kenny to phone me and tell me I'd need to run the rest of the way to the plane,

Kenny said, 'She can't run very fast as she was shot in the leg while trying to rescue children some years ago.'

Looking a bit surprised, the purser relayed this to the captain and a message came back. 'The captain has just googled Miss Becker and he said he'll hold the plane for her.'

When we reached Poland I received a call to say the Kryvyi Rih orphanage was now empty as the residents were on their way to Turkey, thanks to an initiative put in place by President Erdogan's wife. Lesia confirmed this was true, but she also pointed out that there were many more vulnerable children in need of help and arranged for me to meet with Olga Gorb, deputy head of the Dnipro regional administration.

We took the night train from Poland to Kyiv, arriving in the early hours of the morning, and we visited the children's hospital to make a list of paediatric medicines and medical equipment that were now in short supply. Everywhere we went, the bombs fell. Kyiv was attacked because the UN secretary-general Antonio

Guterres was visiting the city, and Moscow openly admitted targeting him.

The following morning we could see huge plumes of black smoke not far from our hotel. The platform for the train from Kyiv to Dnipro was underground, and while we waited for the train there was an air-raid warning, and all the lights went out. I used my phone torch so we didn't inadvertently fall onto the tracks, but it was very eerie down there in the dark. We could hear the distant thump of explosions, the acoustics of the station amplifying and distorting the noise.

Kenny had booked us into the Axelhof Boutique Hotel in Dnipro, which was recommended because it had two electrical inputs with its own transformer substation, as well a generator that ensured the continued operation of the entire building during blackouts.

It was a handsome building, but unfortunately we couldn't appreciate the external architecture in all its glory as the lower front windows were boarded up to protect the hotel's guests from bomb-blast damage. We planned to stay for a few days while Olga, a small, skittish woman in her late thirties with shoulder-length brown hair and soft brown eyes, began to gather a list of orphaned or vulnerable children and their guardians. Once again there was a lot of politics involved, and she appeared to be mired in a mountain of red tape.

While we waited for the list of names, we met with a local businessman called Alexandre, who'd been asked to assist with our mission. Most evenings he'd take us for dinner to his favourite Georgian restaurant, Puri Chveni, where we ate in the vaulted cellar so we'd be protected in the event of a missile attack. He didn't speak much English, but we were often joined by a young soldier called Andreii, who translated for him with an accent that sounded like Arnold Schwarzenegger. Alexandre was a wonderful host, extremely eloquent and with a phenomenal knowledge of literature, art and Western culture. He told us that one of his grandmothers lived in Moscow, while the other hailed from Glasgow and had the surname Johnson. He owned a large construction company that was currently in hibernation after he gave twenty-four of his trucks to the army.

Meals would typically start with a traditional Georgian soup called 'Kharcho', which was fiery and delicious, followed by lamb and beef ribs, which came out sizzling on hot cast-iron skillets, along with a potato and onion side dish. To accompany the food, Alexandre ordered an ultra-sweet pear lemonade. Marino gave up being a vegetarian and decided to overlook his allergies every time we ate there, often suffering for it the following day. Chacha, a Georgian spirit, was served at the end of the meal, but we weren't able to linger too long as there was still a curfew in Ukraine. This didn't bother Marino though, who'd continue the evening with a few glasses of whisky that he kept in his room.

Our hotel was located within fifteen minutes of the River Dnipro (also called the Dnieper), one of Europe's largest, and any attempt to cross it required complex amphibious operations as long-range artillery was often used to target forces and infrastructure on the opposite banks, making it a risky manoeuvre for the armies of both sides.

The three of us were having coffee in the hotel dining room one morning when there was a loud explosion that shook the whole building, rattling the large plate-glass windows beside our table. A missile had just hit the railway station, which would now be out of action for a few days. We needed to continue working, so we relocated to my room, which faced the back of the hotel and would therefore be safer.

Two weeks passed while we waited for details of the women and children who needed to leave, and we were now having problems getting through to Olga. I was becoming incredibly frustrated as we couldn't arrange accommodation in the UK without knowing exactly how many children would be included in the mission.

I contacted Yuri, a former Ukrainian politician who lived in London and was trying to organise medical aid for Ukraine. He had some influential contacts in Kyiv, and when I told him about the problems we were having he offered to set up a call with the deputy prime minister. She was incredibly helpful and clearly wanted to support the mission, and within a few days of that call I received the information we needed. There were seventy-seven orphaned children and their guardians on the list.

I sent their details to Richard Harrington's office in Whitehall, and messaged Tiggy at Virgin Atlantic to ask if they'd consider flying the group to the UK. I also called Aneta who'd arranged the accommodation in Poland for the orphaned children in March. She offered to house the group just across the border at a hotel in Janów Podlaski that had rooms available for five or so days, which would hopefully be enough time to sort out the visas.

Throughout this process I was communicating with Ed Culliney, private secretary to Richard Harrington, who made it clear that before anything could be agreed regarding relocation of the families to the UK, we'd need a letter from the Ukrainian authorities confirming that the children had permission to leave the country. This requirement was clearly to avoid the same problem that we'd had when trying to fly the last group of orphaned children from Poland. At the same time, I was asked to send a letter to the Ukrainian authorities confirming that the children would be cared for in Britain for the duration of the conflict with Russia.

Before I left the UK I contacted Jane Townsend to see if she had any advice regarding accommodation. She told me that most Ukrainians had come to Wales through the 'super sponsor' programme, which simplified entry to the UK. This was launched by the Welsh government as part of the broader UK-wide Homes for Ukraine scheme, and meant that refugees didn't have to secure individual sponsors before applying for a visa. The

Welsh government acted as a 'super sponsor', taking responsibility for their initial accommodation and support.

The only thing that might cause a problem was the fact that Wales was short of appropriate accommodation for large groups. Jane introduced me to the Steve Morgan Foundation, founded in 2001 by businessman and philanthropist Steve Morgan CBE, who had just agreed to provide funds for UARUK to open a Refugee Hub. When Jane told them about our efforts to bring orphaned and vulnerable children to the UK, he offered to help. I was put in touch with his assistant Jane Harris, who confirmed that Steve was willing to fund the cost of food and accommodation for the group for up to six months.

We sent a copy of this letter to the Ukrainian authorities and within days we'd secured permission to move the children to Lviv. Alexandre was working with the authorities to arrange transport for the group to get there, where we'd be joined by families coming from Zaporizhzhia and Mariupol, cities that were under constant attack.

The night before we left Dnipro I found Lyse Doucet, Lindsey Hilsum, international editor for *Channel 4 News*, and Christina Lamb, chief foreign correspondent for the *Sunday Times*, having drinks in the bar. Lyse was her usual warm and ebullient self, and I spent a pleasant evening with these incredibly brave and talented journalists, who represent the pinnacle of British foreign reporting, covering some of the world's most challenging and impactful global events, and bringing them to the forefront of public consciousness.

After we checked out of the hotel the next morning, Alexandre came to take us to the station, where seventy-seven children and their guardians were waiting. Following a number of missile attacks on the station, the evacuation was being carried out in secret to avoid the risk of the train being targeted by Russian forces. We were introduced to the various groups, which included a pastor who was the foster carer of nine orphaned children, an older woman called Svetlana who had six children in her care, a wonderful woman called Lyudmila, who was caring for two teenage boys and her granddaughter. There were also three sisters who had eight children between them. The children weren't orphaned, but the women were poor and didn't have the means to leave Ukraine on their own. They were also determined to remain together, which meant it was impossible for them to apply through the Homes for Ukraine scheme.

Three carriages had been assigned to our group, and we were urged to board the train as soon as possible so as not to attract attention from the air. There was an air-raid warning as we gathered on the platform, which was a bit unnerving, but no explosions.

The carriages were a fascinating mix of Soviet-era design and practical durability, tailored for long-distance travel across the vast country. Open plan, with rows of bunks and overhead storage, all the passengers shared a single communal space; given the outside temperature of 40°C, the lack of air conditioning and the single toilet per carriage made for an extremely uncomfortable three-hour wait in a railway siding. It wasn't even possible to open the windows as they appeared to be nailed shut.

Fortunately, I was able to do some work while we waited as we had Wi-Fi courtesy of Elon Musk's Starlink satellite-based internet service, which he introduced to Ukraine at the start of the Russian invasion earlier that year. Checking my emails, I discovered that Sue Evans had come up against a great deal of red tape when trying to use Bruton School to temporarily house the children and their guardians, with local authorities citing child safeguarding concerns. Fortunately, Steve Morgan had managed to secure accommodation at the Holiday Inn Express Hoylake in Wirral. Just a few hundred metres from the beach, the hotel had fifty-six double rooms, which would be sufficient to house all the orphaned children and their guardians for up to six months.

After three hours there was a low, rumbling vibration that grew louder and louder as the main engine was slowly backed up towards the waiting carriages. Once the engine was close enough, the SA3 couplers automatically locked together with a sharp metallic clank as the engine and the carriages made contact. A safety pin inserted into the mechanism to prevent accidental uncoupling during travel was followed by a hiss of pressurised air as the hoses – part of the train's pneumatic brake system – were connected. This was followed by lots of creaking and groaning as the train finally began to roll out of the siding.

Kenny, Marino and I shared one of the open compartments, with two bunks either side. We watched as the children raced up and down the aisles, excited to be on a train after months living in shelters, but as the sun went down we were told to shut the blinds, and suddenly it was pitch dark.

In the compartment next to ours an older lady called Iryna was looking after two orphaned boys called Illia and Sasha, aged seven and nine. Sasha was incredibly bright and was continually practising his English, while his younger brother had ADHD and kept swinging from the luggage racks and accidently kicking poor Kenny in the face. In the end Marino called out to their long-suffering grandmother, 'How do you say, "Please lock up your monkey" in Ukrainian?'

As we lay there in the dark, listening to the rhythmic clacking of the wheels on the tracks, Marino began to sing a haunting Italian lullaby, which took me by surprise as I'd never heard him sing before. It was incredibly surreal listening to the sound of his deep, throaty voice as we trundled across Ukraine on a train filled with orphaned children.

The journey took a further nineteen hours and was hot, airless and extremely uncomfortable, but there was plenty of food as the guardians had brought sandwiches, fruit, crisps and other treats, and before leaving we'd virtually emptied a small supermarket close to our hotel.

We arrived in Lviv the following afternoon and were met by American volunteers, who ferried us to our accommodation. The building we were staying in was ironically a former institution for orphans that was now just being used to house people who were passing through.

We were allotted the three upper floors, but unfortunately there was no lift and we had to carry our luggage up the stairs. One of the families had a fourteen-year-old daughter called Margherita who had cerebral palsy and was confined to a wheel-chair. Her father was ill, having been diagnosed with metastasising melanoma and was in urgent need of medical treatment, so he couldn't help. Kenny and I had to virtually carry her as she tried to put one foot in front of the other, and our progress was labo-riously slow. I was looking forward to a shower, but much to my disappointment there was no running water. The building obvi-ously hadn't been renovated and the toilet didn't flush. The prison-style, rusty sprung beds with strained horsehair-filled mattresses were incredibly uncomfortable, and I couldn't help imagining the little orphaned children who must have lived here when it was still used as an institution. I also wondered how many of the women must now be regretting their decision to leave Dnipro.

Feeling exhausted after twenty-two hours on a train I soon drifted off to sleep, only to be woken a few hours later by the sound of missiles flying overhead.

'Guys, do you think we should move everyone down to the basement?' I asked.

'The missiles are landing around three kilometres from here,' replied Kenny, 'so I don't think we're in any immediate danger. But don't worry, if they start to fall any closer, I will wake every-one and we'll get them all downstairs.'

We came down in the morning to find a glamorous dark-haired woman called Yulia Gershon, formerly Miss Ukraine, who'd arranged to bring a further thirty women and children with us to

Poland. They were living in areas that were being targeted by Russian forces, and hearing that there might be an opportunity to travel to the UK, they arrived in Lviv that morning.

Two buses were parked outside ready to take us all to Poland and everyone clambered aboard. Both buses were filled to capacity, so Marino offered to squeeze into a seat at the front beside the glamorous Yulia, while Kenny joined the group on the other bus. I was seated beside a young woman called Alina, who was wearing a blue and yellow hat, the colours of Ukraine. She was sitting with a small boy and holding a newborn baby. Standing on the pavement waving was a tall, thin young man, with tears streaming down his face. Alina explained that this was her husband, who was having to stay behind and fight.

Before leaving Britain I'd promised Billie that I'd be back in time for her graduation, which was due to take place on 17 May. In spite of her somewhat traumatic childhood and the fact that I wasn't always there when she needed me, she'd studied hard and was awarded a degree in politics and international relations. It was now the 15th, and I knew that although there was a chance I wouldn't make it to the ceremony, I was determined to try. We spent seven hours at the border while they checked everyone's papers, and by the time we reached Poland it was after midnight. I'd managed to secure a seat on a flight leaving early in the morning, and Marino was also leaving Poland, as he needed to be in Italy for a conference on bone marrow transplants. We'd arranged to leave Kenny in charge of the group and Yulia assured us she had everything arranged at the hotel. The bus dropped us at a small town on the way to Janów Podlaski and fortunately we found a taxi driver who was prepared to take us to the airport. We said a hurried goodbye and I caught my flight to London with minutes to spare. The plane landed in the early hours and then it was a mad dash through passport control.

Finally, I was on the train to Kent with Billie and Heather, and although I knew the women and children would be fine in Poland without me for a couple of days, I couldn't help but feel anxious. This was probably one of the greatest dilemmas I faced in my work, for I was often forced to choose between the people I loved and the innocent victims of war.

Billie was delighted I'd actually made it back this time, though, and as we travelled through the lush Kent countryside I forced myself to stop stressing about something I couldn't change. We went for lunch before strolling through the vibrant and bustling streets, filled with a festive atmosphere that reflected the importance of the occasion. The narrow cobbled lanes that surround the cathedral echoed the charm of Canterbury's medieval heritage, their timeless character enhancing the sense of tradition on this special day.

Billie was preparing to collect her cap and gown from the rental shop when I checked my phone and saw I'd received an email from Steve Morgan. Heather knew from my face that all wasn't well, and she offered to accompany Billie while I figured out how to respond. Having received confirmation of Steve Morgan's offer to accommodate all of the women and children at the Holiday Inn Express Hoylake, Richard Harrington responded by telling him that the Ukrainian government had not approved this movement of their citizens and he wrote, 'as usual with Sally, all is not as it seems and we need to get to the bottom of this.'

I was shocked by his message, for he'd always seemed so supportive of my work. In fact, when we first met at the Home Office to discuss the plight of the Yazidis, he greeted me with the words, 'Prime Minister David Cameron asked me to meet with you. I was told you're an honourable woman.'

Jane assured me that despite Richard's message, Steve Morgan was still very much on board, but I was concerned that if the British government believed that I'd evacuated the women and children without the approval of the Ukrainian authorities, it was unlikely that I'd get permission to bring them to the UK.

I entered our hotel room with Richard's message still going round in my head, and when Billie walked in looking resplendent in her cap and gown with the University of Kent's colours on the sash, she immediately knew something was wrong and I saw her face drop, for once again a major event in her own life was going to be tarnished by my commitment to people elsewhere. Heather did her best to cover for me, enthusing about how wonderful she looked, but I knew it was too late. What should have been a special moment was gone.

The graduation ceremony at Canterbury Cathedral is a deeply moving and historic event, combining centuries-old tradition with modern celebration, and sunlight was streaming through the intricate stained-glass windows as we took our seats. The ceremony began with a formal procession as the staff and dignitaries, dressed in their traditional regalia, walked solemnly down the aisle to their seats off the nave. The cathedral's stunning gothic architecture provided a breathtaking backdrop, imbuing the ceremony with a sense of grandeur and solemnity. The students lined up to receive their degree certificate from the Chancellor and when it was Billie's turn to cross the stage, I couldn't have been more proud.

Before returning to Poland the next day, I sent a copy of a letter from Iryna Vereshuk, the deputy prime minister of Ukraine, to Richard in which she confirmed that she had spoken to me personally about the evacuation of vulnerable children from Ukraine during a conference call and that she had assured me of her government's full support for the mission.

Kenny was needed back in Britain, having been away for nearly one month, so Billie came with me to help with the children. We were also joined by Alex, who'd help with the visa applications, and Iri, who'd be our translator. It was a long drive to Janów Podlaski, and by the time we arrived it was getting dark, but Kenny was waiting at the gate to meet us. He told me that the previous night Yulia had brought some more women and children to the castle, so there were now 167 altogether. Among the group were two orphaned boys travelling with their guardian; the boys had been captured and beaten by Russian soldiers, and were still traumatised.

The Hotel Zamek is located in a beautifully restored castle, blending modern amenities with the charm of its original architecture. Our refugees were housed in two separate buildings directly opposite the castle. All the rooms had modern conveniences like flat-screen TVs and en-suite bathrooms, and a dining room had been set aside for our group in the beautiful grounds where they served a buffet-style breakfast, lunch and dinner.

Tiggy had managed to get approval for another Virgin Atlantic flight that could carry up to 240 people from Warsaw to London, but until we had confirmation of the visas he was unable to confirm the flight. In the meantime, the refugees were enjoying the hotel's facilities and making the most of the wonderful grounds, playing football and strolling along the riverbank and through the woods.

Ed Culliney advised me to communicate with the Ukraine Humanitarian Task Force set up by the British government and led by Ellen Laidlaw. She sent me endless lists of questions and I was advised to complete visa application forms for the whole group before we could proceed any further. When I expressed my concern to Ed regarding the timing, he assured me that once we'd made the necessary applications, he'd do his best to expedite them, so Alex opened his laptop, and we spent the next couple of days filling them in. We'd already discovered that the only way we could bring larger groups to the UK was through the Welsh 'super sponsor' programme, but knowing there was a shortage of suitable accommodation in Wales, we'd need the government to approve the use of the Holiday Inn Express Hoylake in Wirral funded by Steve Morgan.

The days passed with more questions coming from the Task Force, with no indication of whether the applications were being processed. The Hotel Zamek manager was now becoming extremely impatient, as he'd only agreed to house the group for five days; it was now 24 May and there was still no sign of any movement on the visas. Ed assured me that the Task Force was 'working at pace' on the matter, but with no sign of the visas, Tiggy had no choice but to stand down the plane.

I was called to the hotel reception and was told that we'd need to vacate the hotel by eight o'clock the following morning as they were expecting more guests and needed the rooms. We had to get to Warsaw, where those who didn't have international passports could attend the visa hub for their biometrics, but the Wolves Summit were holding the largest tech conference in central and eastern Europe from 24 to 27 May, and all the hotels were full. I called a meeting and addressed the group, explaining about the hold-up with the visas and the fact that we'd have to leave the hotel. A number of them had heard stories about people from Ukraine ending up at the Ptak Warsaw Expo, one of the largest refugee hubs in Poland. With a capacity to host up to 20,000 people, Ptak served as a transit centre where refugees could stay while being relocated to other European countries. A woman called Nina Meshchanova told me that Covid was rife among the refugees at the camp, and children were apparently being 'eaten alive' by bedbugs, so they were understandably horrified at the thought of ending up there, but I assured her this was not part of the plan. Nina who was orginally from Kyiv, had left the city with her two young children Hanna and Seva, who were both traumatised by the constant shelling. Hearing about our mission, she had decided to join us and give her children a chance to live without the constant sirens and the sound of explosions.

I managed to reach someone who ran an NGO helping refugees in Poland, and he told me that the Ministry of Social Affairs was ready to assist. We rented three buses to collect us the following morning and we drove 150 kilometres to the Arena Ursynów, a sports centre in Warsaw that would serve as temporary accommodation for our group while we sorted out the visas. There were two hundred beds in the centre and round-the-clock security, so the mothers agreed that it would be fine for a few days while we sorted out the visas. We sent out for some food, and while I was upstairs meeting with people in charge of the facility, the group were told to gather their belongings and wait outside.

We came back downstairs to find the hall was now empty, and I raced outside to find the refugees were being herded onto buses by men we hadn't seen before. Some of the mothers called out to me, clearly distressed, and a woman whom I later learned was one of the people in charge of Ptak Expo started filming me on her phone. When I challenged her, she just smiled. Billie noticed that the girl with cerebral palsy was being helped into the minibus by her parents, so we quickly ran to the vehicle and jumped in beside them.

We arrived at Ptak Warsaw Expo as the last of our group was entering the building, and as we tried to follow them inside, a policeman appeared and told us that unless we had Ukrainian passports we couldn't enter. The women sent photos of the interior, where thousands of beds were placed side by side in an enormous exhibition hall, and begged me to help get them out as soon as possible.

I received an invitation to attend a Zoom meeting with members of the UK government's Ukraine Task Force that afternoon, so we booked into a small hotel not far from Ptak. During the meeting they soon made it clear that there had been no real progress regarding the visas, that the Task Force wasn't planning to create a special programme for our group and that we'd need to apply for visas through Homes for Ukraine. I pointed out that it was most unlikely that anyone in the UK would be able to host such a large group, but they were adamant that this was the only option.

After several phone calls to the Ukrainian social services, we managed to get the women and children moved to Global Expo, a smaller refugee centre run by Ukrainian volunteers. It was so much better than Ptak, and meals were served buffet-style in a pleasant dining room, with the women and children being assigned a large room of their own. They all seemed much happier now, but a couple of days later I was devastated to learn that Svetlana had left. She had a heart condition and was feeling unwell. Afraid that she might be taken to hospital and separated from the six orphans in her care, she packed up their things and took them on a bus all the way back to Ukraine.

Steve Morgan's generous offer to provide food and accommodation at the Holiday Inn Express Hoylake was rejected by the UK government on the basis that the social services didn't feel there was enough space for the children's leisure activities. Knowing that the hotel was situated so close to the beach, this really didn't make sense to me.

Before leaving, we brought mobile phones for some of the women and older children so they could remain in contact with their families and text us if they needed anything. Back in the UK, I had several remote meetings with the Welsh government, who appeared to be keen to help, but they made it clear that it would take some time to allocate suitable accommodation. They advised me to resubmit all the visa applications through the Welsh 'super sponsor' programme, but they also warned me that the programme was about to be suspended for a few weeks in order to free up some space in their hotels. I called Pernille and she alerted Sue, Jane and her colleagues, who started working on the application forms. These took many hours to complete, and it was well into the night before all the forms were finally ready to upload.

Sadly, just as we were uploading details for the last group, the programme was officially suspended and the portal closed. Sasha got through but Illia didn't, and of course Iryna could not leave without both of them. The same happened to Nina and her children, who were supposed to travel to Wales with her sister-in-law and her nephew. I had no idea what to do, but Jane and her colleagues offered to find suitable sponsors close to Wales so they could apply for their visas through Homes for Ukraine. It took a couple of months but I stayed in touch with our refugees, travelling out to Poland to visit them whenever possible, and sending funds to pay for fresh fruit and medicines that weren't always available at the centre.

Some of the group were understandably becoming despondent and didn't want to wait any longer, and I was really sad when at the end of July, just as the visas were finally granted, I learned that the pastor had already returned to Ukraine with his nine orphaned children. Some of the families were offered private accommodation and decided to remain long-term in Poland, but around seventy of the women and children chose to wait and see, and in August we were finally able to fly them to the UK.

This was one of the most stressful and frustrating missions I've ever embarked on. Having to leave those wonderful women and children in a refugee centre for weeks on end while I struggled to get them permission to come to the UK was incredibly difficult. I'd constantly check to ensure they were all OK and I spent many sleepless nights worrying about them.

I returned to Ukraine once more that year, this time to help a group of thirteen children who were either partially or completely blind and in need of specialist care. They were living in areas that were constantly targeted by Russian forces, and I was asked to help them leave together with their parents and siblings. Marino and Kenny came with me, and we rented a bus and a driver who took us to pick up some of the children and their families from Zaporizhzhia, where the nuclear power plant had fallen into Russian control just days earlier. On our way to Odessa to pick up more families, we passed through a small town called Snihurivka and over a strategic bridge that spanned the Inhulets river. It was pitch dark but we had to travel at top speed, and less than ten minutes after we crossed it was destroyed by the Russians. The city of Mykolaiv was in a real mess, buildings levelled from heavy bombardment and shell craters all over the road, which we had to navigate like Formula 1 chicanes. We crossed another bridge that night in Mykolaiv over the Pivdennyi Buh river, and about eight minutes after we crossed the Russians targeted the bridge and the surrounding area, making the road impassable.

We took the families across the border to Moldova, where they were cared for in a village on the outskirts of Chișinău run by the Baptist Church, and two weeks later we flew with them to Germany on a private jet funded by Ein Herz fur Kinder.

Soon after arriving in Britain, Nina, who had a career as a TV producer in Ukraine, got herself a job as a cleaner at the Holiday Inn Express Hoylake. It was now being used to house male asylum seekers, and I couldn't help wondering if that was why the government wouldn't sanction its use for our orphaned children.

Most of the refugees are still in the UK, waiting for the war to end. I have stayed in touch with some of them, and last Christmas I received a heartwarming message from Nina who was recently reunited with her husband.

Dear Sally

I just want to take a moment to express my heartfelt thanks for everything you've done for us. Your kindness in bringing me and my children, Hanna and Seva, from Ukraine to Britain means the world to us.

Your support and compassion during such a difficult time made all the difference and we couldn't have made this journey without you.

Your selfless dedication has truly inspired us and we will always be grateful for your help.

Thank you for being our angel and making this transition smoother. We appreciate you more than words can say.

Nina

46

On 7 October 2023 the people of Israel awoke to the most horrific terrorist attack in the country's history. Following the launch of a barrage of 4,300 rockets and mortars on towns and military bases, thousands of Hamas-led militants stormed the security fence between Israel and Gaza in a surprise attack. Their intention – to kill as many people as possible in response to Israel's continued occupation of the Palestinian territories and the blockade of Gaza.

Three hundred and sixty-four people were killed at the Nova music festival, many of them teenagers, when armed militants, dressed in military attire and using motorcycles and powered paragliders surrounded the area and fired on anyone attempting to escape. Some of those who were injured were executed at point blank range. Israeli communities were attacked along the border – and some of the women were brutally raped and killed. Many people, including children and babies, were shot, mutilated or burned alive while trapped inside their homes. Amongst them was Vivian Silver, the Canadian-Israeli peace activist who I had the honour of meeting during a visit to Israel in 2014. Vivian founded Women Wage Peace to pressure Israeli Prime Minister Benjamin Netanyahu's government to reach a peace agreement to end the Arab-Israeli conflict and regularly volunteered for the organization Road to Recovery, which provided transportation for sick Palestinians from Gaza to Israel for medical treatment.

On 7 October she reported hearing Hamas militants outside her home in Kibbutz Be'eri. Five weeks later the burned remains of her body were found.

Around 240 individuals, including thirty children, were taken hostage and transported to the Gaza Strip to be used as bargaining chips for the release of Palestinian prisoners held in Israeli jails. A twenty-two-year-old German-Israeli woman called Shani Louk was killed, and her partially clad broken and bloodied body was paraded through the streets in the back of a pick-up truck while armed men around her praised God and spat on her lifeless corpse.

The horror of what happened that day, with 1,195 Israeli people killed and 7,500 injured, will haunt the Jewish people for decades to come.

While most Israelis were still reeling from the attack, the Israel Defense Forces (IDF), which had been caught totally unawares and failed to protect its people, immediately launched an operation targeting Hamas, which had embedded itself in a vast network of underground tunnels, firing barrages of rockets into Israel and using civilians as human shields. Many of the victims of Israeli air strikes were children, their catastrophic injuries caused by one of the most destructive bombing campaigns ever mounted on Gaza. Hospitals were damaged in the Israeli onslaught, and it became impossible for critically injured children to get the treatment they needed.

After seeing a story online about Ahmad Shabat, a little boy who lost both of his legs following an Israeli air strike that also killed his parents, Alisa Kireeva and Nadia Ali teamed up with several other women across the globe, united in a mission to support people in Gaza. They called their organisation Gaza Kinder Relief, and in February 2024 they sent me a list of children in need of specialist treatment abroad and asked if I could help.

Save a Child had recently partnered with Project Pure Hope (PPH), a humanitarian initiative founded by a group of senior doctors and healthcare leaders who were planning to provide life-saving medical care and support in hospitals across the UK for victims of conflicts in the Middle East. They'd already been in discussion with the Home Office, and we decided to work together to try to make it happen.

Having already encountered so many problems with the British government, I didn't have much faith left in the system, so I also began talking to contacts at Interplast Germany. They introduced me to a woman called Kerstin van Ark, managing director of the German Society for Plastic, Reconstructive and Aesthetic surgery, who was very keen to help. She began working day and night to identify hospitals and consultant paediatric specialists across Germany who were willing to offer their services free of charge. With help from the case managers at Kinder Relief, we gathered detailed information on thirty-two of the injured children and began negotiating with the Palestinian Ministry of Health in Gaza, who'd need to authorise the families to leave. We submitted the list to the Israeli Coordinator of Government Activities in the Territories (COGAT) for security clearance, and through Alisa, who'd established a good relationship with Dr Hatem Amer, associate minister of health in Egypt, we managed to get eight of the children and their families moved across the border. After several weeks and many phone calls and meetings, the German government were unwilling to approve the visas and Britain was still dragging its feet. Feeling increasingly frustrated, I called Marino on the off chance that he might be able to help.

'Leave it with me,' he said.

Marino introduced me to Barbara Fari, a woman in her fifties who'd facilitated the evacuation of many chronically ill children from Kurdistan. Barbara, a former nurse at the Burlo Garofolo Paediatric Institute in Trieste, spoke to the institute's director about the possibility of receiving some patients from Gaza. He agreed, and after a great many emails between Barbara and the Italian government, various other hospitals and a company in

Bologna that makes prosthetic limbs, we were finally told that all the relevant authorities had approved the evacuation.

At the end of May I flew to Italy to meet Barbara and Marino, and board the aircraft we'd chartered for the medevac flight. Marino brought the president of the Palestinian community in Padua with them to serve as our interpreter, together with two young doctors. As usual we went right up to the wire waiting for the embassy to approve their visas, but finally at 2 a.m. we received the confirmation we needed. The fifty-seat Embraer executive jet funded by PPH and Direct Relief was waiting on the tarmac, and as soon as the landing slot was confirmed we took off and flew to a military airbase in Cairo. After landing we were taken to a holding room to wait for the families. When I'd first received the case files three months earlier I was shocked by the pictures of their injuries, and now, as the children arrived, it was as if the photos were coming to life.

Ahmad Shabat, who was travelling with Ibrahim, his uncle, was racing around in his wheelchair. Ibrahim was a very personable young man who'd immediately adopted his nephew and brought him across the border to Egypt with his wife and baby. Unfortunately, it wasn't possible for them to travel to Italy, so Ibrahim had decided to leave his young family behind for now for the sake of his nephew. Considering what Ahmad had suffered he was amazingly resilient, and he'd learned how to manoeuvre his wheelchair with great skill, racing around outside with nine-year-old Shaima, who was also in a wheelchair, having lost her left arm and her right leg. She too was travelling with her uncle, as her parents were staying behind with their other children.

There were two young girls, sisters called Jana and Joudi, with thalassemia, both in urgent need of bone marrow transplants, and a three-year-old called Julia who had a cystic hygroma in her neck. As a result of her condition, Julia's tongue was grossly swollen to the point where she couldn't eat solid foods. Despite her condition, she was incredibly sociable and strode about demanding hugs. Julia was profoundly deaf, but she'd created her own sign language, and it was fascinating watching this bright little girl signing at top speed with her chubby little hands. Her mother Weam was just eighteen years old, and I was shocked when Barbara told me she'd just discovered that Weam was pregnant, as her bump didn't show beneath her loose clothing. I was concerned that she mightn't be allowed to fly, as Julia was getting progressively worse by the day and if not treated soon, she probably wouldn't survive.

It was difficult to know what to do, but Weam assured us that she wasn't due to give birth for a while yet, so I left the decision to Barbara, as they'd be her responsibility once we landed back in Italy. Barbara was adamant they should come with us regardless, but one of the men from the Gaza Ministry of Health had overheard the conversation and instructed a female colleague to find out who was pregnant. I could see Weam looking worried, so I hurried her into the bathroom and she waited there until it was time to leave.

Each of the patients was accompanied by their mothers or another close relative and their siblings, so there were twenty-eight of them in all. They were driven to the plane in ambulances overseen by Hatem, who'd played a major part in making this happen. The flight took several hours as we had to stop to refuel in Greece, and when we were finally on our way to Italy, Weam appeared to be in some discomfort. While someone took care of Julia, Barbara helped Weam to the front of the plane and sat down beside her. Later we discovered that her waters had broken, and after twenty-four hours at the hospital in Italy, with Barbara barely leaving her side, Weam finally gave birth to a baby girl.

By the time we arrived in Trieste it was close to midnight, and a fleet of ambulances was waiting on the tarmac to ferry the children to the Burlo Garofolo hospital. It was a joy to see the surprise on the paramedics' faces when Ahmad came whizzing towards them in his electric wheelchair. When the ambulances arrived at the hospital, fifteen-year-old Kamal, who'd lost one of his legs just below the groin, climbed from the vehicle without any assistance. They wanted to carry him into the hospital on a stretcher or in a wheelchair, but he refused, walking along on his crutches, head held high.

'They'll all be fitted with advanced prosthetics made especially for them in Bologna once their wounds are sufficiently healed,' said Marino.

Sadly, hundreds of children were still trapped in Gaza, including some of our own patients. A fourteen-year-old boy called Kareem was badly injured when a shell landed close to where he was standing. His leg became infected and he was in urgent need of treatment, but on 7 May, when he finally received clearance to cross into Egypt, the Rafah border was closed. Despite pleas from his mother to save his leg, the surgeon had no option but to perform an amputation. Afterwards Kareem suffered from depression and refused to eat, becoming severely malnourished. We arranged round-the-clock care for him, making sure he had fresh fruit and vegetables and other nutritious food, and slowly he began to recover but he was still in need of treatment for his leg which kept getting infected since leaving the hospital.

Sky News ran a story about Kareem and another of our patients – Zeina, a little girl just two years old when she suffered life-changing injuries. Zeina and her four-year-old sister Lana had been playing together, when there was an air strike close by. Zeina, terrified, ran clutching at her mother, who was holding a pot of boiling soup which spilled all over her daughter.

'It was a day of nightmares,' said Zeina's mother, describing the moments leading up to her daughter's injury as she was playing in the family's tent in al-Mawasi. 'Her face and skin were melting in front of me. I picked her up and went barefoot into the street.'

Medical services were stretched, but Zeina was eventually treated by the Red Cross doctors at Gaza's European hospital, where she underwent a skin graft from her father's leg. She was at risk of sepsis and in urgent need of further treatment but the Rafah crossing was still closed. Finally with help from our colleagues at Kinder Relief we managed to get Zeina moved across the border to Egypt via Kerem Shalom. Sadly her father wasn't allowed to accompany her and it was heartbreaking for him when they had to say goodbye. She was joined in Cairo by another of our patients called Alaa, a seventeen-year-old girl who was severely injured during an airstrike that killed her father and both of her brothers. It took several weeks to arrange their visas but they were finally flown to Italy for specialist treatment.

After 12 months of war, 45,000 Palestinians were reported to have been killed in Gaza and many more injured. With the Kerem Shalom crossing now open there were regular evacuations and after weeks of negotiation with COGAT and the Palestinian Ministry of Health, we finally managed to get Kareem on a flight to UAE, together with his mother and three siblings. They sent us wonderful photos on their way to Ramon Aiport in southern Israel and again when they landed in Abu Dhabi, far from the horror of the war.

As of 13 February 2025, the ceasefire between Israel and Hamas remains fragile, with regional players like Iran adding complexity to the geopolitical landscape.

The initial phase of the ceasefire is set to conclude in early March, but discussions for subsequent stages, including the release of additional hostages, has yet to commence. However, the current truce has allowed us to send in truckloads of humanitarian aid to Gaza and to evacuate more sick and injured children. Among the most recent group was an eight-year-old boy called Ibrahim who suffered third-degree burns to his face and upper body. Ibrahim was accepted by the same hospital in Padua as Zeina and Alaa but it took several months to finally get him and his mother to Egypt, from where they were flown to Italy on a flight sponsored by the Italian government.

But despite these positive developments, challenges persist. International cooperation is needed to combat terrorism and dismantle the extremist networks, and core issues need to be addressed, like the status of Jerusalem, major security concerns for Israel and a credible political pathway for the Palestinians.

Achieving peace requires collective efforts from individuals, communities and nations, emphasising dialogue, empathy and cooperation over conflict and division. There have to be mechanisms to prevent future escalations, such as international monitoring, and reconstruction of homes, infrastructure and essential services like water and electricity. Lasting peace will require compromise, strong leadership and sustained international commitment and I hope with all my heart that one day it will happen.

AFTERWORD

When I look back over the past three decades and the role I played in various conflicts, there are more questions than answers and I suppose there always will be. I never knew why I was given permission that was often denied to others. I never untangled the web of misinformation and misunderstandings that bedevilled so many missions, and I've never discovered what happened to the £1 million of medical aid and equipment secured in a UN compound in Metković during the Operation Angel mission in Bosnia. I don't know what caused the breakdown in communications between the British government and the UNHCR on the issue of visas, and I still don't understand why the British press withdrew their support.

I certainly never set out to become so embroiled in the Balkans conflict; it just happened that way. Every time I became involved, I found myself making a promise that I felt I had to keep, while at the same time thinking, 'Why the hell did I do that?'; and every time I grew more afraid, knowing what honouring that commitment would entail.

I greatly regret the fact that the UN found it necessary to be obstructive towards me rather than working alongside me. I'm sure that together we could have achieved so much more. Individual officers, soldiers and politicians said supportive things to me in private that they could not say publicly. But the whole is greater than the sum of its parts, and for me the whole represented everything that's bad about bureaucracy: inflexible, impersonal and lacking in imagination. Perhaps it doesn't matter that I've got no answers to my questions: truth, as we know, is the first casualty of war.

Although applauded for my actions, I've also been subjected to a great deal of criticism. I've been accused of being foolish and naive – and no doubt at times I was – but perhaps in part it was my naivety that enabled me to proceed. For had I done as the UN insisted and made applications for visas and hospital beds prior to each mission, some of the children might not have survived.

It seemed that each conflict was followed by another and it was always the children who suffered most. But I'm humbled by resilience of those whose lives I've had the privilege to touch. Their courage in the face of unimaginable suffering has been a source of strength and a constant reminder of why I had to keep going in spite of the obstacles I encountered along the way.

ACKNOWLEDGEMENTS

I would like to thank my mother for her eternal faith in me, and my dear friend Heather James for all her advice and support through these somewhat turbulent years.

Bosnia

My thanks to Brigadier Dr Ivan Bagarić and his colleagues at Bijeli Brijeg who enabled me to help the children on the 'other side', and to dearest Vava (Vladimir Mikulić), my great friend and protector. Lynne Gillette, who made me laugh through difficult times, and Tim Clancy, Tim Higham, Thierry, Paul, Domi, Paddy and Sean. And to Collette Webster, whom we all hold in our hearts.

To the staff at Higijenski, especially Hafid Konjhodžić, Jovan Rajkov and Dragan Milavić, all true heroes who will hopefully one day receive the recognition they deserve.

Thanks to Mike Mendoza for his support throughout the Balkan conflict. To Val Young, Stewart Weir, Justine and Alicia for their help with Operation Angel. Michael Harris, the Imam of Hove, Ansel Harris, Molly Brandl Bowen, Joyce Simpson, Eli Benson, Rita Eker, June Jacobs, Brian Charig and Dr. T. Scarlett Epstein OBE. The *Sunday Mirror*, Sally Line Ferries, Nissan, Trailblazers, Teddies for Tragedies, the Life Foundation, the Variety Club, the Brighton Collection group of hotels and the

Celebrities Guild of Great Britain, BBC's *This Morning*, Meridian TV, Gloria Macari, Roger Ferris, Yolanda Beeny and everyone involved with 'Hear the Children'.

Special thanks to Dr Duncan Stewart, my 'knight in a flak jacket'. To Mick Fegan, Lawrence Le Carré, David and Ashley Rose, teams from the AA, the BRS and the RAC, and all the brave truck drivers, nurses, doctors, ambulance technicians, firemen, police and members of the Territorial Army who gave their time to deliver the aid and help evacuate the children.

I would also like to thank the UNPROFOR soldiers and the UN officers who were involved in what became a very complex mission: Colonel Peter Williams, Major Tohler, Major Need, Sonja Thompson (UN), Jerry Hulme (UNHCR), Danielle (UNICEF), the US Air Force, the British Army and the Royal Navy. Norris McWhirter, Sir John Major and Sir Paddy Ashdown. Tony Redmond and his team from the Staffordshire Hospital in Stoke, the Heartlands Hospital Trust in east Birmingham, the Walsgrave Hospital, Coventry; the Midland Centre for Neurosurgery, Smethwick, and the Groby Road Hospital, Leicester. And a special thank you to the Veterans for Peace and Ronald McDonald House for taking such good care of the children when they arrived in the United States.

Kosovo

To Isa Zymberi, Jak Mita and Marta (Mother Teresa Charity), Ismet Shamolli, Riza Laha, Abedin (Rambo), Chamed and Sadedin (Dino), Gani Shehu and Lum Haxhiu. Colonel John Crosland, Sir Brian Donnelly, Bob Gordon, David Slinn and Bukurie Gjonbalaj. Prime Minister Bukoshi of Kosovo, President Meidani of Albania, and Demetrios Plaits, the Greek chargé d'affaires in Tirana. Her Royal Highness the Duchess of Gloucester, Anne Wood CBE and the myriad charities, organisations and individuals who raised funds and collected aid for the missions, and to all the volunteers who took part in our convoys to Kosovo and Northern Albania.

A special thank you to Liz Dack, who was with me at the worst of times, and to the brave members of the OSCE, especially Pierre Maurer MEP, Phil Figgins, Andrea Shulz, Artan and Benny.

With special thanks to my dear Bill Foxton OBE, who may be somewhere in the Accursed Mountains … laughing.

Iraq

Sarah K. Griffin, Mandeep Mancu, Laura Webster and Graham de Shmidt, who supported our work in northern Iraq and beyond. To Karim Kamal, Dr Sherzad, Dr Hussein, Mourad Mishko, Dr Nabaz and Sista Lesli. With a very special thank you to Marino Andolina, who risked his life to help so many children in so many war zones that I've lost count.

Save a Child

LEO Innovation Lab, Collegium Telemedicus and Happy Porch, Christina Kirk, Miron Derchansky and Pernille Richards. Evelyn Peng Ong, Dr Annemieka Miedema, Ashish Desai, Professor Eitan Kerem and Dr Hashavya for their help in launching our paediatric telemedicine programme. Ehsan Faisal, the Addis Clinic, Clyde & Co., the British Association of Paediatric Surgeons (BAPS), the European Paediatric Surgeons' Association (EUPSA) and all the specialists around the world helping us bring paediatric expertise to doctors treating children in besieged and remote areas.

Ukraine

Tiggy Thiagarajah and Virgin Atlantic, MDAUK and Rob Rinder, Joel Bennet, David Emin, Jane Townsend and her team in Wales. Jane Harris and the Steve Morgan Foundation. The Arche Hotel Group, Alex Ong and Ira. Religions for Peace, United Ukraine Appeal, Franks Family Foundation, Coutts Foundation, M.K. Rose Charitable Trust, Harold Hyam Wingate Foundation.

With special thanks to Marino Andolina, Kenny Green and Alexandre Kirichenko for their help with the evacuations from Dnipro and other front line areas in Ukraine.

Gaza

Children of Peace, Coutts Foundation, Direct Relief, Blue Moon, Kinder Relief and Project Pure Hope. Dr Hatem Amer and the Egyptian Ministry of Health, Federico Novellino and the Italian embassy, Barbara Fari and the Burlo Garofolo Children's Hospital in Trieste.

And lastly to publishing director Ajda Vucicevic and the team at HarperCollins, and to all the journalists and media organisations who have supported my work over the past three decades, helping me to highlight the suffering of innocent victims of war.

PICTURE CREDITS

All photos courtesy of the author with the following exceptions:

p.1, top right: © Tim Higham
p.2, top right: © Ian Derry/Syndication International
p.2, bottom: Tim Ockenden/PA Images/Alamy Stock Photo
p.6, bottom: © Steve Parsons
p.7, top: Cameron Spencer/Getty Images

While every effort has been made to trace the owners of copy-right material reproduced herein and secure permissions, the publishers would like to apologise for any omissions and will be pleased to incorporate missing acknowledgements in any future edition of this book.